The Economics of the Brand

WITHDRAWN

The Economics of the Brand

A marketing analysis

Trevor Watkins

McGRAW-HILL Book Company (UK) Limited

London · New York · St Louis · San Francisco · Auckland
Bogotá · Guatemala · Hamburg · Johannesburg · Lisbon · Madrid
Mexico · Montreal · New Delhi · Panama · Paris · San Juan
São Paulo · Singapore · Sydney · Tokyo · Toronto

Published by
McGRAW-HILL Book Company (UK) Limited
MAIDENHEAD · BERKSHIRE · ENGLAND

British Library Cataloguing in Publication Data

Watkins, Trevor
   The economics of the brand.—(McGraw-Hill
   marketing series)
   1. Marketing—Economic aspects
   I. Title
   380.1   HF5415.125

   ISBN 0–07–084156–X

Library of Congress Cataloging in Publication Data

Watkins, Trevor.
   The economics of the brand.

   (The McGraw-Hill marketing series)
   Bibliography: p.
   Includes index.
   1. Brand choice.   I. Title.   II. Series.
HF5415.3.W38   1986   658.8'343   85–23295
ISBN 0–07–084156–X

12345 WLL89876

Typeset by Styleset Limited, Warminster, Wiltshire, and printed and bound
in Great Britain by Whitstable Litho Limited, Whitstable, Kent

In memory of my father who offered the world the brand name Lamberto's

CONTENTS

PRICING

MK RES

DISTRIB

PREFACE

This book explores the relationship between economics and marketing. It was initiated because I felt, as a trained economist, that the contribution of economics to marketing practice was under-valued, particularly when compared with the contribution from the behavioural disciplines.

The book has turned out to be broader in the scope of input disciplines than was originally intended. It compares economic theory with marketing practice and where necessary encompasses other disciplines.

The views expressed in the book have grown out of over 10 years' lecturing experience in marketing and economics. Although one can never be completely satisfied that one has gone as far as one could, it is hoped that the insights offered will be valuable to students on BEC and BA Business Studies courses as well as on industrial economics and management courses at undergraduate, post-graduate and post-experience levels.

The value of the book is in providing an academic orientation to marketing practice. It provides a balance between the academic and the empirical, and examines the contrasts and comparisons between them. What results is an interesting, readable book which is thought-provoking. Certainly all the answers are not provided but the reader should be provoked into taking a new perspective on marketing both as business practice and as an academic study.

Last, but by no means least, the book has much to offer the marketing practitioner in providing a logical framework for understanding the interrelationships in marketing.

I would like to thank Christine Wadden for her speedy typing, my former colleagues at the University of Nottingham, Mike Wright and Professor Brian Chiplin for their encouragement and stimulation in the preparation of the drafts of this book; also many past students who unwittingly acted as guinea-pigs for material which now forms part of this book.

Finally, thanks and my love to my wife Val and my daughters Jane, Francine and Anna for the support they have given me.

Trevor Watkins
Dorset Institute of Higher Education

I acknowledge with thanks the permission granted by Media Expenditure Analysis Limited to use the data in Table 3.1, and by the Market Research Society and Audits of Great Britain Limited for the use of data in Table 2.1.

ONE
THE BRAND

1.1 THE SCOPE OF THE BOOK

This book explores the relationship between economics and marketing. Because marketing involves applications of theoretical concepts, principles and techniques, the focus of inquiry is *the brand* which is at the heart of marketing practice. Thus economic influences on the brand are examined, along with other practical and theoretical influences, in a modern competitive business environment.

The reason for taking this approach is to attempt to bridge the gap between economic theory and marketing practice, using the brand as the level of analysis. To some extent this assumes that marketing can be viewed as a sub-set of industrial economics and the book examines the areas of maximum relevance to an explanation in microeconomic terms of marketing phenomena. This reflects a widespread impression that marketing practitioners undervalue the contribution of economics. However, as the book unfolds it becomes clear that economic influences alone cannot sufficiently explain marketing practice and a broader range of influences is referred to, although the emphasis remains economic.

This is not an economics textbook. It is a view of marketing practice from an economic angle. It assumes a knowledge of elementary economics but no specific knowledge of marketing beyond an appreciation of commercial practice.

1.2 THE RELATIONSHIP BETWEEN ECONOMICS AND MARKETING

Economic theory has always had difficulty in incorporating the brand into analysis. There is a tendency to assume that competing brands are different products, but consumer choice between essentially (physically) similar brands is not really explained by traditional economic theory: it is subsumed into a rather nebulous variable usually named 'consumer tastes'. At the industry, product group or similar level of aggregation, brand differences can be conveniently treated in economic analysis as one form of competition. In marketing practice the brand is central to the success of the company. A further problem is that much theoretical economic analysis is static, or at best concerns comparative statics, whereas marketing practice is dynamic: decisions in one period have effects in successive periods, perhaps at an increasing (or decreasing) rate. Effects of multiple, interrelated decisions by a firm and its rivals become intertwined over time, making it difficult for the economic analyst to disentangle them. There is a need for a bridge between the two levels of concern, and this book attempts to provide at least stepping stones between economic theory and marketing practice.

As the emphasis in marketing is on meeting company objectives (usually involving profit-making) through the provision of customer satisfaction, the starting point for the book is demand analysis and this is covered in Chapter 2. This chapter considers demand forecasting and introduces Lancaster's characteristics approach which is thought to be a useful method of analysing brands in economic theory terms. This chapter also examines economic influences on demand. It contrasts the traditional economics 'aggregation' approach to the study of demand with the more usual 'individual' level of analysis in marketing practice, which draws on behavioural influences primarily from the disciplines of sociology and psychology and their offshoots.

Indeed, the demand-side bias is continued throughout the book. The traditional economic pre-occupation with costs and other supply-side factors is not a central concern of the book, being seen as a constraint on demand-side influences rather than of primary concern in themselves.

The economic approach is continued into Chapter 3 in which its relationship with marketing practice is explored in the context of the industrial economic concept of market structure. Here the role of marketing in conditions of perfectly competitive, monopoly, and imperfectly competitive market structures is considered. This can be seen as setting the competitive framework for marketing practice.

The relationship between economics and marketing is examined in a practical context in the two chapters (4 and 5) on market conduct which follow. The first of these conduct chapters considers price competition and examines the role of price as a brand-marketing variable in a competitive environment. Both economic and non-economic influences on pricing research are examined, in particular the use of conjoint measurement in pricing research. The second conduct chapter considers non-price competition, in particular in the creation of brand image through advertising and other promotional activities. Campaign planning and the role of advertising effectiveness are examined, involving both economic and non-economic influences.

As the focus of the book is the brand, the next two chapters (6 and 7) consider this central element of marketing strategy. The first of these chapters considers brand policy which examines the concept of the life cycle of brands and the role of the brand as a part of a multibrand company's product policy. As this discussion highlights the importance of new brand development, the next chapter examines the marketing aspects of the new brand development process. Again following the demand-side emphasis, this chapter concentrates on the role of market research in ensuring that new brands launched will be successful.

Chapter 8 examines the distribution of brands, looking at the economic influences on the choice of distribution channels for brands, the alternatives of direct and indirect routes to the ultimate consumer and the relationship between the brand's manufacturer and independent intermediaries.

Where relevant, specific examples of marketing practice are given not only for consumer goods marketing but also for services marketing which is a major growth area in terms of the usage being made of marketing techniques.

The final chapter draws the threads together by examining the economics of marketing variables of price, promotion, brand quality and distribution to produce an integrated marketing strategy. This provides insights into optimum marketing-budget allocation. The chapter concludes with a brief examination of future trends for brands, in particular the growth of marketing information systems and the concept of global brands.

The book as a whole explores the relationship between economic theory and marketing practice at a microeconomic level of analysis through the medium of the brand. Where necessary wider influences are included especially market-research-based influences, but essentially the book evaluates the role of economics in marketing practice. The book is primarily concerned with demand-side influences and the underlying assumption is that a brand can only be successful if these demand influences are fully taken into account. Only then do supply-side factors become important.

The rest of this chapter examines the concepts of the brand, of the manager and of elasticity measures, which underpin the discussion in the rest of the book.

1.3 THE BRAND

1.3.1 The concept of the brand

It is difficult to define the concept of the brand but the essence is that a brand is an identifiable version of a product which a consumer could perceive as being distinctive in some way from other versions of the product. Usually a brand will have a name which attempts to encapsulate the distinctiveness of the brand. The consumer orientation in the definition reflects the primary concern of effective marketing executives — meeting company objectives through customer satisfactions in a competitive environment. A brand can be based on a name, symbol, design or other aspect which distinguishes a company's offering from its rivals'. A brand name is that part of the brand image which can be vocalized, and should suggest the brand's personality; a brand mark should offer visual appeal and, on trade marks, offer legal protection.

Successful branding makes the brand equivalent to a product in that consumers do not perceive rival brands as acceptable alternatives. The brand name can become generic, it can be used by consumers when referring to the product type. In the UK, Hoover, a brand name, is often used in place of 'vacuum cleaner', the product. If this is carried through into purchasing it puts the brand into an extremely strong position in the market — the equivalent of a monopolist in some cases. As a working definition, it is feasible to tell one brand from another in a multibrand company by using the criterion of whether or not each have separate brand names. Thus a new brand can be separated from a rejuvenated existing brand by the test: does the 'new' brand have a new name? For example, on this definition the Ford Cortina Mark 1 to Mark 5 was a brand which was continually rejuvenated; the replacement, the Ford Sierra, is a new brand (with a new name).

In their 1984 annual report, Saatchi and Saatchi Compton Worldwide, the advertising agency, recognized the importance of the concept of the brand as perceived by consumers. They assert that:

> when probed deeply, consumers describe the products that they call brands in terms that we would normally expect to be used to describe people. They tell us that brands can be warm or friendly; cold; modern; old fashioned; romantic; practical; sophisticated; stylish and so on. They talk about a brand's persona, its image and its reputation — and this 'aura' or 'ethos' is what characterises a brand.

The relationship that consumers enjoy with brands is therefore a complex mixture of rational and emotional factors. The balance varies, brand by brand, product category by product category. They conclude that:

> It follows that all brands, like all people, have a 'personality' of one kind or another. But like the strongest individuals, the strongest brands have more than mere personality — they have 'character' — more depth, more integrity, they stand out from the crowd.

1.3.2 Marketing complexity and the brand

The brand should be capable of personalization in the way it is presented so as to encourage consumers to identify with it. The brand should communicate a distinctive value to potential consumers through using such variables as the name, package, physical product and/or service provided, colour, shape, size and price, through the promotional appeals made and the distribution and display processes. The key to success is in the combination of these elements of the marketing mix to form a whole which is meaningful to consumers. Table 1.1 gives a fuller identification of the elements of the marketing mix — the variables available to the manufacturer of a brand which can be combined in presenting a brand to the market. Clearly this is a complex practical process. The process can be seen as a sub-set of industrial economics in that it is about how modern business firms compete in the market-place and is thus highly relevant to the scope of this book.

It is important to note this empirical complexity at the outset. Kotler[1] identifies a number of

Table 1.1   Elements of the marketing mix of manufacturers

Product planning—Policies and procedures relating to:
    Product lines to be offered – qualities, design, etc.
    The markets to sell to – whom, where, when and in what quantity.
    New product policy – research and development programme.

Pricing—Policies and procedures relating to:
    The level of prices to adopt.
    The specific prices to adopt (odd/even, etc.).
    Price policy – one price or varying price, price maintenance, use of list prices, etc.
    The margins to adopt – for the company; for the trade.

Branding—Policies and procedures relating to:
    Selection of trade marks.
    Brand policy – individual or family brand.
    Sale under private brand or unbranded.

Channels of distribution—Policies and procedures relating to:
    The channels to use between plant and consumer.
    The degree of selectivity among wholesalers and retailers.
    Efforts to gain co-operation of the trade.

Personal selling—Policies and procedures relating to:
    The burden to be placed on personal selling and the methods to be employed in
        (1) The manufacturer's organisation.
        (2) The wholesale segment of the trade.
        (3) The retail segment of the trade.

Advertising—Policies and procedures relating to:
    The amount to spend – i.e., the burden to be placed on advertising.
    The copy platform to adopt:
        (1) Product image desired.
        (2) Corporate image desired.
    The mix of advertising – to the trade; through the trade – to consumers.

Promotions—Policies and procedures relating to:
    The burden to place on special selling plans or devices directed at or through the trade.
    The form of these devices for consumer promotions, for trade promotions.

Packaging—Policies and procedures relating to:
    Formulation of package and label.

Display—Policies and procedures relating to:
    The burden to be put on display to help effect sales.
    The methods to adopt to secure display.

Servicing—Policies and procedures relating to:
    Providing service needed.

Physical handling—Policies and procedures relating to:
    Warehousing.
    Transportation.
    Inventories.

Fact finding and analysis—Policies and procedures relating to:
    The securing, analysis, and use of facts in marketing operations.

Source: Adapted from Neil H. Borden, 'The concept of the marketing mix' in George Schwart, *Science in Marketing*, (John Wiley and Sons, New York), 1965, pp. 389–90.

factors which add to the difficulties of decision-making in marketing practice. As applied to brand marketing these include:

1. *Estimation of the sales response* to changes in overall marketing expenses. At the brand level of analysis it is difficult to predict the effect on sales from adjustments in marketing expenditures because the isolation of the effects from other activities in the market-place such as competitive effects and other exogenous events is complex.

2. *Marketing mix interaction*: As already noted it is not sufficient to decide on the most appropriate level of each of the marketing mix variables in isolation. The interaction of the variables must also be taken into account. For example, an advertising claim of high quality combined with a relatively low price may confuse consumers and lead them to disbelieve the quality claim. The elements must be consistent and form a credible, valuable brand image which appeals to consumers.

3. *Competitive effects*: A theme of this book is marketing practice. The brand is seen as a competitive weapon. In chapter 3 in particular the use of brands as part of competitive strategy is considered. What is clear from this analysis is that competitors are likely to react to changes in a company's brand-marketing strategy; these reactions make the prediction of effects all the more difficult. Of course these competitors will also initiate action using their own brands and the company may need to react to these changes in ways which it would have preferred to avoid, given an unconstrained choice.

4. *Delayed response*: When changes in the brand-marketing strategy are planned and then executed, market reactions may be delayed by an unpredictable period of time. An individual example illustrates this point. Suppose that an advertising campaign for a brand is planned. There will be a delay before the planned advertisement is produced, then before it appears, then before it is perceived by a reader (viewer or listener). This reader may take in the message and remember it but may react to it only, say six months later, when a need for the brand arises. Thus, although the sale may then be caused by the original advertisement, the measurement of the advertisement effect is made extremely difficult. Moreover the reader may remember the advertising message but forget the source, so that if questioned at the point of sale may not recall having seen the advertisement. Linking advertising expenditure to sales response is complex and exacerbated by the likelihood of delayed effects.

   A further complication can be that short-term responses may differ from longer-term reactions. For example, when the British Post Office put up the cost of sending letters there was a strong public outcry with much adverse publicity. When the change occurred the initial response reduced the volume of mail sent to about 80 per cent of the original amount. However, over the next few months this proportion gradually increased to over 93 per cent as people became used to the change and the initial response gradually faded.

   The opposite effect can also occur. When a bad harvest of potatoes occurred in the UK in the late 1970s the price of potatoes rose rapidly. However, the initial reaction was to continue to buy them at the higher price as it was felt that potatoes were an integral part of the British diet. Only slowly did alternative food (such as rice and spaghetti) grow in popularity. When, in the next year, the price of potatoes returned to a lower level, demand was lower than expected as people had adapted to their alternative diets and were again slow to readjust.

   Thus habits can lead to a delay in the reaction to marketing changes: the more deeply ingrained the habits, the slower the response change. There may be different short-run and long-run reactions to marketing changes. A short-run monopoly may not last into the longer term as people are able to adapt more and perhaps are more likely to change their habits in the longer term when market conditions change.

5. *Multiple markets*: Modern business is increasingly internationalized. The concept of the global brand is discussed in the last chapter of this book. If a brand is to grow, in sales terms, it may

need to be made available to more and more markets (or further segments of existing markets). As different markets are likely to have different characteristics, this complicates the marketing task still further and may involve the brand being produced in slightly different versions for each market. Certainly language differences need to be considered, as do cultural differences and distribution requirements.

6. *Co-ordination of intra-company brand activity*: The next section considers the role of the brand manager in the organization. In many organizations there are likely to be inter-departmental conflicts which, if not checked, can lead to sub-optimization of objectives. For example the production department may wish to produce long runs of standard versions of the brand to minimize unit costs and maximize quantity discounts received on the raw materials bought in. In contrast the brand managers may wish to have short runs of a variety of colours, shapes and sizes of the brand. The need for negotiation complicates the brand marketing task.

Objectives for the brand may also differ within the organization. Although shareholders wish to make high profits on their investment this may be seen as a constraint rather than an objective by top management interested in their individual power, obtained via take-over or mergers. Brand managers may expect to gain more importance in the organization from sales maximization or market-share maximization (especially if the brand is market leader). These individual objectives must be balanced with departmental and corporate objectives.

7. *Environmental uncertainty*: Quite outside the control of the company, changes can occur which affect the market response to the brand-marketing strategy. Economic conditions change and legal, social and technological changes can all occur independently of the company. For example legal controls on advertising content may affect advertising claims for the brand. Social trends such as consumerism may put pressure on the company to use certain ingredients in the brand for health reasons, or certain types of packaging to avoid environmental pollution. In some situations this can have a major effect on a brand.

1.3.3 Brand decision-making approaches in complex empirical situations

Taken together these factors make the brand image creation process and the planning and implementation of a brand-marketing strategy complex and require a dynamic, flexible approach to optimizing brand performance. In practice this complexity can be dealt with on the basis of:

1. *Past experience*: A manager's accumulated experience can be used as the basis for making future decisions. This is perhaps the simplest approach but has little to commend it without further inputs to the decision process.

2. *Company operating procedures*: In a sense this is formalized past experience application. It may lack flexibility to change to meet changing market conditions. Nevertheless, this can produce a more standardized approach than allowing individual brand managers to make decisions in isolation.

3. *Market research*: This can be used as a decision input but not to make the decisions themselves, although recommendations may direct action. It seems sensible, if a marketing approach based on customer satisfactions is to be applied, to use as much relevant marketing intelligence as can be cost-effectively assembled in time. This book examines various application areas of market research in brand marketing, particularly in new brand development, but also in pricing and advertising research.

4. *Models of market response*: This book examines a number of economic models which could be applied in a practical context or which provide a valuable theoretical underpinning of marketing practice. If models are to have practical value they must be accepted by brand managers and those models which are presented are critically appraised from this viewpoint.

1.3.4 The brand decision process

The brand manager needing to deal with the brand in a complex market environment needs a decision-making process for each situation which arises. A standardized approach could be to:

1. *Define the opportunity/problem which has arisen*: This would involve a careful statement of exactly what is involved in the decision to be made.
2. *Analyse the decision requirements*: This would include the likely effects of making the right or the wrong decision. The relationship of the decision to the company and the brand objectives needs to be identified and if necessary clarified. It would also include an identification of the information needs in making the decision. Alternative solutions may be identified at this stage and criteria for the choice of the best alternative determined.
3. *Collect information*: The specified information can then be collected. This may involve a market research agency or in-house specialists. It may utilize existing company data, published statistics, trade, government or media sources or a range of other sources. The cost of the information must be balanced against the need for accuracy and speed and the importance of the decision. The information collection must be cost-effective. If a model is to be used then the information inputs for the model must be obtained.
4. *Analyse information*: The collected data must be assembled, edited and analysed in appropriate ways. This may involve representing the data in a different form and tabulation and cross-tabulation of the data. Statistical tests may be necessary in the interpretation of the data.
5. *Develop alternative solutions*: Once the data have been analysed, the alternative solutions can be tested and developed and related back to the objectives of the decision.
6. *Select and apply the best solution*: After fully considering the alternatives the best solution should be chosen on the specified criteria and related back to the original opportunity or problem. The solution should then be applied and progress monitored, so that any deviations from the expected results can be reacted to.

Of course, the above decision structure is a generalization by nature. The type of decision which could affect a brand may include:

1. Whether or not to develop a new brand.
2. Whether or not to introduce the brand in a new market.
3. Whether or not to rejuvenate an existing brand.
4. How to react to a new brand from a competitor.
5. How to react to new government legislation affecting the brand.
6. How to react to changes in consumer requirements.

This decision framework is a useful, logical way of approaching complex issues but may need to be compressed, amended or expanded in particular applications.

1.4 THE BRAND MANAGER

In a business organization the brand manager is the individual with the responsibility and accountability for marketing the brand so as to meet company objectives, usually in the form of planned absolute or relative sales and/or profit targets. This manager, usually one of a team of brand managers under a product group manager, can draw on specialist expertise from promotional, market research and sales executives. The brand manager is the organizational focus for the brand dealing with a plethora of departments within the firm so as to optimize the brand-marketing strategy and tactics.

This role is not a 'line' function but a planning function taking into account market needs and competitive action with the vital co-ordination and control roles incorporated. The brand manager must:

— Plan the marketing strategy for his brand(s).

— Co-ordinate the implementation of this strategy so as to form a brand image which is valued by consumers.

— Control the implementation of the brand-marketing strategy so as to ensure that the planned objectives are met, especially in the light of competitive action and reaction to the brand. This implies the need to retain flexibility to change plans at short notice should competitive conditions dictate.

The role has many economic influences. In practice the profit aim incorporates sales and cost aims. As Bureau[2] has written:

> The brand manager 'makes' nothing, sells nothing, buys no raw materials, creates no advertising. He is hired specifically on the basis that, being uninvolved in administering and controlling the 'doing' functions of the company, and of the people who do it, he may bend all his energies to planning and controlling the execution of those plans. The creation of the brand manager concept rests first and foremost on the belief that planning the revenue-earning competence of a product in the market place is vital to the company.

The advantage of a brand-management organization structure is that one individual can be made responsible for harmonizing the marketing programme for the brand and should spot market trends as they develop more quickly than with any other structure. Small brands are not ignored but can be represented in the organization by the responsible brand manager. The brand manager should receive excellent training for promotion as all parts of the organization are likely to be contacted by the brand manager in his work.

It is important that the brand manager is given authority to effectively carry out these functions. It is quite possible for inter-departmental rivalries to lead to conflict and frustration. The brand manager may become a 'jack of all trades but master of none' without specialist abilities in any one marketing function. He must be a good persuader and communicator to get his way.

The nature of the job leads to a tendency for a high staff turnover. Continuity may therefore be lacking and a newly appointed brand manager may initiate change for the sake of change purely to establish his presence in the organization. If there is a low staff turnover another problem can result: brand managers may become too closely identified with the brand and cease to make rational decisions. In particular, dropping a brand may be avoided as the brand manager's responsibilities will be reduced and no one wishes to be associated with the stigma which can attach to a 'failure'. Old brands may therefore be supported beyond their useful life.

If the brand manager is to be seen as a profit centre then a formalized authority level must be established to enable the responsibility to be dispatched effectively. Only then can results in profit terms be seen to reflect the performance of the brand manager.

Alternative organizational systems can be used, such as having a team of specialists reporting to an overall marketing manager, or having a series of geographical regions each with a marketing manager, or in particular a marketing manager responsible for a particular type of customer. This latter system reflects the importance of the consumer in the organization but does not necessarily have the advantages which the brand manager system has.

If the brand management system of organization is to work effectively then clear delineations of responsibility are necessary along with formal lines of communication and authority. This approach must be costed against alternatives to find an optimum number of brands per manager so that each receives the necessary and economically justifiable level of attention from the brand manager.

1.5 ELASTICITY

Much of this book is concerned with the effects of changes in marketing variables on demand, expressed in terms of unit sales. It is clear that measurement of these effects is important and it is necessary to derive some indicator of responsiveness that is unaffected by the particular units of measurement chosen, so that effects of changes on each of the variables can be easily compared. The simplest approach is to work in proportionate changes and this is exactly what the economist's concept of elasticity does. Usually in economic theory, the major use of the concept relates to price elasticity but each of the other marketing variables has elasticity measures which can be associated with it. Price elasticity will be considered first.

The (own) price elasticity of demand represents the proportionate change in quantity demanded resulting from a small change in price. This can be expressed as

$$e_p = \frac{\Delta Q/Q}{\Delta P/P}$$

where e_p = price elasticity of demand

Q = sales

P = price

Δ = a small change in

In terms of calculus:

$$e_p = \frac{dQ}{dP} \cdot \frac{P}{Q}$$

Technically, this is known as point elasticity and applies only to small changes around a defined point on the demand curve, but the point can be located anywhere on the demand curve.

It is immediately clear that price, P in the above equation, can be replaced by A (for advertising), R (for product quality) or D (for distribution effort), S (for service effort) and so on for other marketing variables so as to derive equivalent, comparable elasticity measures. An important distinction is that usually a price fall leads to a demand *increase* (given a downward sloping demand curve) whereas a decrease in any of the other marketing variable settings, say advertising, usually leads to a demand *decrease*. This is expressed in the calculations through e_p having a negative value whereas the other elasticity measures, say e_A, have positive values. However, in marketing terms a price fall can be viewed as spending part of the marketing budget on the price variable, that is, on a (temporary) reduction in the 'normal' level of price for sales promotion reasons. In this sense increasing the marketing expenditure on the price variable (thus reducing price) should change demand in the same direction, as would an increase in marketing expenditure on other variables.

A further point that should be noted is that price elasticity is strictly own-price elasticity and it is possible to define a price elasticity measure to cover the effect on the demand for brand A from changes in the prices of competitive brands B, C, D and so on, in exactly the same way. Indeed this concept can also be used to cover changes in a firm's other brands' prices and their effects on the demand for brand A. In this latter case the elasticity measure will be negative if the brands are complements and positive if the brands are substitutes. These measures are known as cross-elasticities of demand.

A unitary value for own-price elasticity of demand implies that total revenue will remain constant for a small change in price, as quantity demanded changes in the same proportion as the change in price. Demand changes which are proportionally greater than the price change (in the opposite direction), known as price-elastic demand, would lead to an increase in sales revenue for a small decrease in price and a reduction in sales revenue for a small increase in price. Demand changes which are less than the price change (in the opposite direction), known as price-inelastic demand, would lead to an increase in sales revenue for a small increase in price and a reduction in sales revenue for a small decrease in price.

In practice, measurement of elasticity of demand is very important although difficult:

> All businessmen would be expected to know something about the likely effect of price changes on the demand for their product even though they would rarely express their knowledge in terms of the elasticity of demand: but it is noticeable to the outside observer that several business decisions pay insufficient attention to the elasticity of demand for the product. When costs are rising it is tempting to try to pass on the cost increases by increasing the price to the consumer, and if demand for the product is relatively inelastic, this measure may well succeed; but when as for example in the case of rail transport there are many substitutes and the demand is relatively elastic, increasing prices may well lead to a reduction in total revenue rather than an increase. Because of declining use of off-peak trains British Rail has, in fact, introduced a wide range of low price special fares.[3]

The attempts to measure elasticity in practice have been primarily concerned with price elasticity but more importantly with product groups rather than brands. The great difficulty is to isolate the demand effects of price (or other marketing variable) changes from environmental 'noise' caused by exogenous variables such as competitive action. For the level of analysis in this book, the brand, this is a major problem.

Lambin[4] studied individual brands in a number of European countries and found significant negative price effects for 37 out of 43 equations estimated. In 23 cases demand was price elastic. Lambin was primarily concerned with advertising and the brands used were highly advertised which may be interlinked with price effects, making the individual effects very difficult to separate and probably reducing the e_p value. In other words brands not so heavily advertised, i.e., where the brand image is not so well developed and brand loyalty is lower, may have higher e_p values. It is usually assumed that own-price elasticities will be greater the more specific the commodity group analysed, i.e., brands are more price elastic than product groups if only because there are likely to be more alternatives available to the buyers. Accurate measurement of the elasticity measures is difficult in practice but can be estimated using econometric methods. As already noted the great difficulty is to isolate the separate and joint effects of each of the marketing variables. Nevertheless, the concept is very important and brand managers are likely to have implicit estimates of the various elasticity measures when making budget allocation decisions.

In subsequent chapters each of the marketing variables is considered, after which the final chapter returns to the budget allocation issue and the importance of elasticity measures in this concept.

REFERENCES

1. Kotler, P. (1971) *Marketing Decision Making – A model building approach*, Holt Rinehart and Winston, New York.
2. Bureau, J. R. (1981) *Brand Management*, Macmillan, London, p. 3.
3. Chiplin, B. (1982) 'The market' in *Business Economics*, J. Bates and J. R. Parkinson (eds), Blackwell, Oxford, pp. 76–7.
4. Lambin, J. J. (1976) *Advertising, Competition and Market Conduct in Oligopoly over Time*, North-Holland, Amsterdam, p. 103.

TWO

DEMAND ANALYSIS

2.1 INTRODUCTION

This chapter attempts an objective analysis of the contribution of economics to practical demand analysis at the brand level. It attempts to show that economic theory can explain marketing practice despite the recent concentration by marketing practitioners on other disciplines for inspiration. The discussion begins with a consideration of the concept of rationality followed by an analysis of the contribution of Kelvin Lancaster to this discussion and concludes with an examination of the similarities in approach of economics and market research practice.

2.2 RATIONALITY

The brand manager with his practical business problems to solve would seem, at least from the evidence of much recent marketing literature relating to buyer behaviour, to be much more likely to refer to sociological and psychological disciplines for inspiration, rather than to economics. The reason often given for this is the failure of economic theory to provide sufficient practical insights into consumer behaviour or practical tools with which to measure demand.

Traditionally, economics has been concerned with products and can deal with brands only as different products. Also, allegedly unrealistic assumptions about an individual's rationality have been made. Palda[1] has argued that the economist's assumption of rationality is not unduly restrictive especially when revealed preference theory is applied. Rationality is assumed in revealed preference theory when the following conditions hold:

1. *Consistency*: If Brand A is bought rather than Brand B, the consumer is inconsistent if he later buys B not A, assuming income and tastes are unchanged and the cost of $B \leqslant A$.
2. *Transitivity*: If Brand A is revealed preferred to Brand B which is revealed preferred to Brand C then Brand C must not be revealed preferred to Brand A, with assumptions above.

Revealed preference occurs with the actual purchase decision. The limitations lie inevitably with the assumptions made. Situations such as impulse buying (random choice) would not be covered by these conditions (i.e., would be classed as irrational). Within the limitations set, the rationality definition is easy to meet. Any apparent deviation from it could be put down to a change in tastes, for example.

However, in practical terms this approach does not help with, for example, sales forecasting. It would seem to have limited practical applicability.

The individual is assumed to allocate his resources in such a way as to maximize his utility, subject to his budget constraint, given that he has perfect knowledge of his wants and the means of satisfying them (the range of brands available). The issue of perfect knowledge is complex. More recent work in economics has incorporated the cost of search for information into the analysis[2] and much debate on the economics of advertising has focused on the effect of advertising on the (mis)allocation of resources.[3] We will return to this point.

The psychological view of rationality is much broader than that normally associated with economics.[4] This viewpoint involves looking at people from an external, objective point of view. Their behaviour may seem irrational because of their unique experience of the psychological fields. At the instant of behaving, psychologists would argue, the actions of each person seem to him the best and most effective acts he can perform under the circumstances. If at that instant he knew how to behave more effectively, it could be argued that he would do so. Under this definition all consumption decisions are rational at the time they are made. In itself however it is of little practical value in analysing demand, although it may direct research attention to the 'psychological fields' and the 'circumstances' of the consumption decision.

The economist's approach to rationality seems to be based on objective and measurable factors rather than incorporating emotional factors into the broad definition of rationality used by psychologists. From a practical point of view, however, it is clear that much advertising of brands relies on not just rational (objective, measurable) claims but also emotional claims aimed at personalizing the brand and its appeal.

2.3 THE OBJECTIVES OF DEMAND ANALYSIS

The above discussion indicates that, from a practical viewpoint, if an individual consumer is to be studied then it is hard to carry out an analysis purely in economic terms when the brands involved in the choice decision involve emotional as well as rational appeals.

The economist's solution to this dilemma would perhaps be to argue that the individual consumer is of little interest to management. It is, this argument would suggest, only an aggregation of consumers that is of interest. Although it may not be possible to forecast what brand an individual consumer would buy next, for example, an economist may concentrate on forecasting how consumers in aggregate will choose, thus providing a market forecast by brand and by implication, a probability that a typical individual will choose a particular brand.

Clearly then the objectives of making a demand analysis have a vital role to play in this discussion. Why is the analysis to take place at all? If the interest in demand is at a sufficiently high level of aggregation to allow this forecast of sales or brand share to be made without considering the individual idiosyncrasies of consumers then an econometric-based forecasting method may be valid.

Palda,[5] for example, produced a single equation model to forecast the sales of Lydia Pinkham's Vegetable Compound in the US between 1908 and 1960. This model used OLS to give the following results:

$$R_t = 3649 + 1180 \log_{10}(A_t) + 774(D) + 32(T) - 2.83(Yt) + 0.665\,R_{t-1}$$

giving a value of R^2 of 0.941 and a low value of the Durbin–Watson d statistic of 1.59 where

R = sales revenue
A = advertising expenditure
T = time trend (1908 = 1, 1909 = 2, etc.)
Y = total personal disposable income in current prices

D = dummy variable = 1 for 1908–25 and = 10 thereafter, to measure the impact of an order by the Food and Drug Administration in 1925 requiring the company to reduce its claims for the product.

While this model has been criticized for the lack of a price-based independent variable and for failing to take into account the likely two-way causation between advertising and sales (see Section 5.5.1), it nevertheless illustrates the production of an effective forecast without the need to study the individual consumer.

Becker[2] in discussing types of irrationality, argues that both impulse buying (unplanned choice at random) and inert buying (habitual brand choice) can be dealt with at the aggregate level, and much of the work by Ehrenberg,[6] studying brand choice, is based on past brand choice patterns translated into probability form.

What this means is that in situations where a study of demand is undertaken to forecast the total size of the market then it would seem theoretically acceptable to use an economic-based approach.

It is in circumstances where demand is being studied to shed light on individual consumers that the need for the disciplines of sociology and psychology have a much stronger claim. If, for example, the motivation of individual consumers is important in planning the content of an advertising campaign, then it is necessary to delve into the psychology of the individual consumer. A recent case study of the fresh cream cake market[7] reports that qualitative group discussions showed that housewives had guilt feelings when buying the product, which they saw as being a luxury item; this led to the use of the copy line 'Naughty . . . but nice' with TV-personality backing within the advertising campaign to persuade people to overcome these guilt feelings and buy the product.

Obviously economics cannot provide such insights into the motivation of individual consumers in brand choice. The closest approach which is made is that by Kelvin Lancaster in his characteristics approach to demand theory.[8]

2.4 LANCASTER'S CHARACTERISTICS APPROACH TO CONSUMER THEORY

The traditional approach to consumer theory explains how a consumer with a limited budget allocates his expenditure between different commodities so as to *maximize the utility* or satisfaction he receives from consumption. In this approach it is the commodities themselves that have the power to yield utility and they are bought for that reason.

The essential feature of the Lancaster approach is that the consumer's relationship to the goods he buys has two stages. The goods are no longer the immediate source of utility or satisfaction, or the basis of the consumer's choice, but they do provide 'characteristics' when consumed which are the source of utility and satisfaction. It is these characteristics, according to Lancaster, that are demanded by the consumer; it is they that yield satisfaction and it is this satisfaction that is maximized. In consumption the goods possess qualities only as inputs, the demand for them is only a derived demand arising from their ability to provide 'characteristics'.

Each consumption activity can be defined by its inputs and by the characteristics that form its output. There is no unique relationship between the number of goods and the number of characteristics. A single good will generally have more than one characteristic and a single characteristic may be obtained from more than one good. The number of goods may therefore be equal to, greater than or less than the number of characteristics produced. Further, goods in combination may possess characteristics different from those pertaining to the goods separately and there may be several combinations of goods that give rise to the same bundle of characteristics.

According to Lancaster, characteristics yield utility. They are intrinsic and objective properties of goods, observable and measurable. The characteristics possessed by a commodity are the same for all consumers and present in the same quantities.

Consumer choice arises between characteristics, not in allocation of characteristics to goods.

Diminishing marginal utility is reflected in the preference ordering of the characteristics vectors, not in the relationship between goods and characteristics.

Lancaster's approach — at least for marketing applications — is of most interest at the individual-brand level of analysis, which in itself is a step forward towards applications. Economic theory has found difficulty in dealing meaningfully with brands rather than distinct and separate products. The question of defining separate products is neatly side-stepped by the concentration on characteristics in Lancaster's analysis. This is a move nearer to the marketing man's concepts of consumer satisfaction and can be of more value in explaining brand choice than is traditional consumer theory. Lancaster's approach also makes dealing with the introduction of new brands into a market easier in traditional economic demand theory.

Traditional economic theory would define two brands of, say, baked beans as different *products* for the purposes of analysis. In Lancaster's approach the two brands may differ in terms of the amounts of one or two characteristics which are possessed by each of the brands, e.g., calorie content, number of beans per ounce. Indeed, Lancaster would argue that a brand could not survive in the market place unless it possessed at least one characteristic in greater quantities (or less if it were a negative characteristic) than its competitors, per unit of the brand. This is not far removed from the marketing concept of the unique selling proposition, the unique appeal of a brand.

In summary then, according to Lancaster the demand for goods by consumers exists only because the goods yield characteristics. A particular model of a car will yield a specific combination of a variety of characteristics such as acceleration rate, economy, seating capacity, load-carrying capacity, service requirements, etc. Lancaster then reconsiders traditional demand theory in terms of his unique selling proposition, the insertion of 'characteristics' between 'goods' and 'utility'.

From a practical viewpoint, Lancaster distinguishes between the perceptions of consumers and their preferences. This is an important move towards marketing theory. Lancaster assumes that all consumers perceive characteristics in the same way, i.e., they are objective and measurable. In choosing between goods (in terms of the characteristics possessed) consumers express their preferences which are subjective, and this choice is made to reflect the consumer's attempt to maximize utility subject to his budget constraint. In marketing practice it would probably be assumed that both perception and preference were subjective.

The practical differences then relate to the concept of perception in this content. In psychological research exploring how the individual consumer perceives brands, it is often answered that the process of perception is subjective not objective. The subject is explored in detail by Delozier[9] and by Engel and Blackwell.[10] For example, recent research by the author shows that users and non-users of new and established brands of chocolate confectionery perceive the characteristics of the brands in different ways. The 'brand image' of each brand on twenty scales of the average user and non-user is shown in Figures 2.1 and 2.2. This and much more research indicates that individual consumers do view brands in different ways.

Lancaster's approach to perception assumes that each consumer perceives the characteristics the brand possesses in the same way. This assumption is necessary if it is to be possible to produce a 'standard' relationship between brands and characteristics for all consumers. Thus the relationship of a brand to its characteristics can be expressed as in Figure 2.3.

Because Lancaster assumes that characteristics are additive, the more units of Brand 1 or 2 purchased, the more of the two characteristics assumed to be possessed (A and B) are obtained. Brands can be expressed as rays in characteristics space.

2.5 CONSUMER EQUILIBRIUM IN LANCASTER'S APPROACH

Assuming that:

1. Two brands exist, both providing combinations of two characteristics in given proportions;

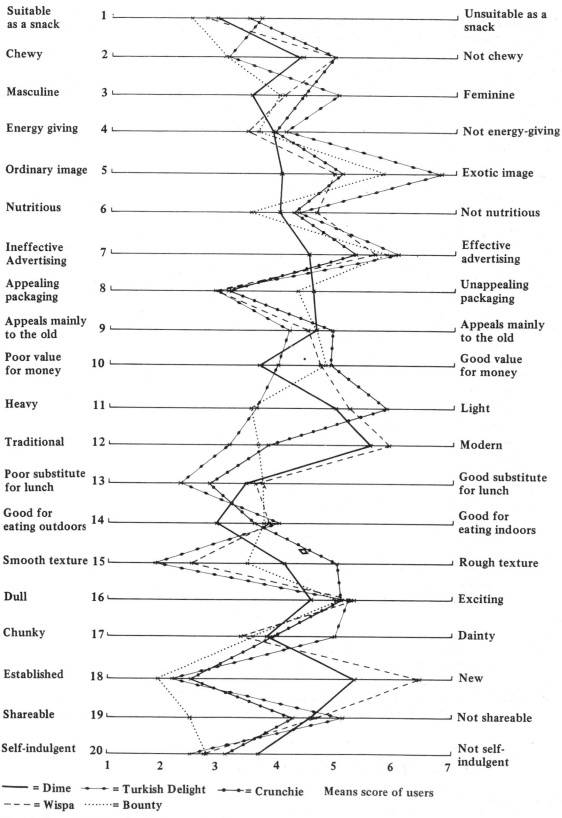

		Suitable as a snack							Unsuitable as a snack

Suitable as a snack — 1 — Unsuitable as a snack

Chewy — 2 — Not chewy

Masculine — 3 — Feminine

Energy giving — 4 — Not energy-giving

Ordinary image — 5 — Exotic image

Nutritious — 6 — Not nutritious

Ineffective Advertising — 7 — Effective advertising

Appealing packaging — 8 — Unappealing packaging

Appeals mainly to the old — 9 — Appeals mainly to the old

Poor value for money — 10 — Good value for money

Heavy — 11 — Light

Traditional — 12 — Modern

Poor substitute for lunch — 13 — Good substitute for lunch

Good for eating outdoors — 14 — Good for eating indoors

Smooth texture 15 — Rough texture

Dull — 16 — Exciting

Chunky — 17 — Dainty

Established — 18 — New

Shareable — 19 — Not shareable

Self-indulgent — 20 — Not self-indulgent

1   2   3   4   5   6   7

—— = Dime   —•— = Turkish Delight   —•—• = Crunchie   Means score of users

– – – = Wispa   ·······= Bounty

Fig. 2.1 Competitive brand analysis – brand image profiles (users)

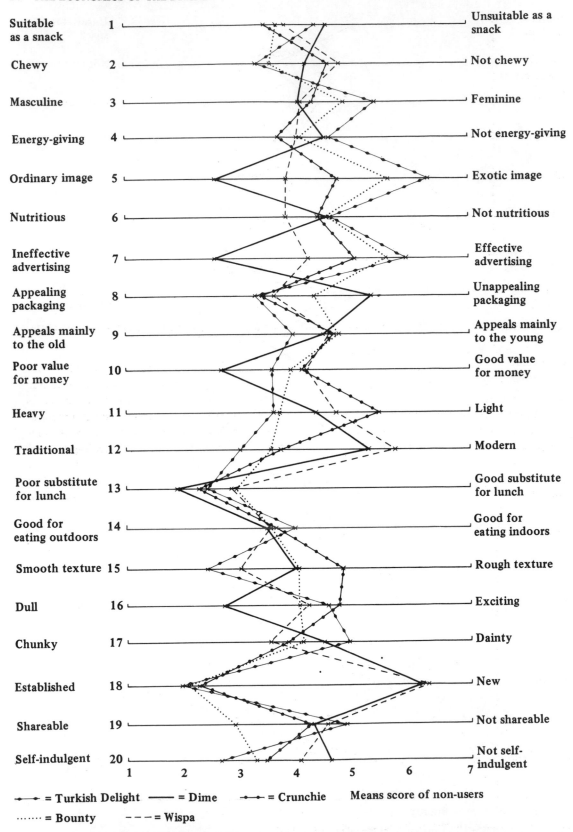

Fig. 2.2 Competitive brand analysis — brand image profiles (non-users)

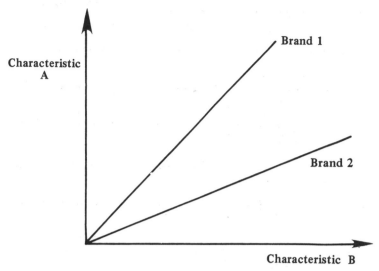

Fig. 2.3 Relationship of a brand to its characteristics

2. Income is represented by the budget constraint and prices (and therefore relative prices) are given;

Consumer preferences may be expressed in the form of an indifference map.

In Figure 2.4 point *A* represents the vector of characteristics attainable by spending all income on Brand 1; point *B* represents the vector of characteristics attainable by spending all income on Brand 2; *AB* is the efficiency frontier. This consists of points representing the characteristics vector attainable resulting from the consumption of each of the brands separately (at *A* and *B*) and consuming them in linear combination (those points between *A* and *B*). Thus *Q* represents the sum of the characteristics attainable from the consumption of Brand 1 yielding *OR* characteristics or Brand 2 yielding *OS*. *AB* therefore represents the maximum amounts of characteristics *A* and *B* obtainable from Brands 1 and 2, given prices and incomes. *OAB* is the set of all characteristics available from Brands 1 and 2. The shape of the efficiency frontier *AB* will be the same for all consumers. Differences in incomes will

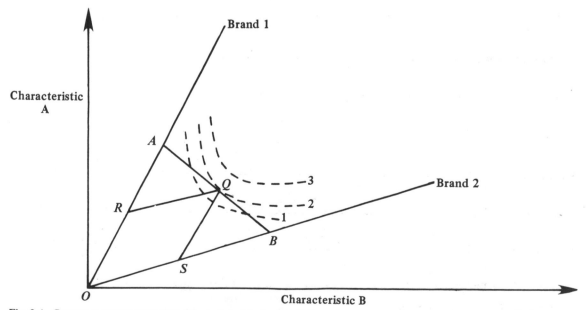

Fig. 2.4 Consumer equilibrium with 2 brands and 2 characteristics

result in the frontier being further out or closer in but its shape will remain the same, given relative prices and a fixed number of goods. It will change if relative prices alter or may do so if new goods are introduced or existing ones withdrawn.

If we add a consumer's indifference map to the information we have, we find the consumer's optimum position is at Q which is the point of tangency between the efficiency frontier and indifference curve 2. At this point the marginal rate of substitution of the characteristics in consumption is equal to their price ratio. With a different indifference map the optimum point could be at A or B or at any point on AB.

Each consumer thus faces two choices: an efficiency choice in rejecting all those combinations of characteristics (and indirectly goods) falling within the characteristics set OAB which are not on AB, and a preference choice in selecting a point A or B or between A and B on the efficiency frontier.

Whereas the efficiency choice is an objective choice and will be common to all consumers, the preference choice depends upon the preference of the individual consumer.

2.6 LANCASTER'S APPROACH – A PROPOSED EXTENSION

Because of the assumption of objective perception these rays are in standard positions for all consumers. If we were to relax this assumption of objectivity then a modification to Lancaster's approach could be considered.

The modification to Lancaster's model that the above analysis suggests is that instead of the characteristics set of the brand applying objectively to all consumers, it applies subjectively to each consumer. Thus, taking the case of a brand with two characteristics (A and B) and three consumers (X_1, X_2, X_3), then if the consumers' perceptions of the ratio of characteristic A to characteristic B obtained from the brand differ, the rays X_1-X_3 could represent the perceived amount of each characteristic obtained from units of the brand by each of the consumers. This is illustrated in Figure 2.5.

Further, it is likely that for different brands and products the variations between different consumers' perceptions will themselves vary. This variation may be seen to be a function of:

1. The number of characteristics which the brand possesses.
2. The range of uses to which the brand may be put.

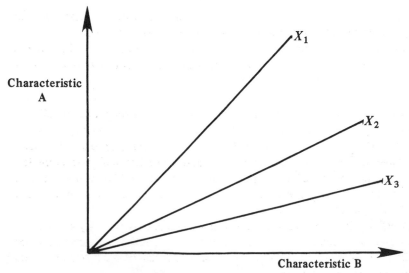

Fig. 2.5 Consumers' perceptions of a brand in characteristics space

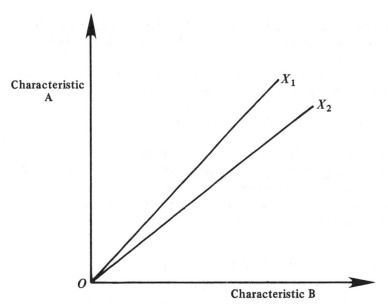

Fig. 2.6 Consumer brand perceptions in characteristics space: consistent values

3. Consumers' perceptions of the brand image as created by promotional activity.
4. Variations in types of consumer and their exposure to promotional activity.

For some brands therefore it may be possible to reach the position illustrated in Figure 2.6 where, again in the two-characteristic case, 95 per cent of individual consumer perceptions fall into the area enclosed by OX_1 and OX_2 for the brand. This area will be smaller in situations where:

1. The brand has few, distinctive characteristics.
2. The brand has a definite usage.
3. The brand image created by promotion is unambiguous and precise.
4. The brand is purchased by similar types of consumers.

With other brands the position illustrated in Figure 2.7 may be more appropriate where 95 per cent of individual consumer perceptions fall into the wider area enclosed by OX_1 and OX_2.

With these assumptions the analysis of demand theory by Lancaster would apply, but to the individual rather than the market as a whole. It would bring the analysis by Lancaster much closer to the approach used in market research practice. This will be discussed later.

It should be noted that criticisms of Lancaster's approach have been made by Auld who introduces the concept of negative characteristics.[11] These can be incorporated into the model as follows: if the characteristic has objectively negative utility, e.g., the effects on health from smoking particular brands of cigarette (as expressed for example by tar content) it is no longer realistic to assume that a brand with more of all characteristics is objectively preferable to a brand with less of all characteristics. The shape of the consumers' (subjective) indifference curves will also change. This would seem to reduce the value of the model in that the practical applications proposed by Lancaster are invalidated if the shape of the efficiency frontier cannot be presumed.

However, by taking the inverse of the utility value of the negative characteristic (or by subtracting the amount of the negative characteristic possessed by a particular brand from the maximum possible) a positive scale can be established and the problem overcome. That is, the less of the negative characteristic possessed, the more the positive scale will read.

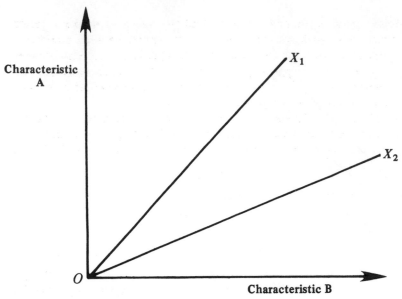

Fig. 2.7 Consumer brand perceptions in characteristics space: disparate views

Hendler has also criticized Lancaster's model.[12] His criticism is based on the assumption made by Lancaster that:

> the characteristics possessed by a good or a combination of goods are, in principle at least, objective and the same for all consumers. The utility derived by the consumer on the other hand, is subjective and depends on his preference function.

Hendler refutes the implicit Lancaster assumption of non-negativity of marginal utility which he states is:

> a very restrictive assumption which transcends the assumption that the marginal utility of a good is always positive . . . Lancaster's model . . . precludes the possibility that a generally desirable characteristic may at some subjective point contain negative marginal utility but at some subjective stage consumers obtain negative marginal utility from extra units of the characteristics; this must be incorporated into the shape of the consumer's in-difference curve.

Incorporating negative characteristics is important if the model is to have marketing applications, as it can be argued that most brands contain negative characteristics which must be outweighed by positive characteristics if the brand is to be purchased.

2.7 LANCASTER'S APPROACH AND MARKET RESEARCH PRACTICE – A COMPARISON

On balance, Lancaster's approach is important because it moves economic theory a step closer to practical application. One can see the links with marketing practice for brands. This link was seen by Ratchford who concludes his discussion by stating that, using Lancaster's approach, 'sales and brand shares could be estimated for the simulated efficiency frontier by cumulating estimates of the most preferred brands appropriately weighted by expenditures across consumers'. This 'differs little from current practice in market research'.[13] Thus he states that 'given a distribution of preferences estimated for a representative sample, reactions to price changes, changes in brand attributes, or the appearance of new brands could be stimulated by varying the efficiency frontier to represent each of these changes and estimating the corresponding change in brand preference.'

If we consider, as an example, brand positioning, then we find that much of market research practice involves identifying dimensions which consumers use to differentiate between brands and trying to measure individuals' perceptions of these dimensions and their preference patterns between them.[14] Data reduction methods such as factor analysis are used to attempt to find the most meaningful dimensions.[15] Shocker and Srinivasan refer to relevant dimensions as 'actionable', that is, those connected with product characteristics which are of use in product development.[16]

Gap analysis is used to identify gaps in characteristics space, often in relation to ideal brands where new brands could be positioned. Non-metric multidimensional scaling[17] using perceived attributes as dimensions in a perceptual map, again using ideal brands, can identify for an individual consumer:

1. Which dimensions are used to make similarity judgements.
2. How each brand is perceived relative to others along these dimensions.
3. What is the location of the ideal point.

Thus both perception and preference measures are taken for the consumer, leading to the identification of market opportunities for new brand positioning. The aim of multidimensional scaling is to determine the underlying structure and dimensionality of a market. This is attempted by collecting simple ordinal data from which is derived a perceptual map. The dimensions of this map are named outside of the methodology by referring to the brand projections of the axes. This makes an interesting comparison with Lancaster's approach to applying his model which compares brands in identified measurable characteristics without researching the relevance of those characteristics to individual consumers.[8]

From the brief description of the market research techniques of use in brand positioning studies, there are obvious similarities between the terms used and approaches taken in these studies and those in Lancaster's theory. The major difference would seem to be that market research 'dimensions' are not necessarily objective and measurable as Lancaster's characteristics are, but are individual subjective perceptions of brand identity, capable of expression in both rational and emotional terms.

There would seem to be close similarities between Lancaster's approach and practical market research, especially if Lancaster's assumption of objective and measurable characteristics were to be amended as outlined above.

2.8 THE ECONOMIC DETERMINANTS OF DEMAND

The following aspects of demand can be isolated when examining the economics of consumer behaviour:

2.8.1 Price

The economists' demand curve refers to the relationship between quantity demanded and price.

Price is of paramount importance in the treatment of demand by economists. As we shall see in Chapter 4 on price competition, price as a competitive tool is quantitative, unambiguous and unidimensional. Other competitive tools, such as advertising, are qualitative, ambiguous and multidimensional in their effects on consumers. Price has a direct impact on sales revenue which cannot be ignored. The indirect effects of other competitive tools explain in part the concentration on pricing in many economic treatments of demand. It can also be assumed that other competitive effects have a pricing implication, i.e., can be translated to a price adjustment and hence treated within price. However, psychological effects of price such as odd-number pricing, e.g., setting a retail at £5.99 rather than £6 because of the supposed effect on demand, are difficult to treat from an economic point of view. These issues will be covered in Chapter 4. The economist's treatment of demand does not take account in itself of the practical complexity of the price including:

— Changes over time (e.g., the expectation of future price changes which can affect current demand).
— Pricing aspects other than recommended price, e.g., special offers, quantity discounts, credit, trading stamps.
— The use of price as a marketing weapon.
— Objectives other than short-run profit maximization.
— The quality implications of price.

If these factors could be taken into account then economic theory could become more realistic in accounting for practice phenomena such as:

— Market penetration pricing.
— 'Skimming' pricing.
— 'Odd-number' pricing.
— Positive-sloping demand curves.

In practice some form of value-for-money comparison is necessary to take account of high levels of brand differentiation which occur in practice. This is discussed in the chapter on price.

2.8.2 Pricing of other products

Some account needs to be taken of the prices of competitive products. Economic theory provides the measure of cross-elasticity. It can be argued that all goods compete for a larger share of an individual's limited budget, although in practice only similar goods will probably influence each other's demand by price changes.

Again, as will be seen in Chapter 4, goods which are substitutes will have a positive cross-elasticity measure and complements will have a negative value. It is the range of brands which a company provides that is of importance in marketing strategy. Attempts will be made to maximize profits (or meet alternative company objectives) by manipulation of price across the range of brand options. This is likely to take the effect of company estimates of consumer price reactions bearing in mind competitive pricing policies.

2.8.3 Income

Engel curves are used to link changes in income level with quantity demanded. This measurement device can be used in practice through either cross-sectional analysis or time-series analysis. In marketing terms this is a very helpful link for product groups but not necessarily for individual brands. Much market research data are available from a variety of sources which use cross-sectional analysis and influence on demand for goods.

An income elasticity measure is used to link changes in income with changes in demand. A particular problem exists with durable goods because of their indivisibility, as families are only likely to buy one item. It is the threshold level which is important in practice.

If a crucial threshold-level income can be identified (*OA* in Figure 2.8) then a target group is specified to which marketing action can be directed. Again market research data provide information on penetration levels of different consumer durables by households. Table 2.1 illustrates the time trend of this penetration. If such data were further analysed by income level of households then it would provide detailed Engel curve information and may lead to the identification of a threshold income level for the purchase of each consumer durable.

In practical terms, what is much more likely is that income is one of a number of factors affecting

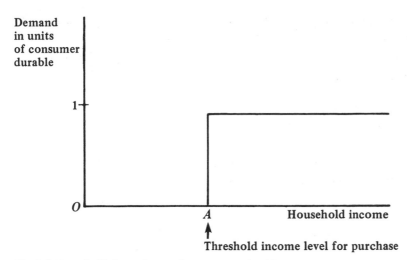

Fig. 2.8 Household demand curve for consumer durables

demand. The link between income and demand also needs to take account of:

— absolute level of income
— relative level of income
— expectations about future income levels

if it is to have practical usefulness. In other words, the social implications of income need to be taken into account in explaining the effect of income levels on demand.

2.8.4 Tastes

Economists treat those factors that shape consumer preferences under the generic title of 'tastes' and assume that any change in tastes is likely to occur only slowly and hence can be assumed constant in the short term, or when dealing with aggregates.

However, for individual brands it is not practical to assume that tastes do not change. Here economists try to link tastes with external observable and measurable characteristics such as age-group, house ownership, etc.

As noted above, it is in the area of tastes that the economic approach to demand analysis is perhaps most tenuous. Lancaster's approach, for example, would be difficult to apply to brands in competition in a market which have very similar objectively measurable characteristics but which make subjective emotional appeals in brand image creation through advertising. Studies have illustrated the lack of discrimination between brands by consumers in 'blind tests' in which the brand name is withheld from the respondents.[18] The differentiation between brands is achieved through subjective rather than objective means. Traditional economic analysis would find this extremely difficult to deal with in any meaningful way.

A further complication in practical demand analysis is the issue of brand loyalty. Inert buying, i.e., buying the same brand repeatedly over time is known as brand loyalty. Brand-loyal buyers are obviously desirable from a marketing point of view. The correlates of brand loyalty will vary with the type of product but would be expected to include satisfaction with the brand, which precludes the search for alternatives. This can be seen as a risk-aversion strategy by consumers: if they feel that the current brand bought meets their needs they can avoid the risk of potential dissatisfaction with an alternative brand by repurchasing the same brand repeatedly.

Repeat buying is of vital significance in practical brand-marketing analyses. For so-called fast-moving consumer goods, success depends on repurchase rather than, as with consumer durables, on

Table 2.1 Household penetration of consumer durables 1971–82

	1971	1972	1973	1974	1975	1976	1977	1978	1979	1980	1981	1982
No of households in Great Britain at 30 June each year (units in '000s)	18 315	18 560	18 800	19 000	19 155	19 310	19 465	19 620	19 775	19 958	20 135	20 270
White goods & major consumer durables	%	%	%	%	%	%	%	%	%	%	%	%
washing machine (i)	66	67	68	70	71	73	75	76	75	77	80	80
clothes dryer (i)	25	26	28	30	31	31	32	34	33	38	37	38
vacuum cleaner (ii)	84	85	89	89	90	90	91	92	94	93	94	95
freestanding gas cooker (i)	59	58	58	57	57	57	56	55	56	53	55	55
freestanding electric cooker (i)	40	41	42	43	43	43	43	43	41	42	40	39
single door refrigerator (i)	NA	NA	NA	NA	75	75	75	74	75	72	71	69
fridge freezer (i)	NA	NA	NA	NA	5	8	10	13	15	19	22	24
separate freezer (i)	3	5	8	10	13	16	20	24	25	28	29	31
Heating insulation/ bathroom fitments												
central heating system (iv)	34	38	40	46	49	51	54	54	56	58	59	61
electric space heating (i)	84	86	84	83	80	75	73	70	65	63	59	59
gas space heating (i)	34	36	37	39	41	42	44	44	45	47	45	49
oil/paraffin heater (i)	28	28	28	26	23	22	21	21	20	16	13	12
water heating (i)	96	97	97	98	98	98	98	97	97	97	96	97
double glazed windows (iv)	NA	5	6	8	9	10	11	14	15	18	21	23
loft insulation (iv)	NA	NA	NA	32	38	38	42	45	51	54	60	63
cavity wall insulator (iv)	NA	NA	NA	2	2	3	3	3	5	6	6	7
shower fitment (i)	NA	NA	NA	NA	NA	NA	12	17	21	22	23	24
DIY and gardening (iii)												
powered tools (saw/sander)	NA	NA	NA	NA	NA	NA	7	10	8	13	15	18
electric drill	NA	NA	NA	NA	NA	NA	36	37	40	41	44	51
power lawn mower	14	18	22	27	30	32	35	36	40	41	42	48
hand lawn mower	38	36	33	30	29	27	25	24	20	21	19	21
Television/video												
colour television (ii)	6	17	30	39	45	51	58	67	69	73	78	78
colour and/or monochrome television (ii)	94	95	95	97	96	96	97	97	96	97	97	98
video recorder (iv)	NA	NA	NA	NA	NA	NA	NA	NA	1	2	6	13

Note: as at (i) 31 March (ii) 30 June (iii) 30 September (iv) 31 December   NA = not available

Sample size: 25 000 households in Great Britain

Source: AGB Home Audit, Audits of Great Britain Ltd. Quoted in *Market Research Society Yearbook 1984*

penetration levels. In some markets consumers will have a shortlist or repertoire of brands they will consider buying on each repurchase occasion. This is not complete brand loyalty but it is, nevertheless, of great importance to marketing practitioners. If a brand does not appear on this shortlist, it has no chance of purchase. In this situation, it is not feasible to forecast the next brand purchased accurately but the probability of repurchase can be estimated from past purchasing activity.[6] This gives an insight into the practical complexities of brand choice. Different consumers will have different repertoires of brands which makes the market definition from a consumer viewpoint extremely difficult.

It is beyond the scope of this book to examine in detail the non-economic influences on demand. It should be noted that tastes in particular have a vexing role to play from the economists' viewpoint. Texts which specialize in examining choice behaviour such as those by Tuck[19] and Foxall[20] in the UK and by Engel and Blackwell[10] and by Howard and Sheth[21] in the US emphasize the difficulties involved in the individual's choice process. An example will illustrate this point. If one is considering consumer choice of brands of chocolate confectionery for, say, a snack between meals then in practice different consumers will consider different alternative choices. Each will have an evoked set — a shortlist of alternatives considered. The wide range of possibilities of brands for inclusion on this shortlist may well extend beyond other chocolate confectionery brands. One consumer may also consider a packet of crisps, an apple, a yoghurt, as alternatives, for example. In other words the market as defined by consumers may extend across traditional product boundaries. The concept of 'anytime food' accepts this wide-ranging choice. However, to construct any type of model to simulate such a choice process would be extremely difficult at the individual level.

As noted above, the concentration in economic analysis on a higher level of aggregation neatly side-steps this problem. The most important question to be answered at the outset of demand analysis must be: what is the paramount reason for studying demand at all? The answer to this question will guide the methodology to be used.

2.9 SALES FORECASTING

The above discussion of the difficulties in demand analysis can be summarized by an examination of one reason for undertaking a demand analysis, that of sales forecasting.

Quantification of demand may be required in order to plan production, to decide whether or not to introduce a new brand or drop an existing brand, or to identify the potential market size, for example. The bases for the forecast can include past sales level projected into the future (time-series analysis,[22] econometric models[23]) or market research surveys of buyer intentions[24] or from opinions, e.g., of the sales force or distributors or outside experts or consultants.

In economic analysis the emphasis is heavily on the first of these types: projecting past data into the future using regression analysis.[25] Concentration has been on industry-level studies or product-group studies rather than on individual brand analyses. One major reason for this is the lack of sufficient past data. Brands have short lives when compared with product groups — the Lydia Pinkham's Compound example of Palda[1] can be considered an exception. This means that only short data series are available which leads to a difficulty in producing accurate regression models for future extrapolations. As we shall see when considering new brand development, there are great difficulties in forecasting likely sales for specific brands using traditional time-series analyses unless a comparison can be made with an existing product in the market or with the same brand in an existing (e.g., overseas) market. This can lead to accuracy problems if the same approach is applied in a different market setting in which demand characteristics may be very different.

Existing brand sales forecasts need to take account of competitive marketing activity as well as assuming a particular level of marketing expenditure on the brand to be examined. In practice, the use of marketing research techniques tends to concentrate on the individual consumer and to attempt to assess from this study the probability of purchase which can be scaled up to provide a sales forecast. The emphasis is on the individual response to a brand. In contrast an economic study of a market may begin with the overall sales potential (number of potential customers x average purchase rates) to be scaled down by assessing the market share which a brand could be expected to attain in a competitive situation. By taking this aggregation approach, the individual consumer response is not specifically assessed, but rather the average response is the emphasis of study.

Thus in sales forecasting practice use can be made of an economic approach but this will often be of limited value in assessing the market response to a specific brand and its idiosyncrasies.

2.10 SUMMARY

This chapter has set out to defend the contribution of economics in demand analysis which seems to be underrated and unfashionable. The starting point of the criticism, the concept of rationality, is shown to be very wide ranging, in practice encompassing most purchasing behaviour.

Lancaster's approach is considered in some detail especially in relation to the similarities and differences in approach with market research practice.

The level of aggregation of the study of demand is considered and the contribution of economics is considered at each level.

Sales forecasting is taken as an example of a practical application in which it is possible to study demand either at the individual consumer level or in aggregate.

REFERENCES

1. Palda, K. S. (1969) *Economic Analysis for Marketing Decisions*, Prentice-Hall, Englewood Cliffs, New Jersey.
2. Becker, G. S. (1971) *Economic Theory*, Knopf, New York.
3. Koutsoyiannis, A. (1982) *Non-Price Decisions*, Macmillan, London, pp. 118–49.
4. Douglas, J., G. A. Field and L. X. Tarvey (1967) *Human Behaviour in Marketing*, Charles Merrill, Colombus, Ohio, Ch. 4.
5. Palda, K. S. (1964) *The Measurement of Cumulative Advertising Effects*, Prentice-Hall, Englewood Cliffs, New Jersey.
6. Ehrenberg, A. S. C. (1972) *Repeat Buying*, North-Holland, Amsterdam.
7. Dickens, J. (1982) 'The fresh cream cakes market: the use of qualitative research as part of a consumer research program; in *Applied Marketing and Social Research*, U. Bradley (ed.), Van Nostrand Reinhold, Wokingham, pp. 4–43.
8. Lancaster, K. J. (1971) *Consumer Demand: A New Approach*, Columbia University Press, Columbia.
9. Delozier, M. W. (1976) *The Marketing Communications Process*, McGraw-Hill, Kogakusha, Tokyo.
10. Engel, J. F. and R. D. Blackwell (1982) *Consumer Behaviour*, 4th ed, Dryden, Hinsdale, Illinois.
11. Auld, D. (1972) 'Imperfect knowledge and new theory of demand', *Journal of Political Economy*, **80**, 1287–94.
12. Hendler, R. (1975) 'Lancaster's new approach to consumer demand and its limitations', *American Economic Review*, **65**, 1, 194–9.
13. Ratchford, B. T. (1975) 'The new economic theory of consumer behaviour, an interpretive essay', *Journal of Consumer Research*, **2**, 3, 65–75.
14. Fitzroy, P. T. (1976) *Analytical Methods for Marketing Management*, McGraw-Hill, Maidenhead, Ch. 2.
15. Aaker, D. A. (1971) *Multivariate Analysis in Marketing*, Wordsworth, New York.
16. Shocker, A. D. and V. Srinivasan (1974) 'A consumer based methodology for the identification of new product ideas', *Management Science*, **20**, 921–37.
17. Green, P. E. and V. R. Rao (1972) *Applied Multi-dimensional Scaling*, Holt Rinehart and Winston, New York.
18. Allison, R. I. and K. P. Uhl (1964) 'Influence of beer brand identification on taste perception', *Journal of Marketing Research*, **1**, 3, 36–9.
19. Tuck, M. (1976) *How do we Choose?*, Methuen, London.
20. Foxall, G. R. (1983) *Consumer Choice*, Macmillan, London.
21. Howard, J. A. and J. N. Sheth (1969) *The Theory of Buyer Behaviour*, Wiley, New York.

22. Thomopoulos, N. T. (1980) *Applied Forecasting Methods for Management*, Prentice-Hall, Englewood Cliffs, New Jersey.
23. Stewart, J. (1976) *Understanding Econometrics*, Hutchinson, London.
24. Crimp, M. (1981) *The Market Research Process*, Prentice-Hall, London.
25. Savage, C. I. and J. R. Small (1967) *Introduction to Management Economics*, Hutchinson, London, Ch. 8.

THREE
MARKET STRUCTURE AND THE BRAND

3.1 INTRODUCTION

This Chapter sets the scene for the discussion of market conduct which follows in Chapters 4 and 5. It examines the relationship between the brand and market structure, and addresses the question: 'Does the competitive role of the brand vary with market structure?' This is approached firstly by an examination of the role of the brand in each major type of market structure and secondly by exploring the impact on the brand of a number of structural considerations. Thus the economic concept of market structure is linked to practical brand-marketing strategy.

3.2 BRAND POLICY UNDER CONDITIONS OF PERFECT COMPETITION*

In theory there is no need to consider the relationship between the brand and a perfectly competitive market structure — there isn't one! The features of perfect competition include:

1. Many firms, each with a small proportion of the total market share (i.e., very low concentration ratio).
2. No barriers to entry or exit from the market, subject to finding a seller or buyer.
3. Homogeneity of products — hence no opportunity for branding.
4. Perfect information about suppliers, products and prices.
5. Independent decision-making with no collision.

These conditions would lead to a perfectly elastic demand curve (i.e., horizontal). There would be no point in trying to create a brand image because of features (3) and (4).

We can create a slightly more practical situation by making minimal changes to the above features as follows:

(a) Retain features (1) and (2).
(b) Assume homogeneity of *physical* products only.
(c) Drop feature (4).

---

* The theory of market structure is not considered here. Readers are referred to Baumol[1] or Pickering[2] for a detailed discussion of the economics of market structure.

(*d*) Change from the static analysis of perfect competition theory to a more realistic dynamic analysis, i.e., introduce time as a feature. Barriers to entry could develop over time.

Using these amended assumptions it is feasible to examine the relationship between the brand and this market structure.

Firstly, a role can now be defined for promotion. A firm would need to inform potential clients of its existence and about existing and new products. In economic terms this is valuable to consumers as it reduces the cost of searching for information. Stigler defines identification as one of the major costs of search.[3] In practice, as noted by Lambin,[4] it is difficult to differentiate informative from persuasive advertising, as will be discussed in Chapter 5.

Secondly, it may be feasible to differentiate a product from its competitors, using non-physical product features as the basis for brand creation. Emotional benefits or other psychological appeals could be used. In practice there is almost always some service as well as product aspect to a transaction. This service component can be used to differentiate a firm from its rivals.

Thirdly, developing this service aspect, the use of effective personal selling and public relations techniques and wider or more efficient distribution of the product which provides increased customer convenience are methods which could be used to differentiate one firm's product from its rivals.

Over time, the above factors could lead to higher prices as the same physical product is supplied with differing service mixes by different suppliers. If customers appreciate, and are willing to pay for, higher levels of service then price levels may vary. This could involve the creation of brands or may be based on the firm's name and reputation. Over time, these factors could lead to the formation of brand images using marketing techniques.

Thus by considering the role of the brand in a market structure which, although based on perfect competition, involves some relaxation of assumptions, it is seen to be possible to postulate a role for the brand.

Another way of approaching this issue would be to concentrate on feature (1) of perfect competition listed above, which implies a low degree of market concentration. A practical situation analogous to this would be the role of marketing in the small firm in an industry of small firms.

Much attention is being lavished on the generation of new small businesses which is heralded as a solution to unemployment problems and to the regeneration of economic activity. If failure for many small businesses is to be avoided, the business initiator needs to possess or develop a whole range of business skills.

When a small business starts, the driving force behind it is often the need of the initiator to avoid unemployment, funded by redundancy payments, or the need for independence. Usually the initiator has a specific skill to exploit. In most cases this skill is production-related. It is often craft-based or has been developed during the previous working life or has been a hobby or an interest of the initiator. This means that the initiator has to develop a wide range of other skills in order to manage the development of the business effectively. Very often the initial business problems concern finance and cash flow, problems which often remain paramount during the early life of the business. Form-filling can very easily become a way of life, with the administrative need for VAT returns, PAYE returns, National Insurance forms, etc.

The major gap in the initiator's developing abilities is often a lack of marketing skills. Besides producing and financing goods or services, the new business has to market this produce profitably. This does not just include selling, but a whole range of activities such as packaging, advertising, sales promotions, public relations, market research, pricing and distributing the produce as well. Each of these activities needs to be combined to form a comprehensive, actionable marketing plan which will integrate with the other skills within the business to enable it to compete effectively in the market place. For example, market research can be used to identify and to explore the needs of potential customers, to determine perceived weaknesses in competitors' produce and to forecast likely demand. Examples of the problems which occur when marketing skills are lacking in small businesses can be found in a range of business types which are illustrated by recently undertaken consultancy work.

Case 1 A long-established builders' merchant had decided to try to cash in on the rapidly developing retail DIY hypermarket trend without any real experience of retail marketing skills. Consequently, some of the decisions made led to longer-term problems. In particular, the siting of the retail store and the advertising strategy used were not having the desired effect on sales against the intensive advertising campaigns mounted by the large national chains established in the market. These decisions were made without a wide consideration of their longer-term implications especially in the site choice, which was almost irreversible without a very high cost. Advertising decisions were made on a week-to-week basis without an overall theme. This *ad hoc* basis was the result of a lack of development of an advertising strategy which could have directed the company effort. Decisions were made after a simplistic consideration of limited insights by the managing director. Expenditure on consultancy was needed to attempt to put the business back on the tracks.

Case 2 A small retail outlet had obtained an agency for a high-quality imported range of furniture. While the company had salesmen highly skilled in personal selling and closing a sale, they lacked the wider range of marketing skills necessary to create a high level of confidence among discerning potential purchasers about the ability of the agency to meet sales and servicing needs in a highly competitive business and to generate the quality image required to match the manufacturer's national advertising campaign. Again, consultancy provided a range of sales promotions and media advertising which were based on market research findings from a survey of past customers. The agency was able to make a much more positive impact on customers by the resulting marketing approach.

Case 3 A theatre company were persuaded to have an audience research study carried out to investigate how ticket receipts could be increased. The study provided detailed background data on the audience constitution with actionable recommendations. However, because of the lack of marketing expertise within the management team of the theatre company, there was great difficulty in the implementation of the findings. The strength and interest of the management team lay in the artistic aspects of the theatre company rather than the marketing aspects. The basic marketing premise of meeting customer needs was greeted with much suspicion by the management team who worked to the principle of 'art for art's sake', customers' needs being of secondary importance. Audiences were not, therefore, increasing in size.

The message from these varied examples is clear. A lack of marketing skills leads to costly mistakes being made and/or a failure to make the most of sales opportunities. There is a need therefore for the management of a small company to be educated in marketing techniques and applications before it commits itself to major decisions which can lead to costly, irreversible mistakes being made.

The areas of marketing which need to be developed seem to be logically considered in the following sequence:

1. As marketing can be defined as meeting the consumer needs profitably, the first step is to consider these needs. This can be done by market research, using all sources of information available to understand the customer better. These sources could include: salesmen's contacts with customers, distributors, or a more systematic survey of customers and their needs. Above all it involves the development of empathy: seeing the company and its products from the customers' point of view. These data can be collected at low cost.[5]

2. The second stage is to use this intelligence in the making of marketing decisions. An identification of customers and their purchasing habits, attitudes, characteristics, etc., leads to a fuller under-

standing of the need for:

(a) An advertising strategy to inform, persuade and reinforce views held as necessary to create a successful image of the company and its products in the minds of the consumers.
(b) A profitable pricing policy based on demand factors as well as competitive and cost influences.
(c) A distribution strategy which takes into account the customers' purchasing and shopping habits.
(d) A sales and sales promotion strategy which presents the product as part of an overall appeal which is likely to persuade the prospect to buy.

3. A review or feedback system to examine the effectiveness of these decisions in the light of sales attainments, customer and distributor reaction and competitive response. The marketing process is a dynamic interactive one which requires constant attention. It must be fully integrated into the business philosophy and activity rather than treated in a piecemeal way using *ad hoc* considerations.

3.3 BRAND POLICY IN A MONOPOLISTIC MARKET STRUCTURE

In theory, features of monopolistic market structure include:

1. The firm is the industry (hence the brand is the product).
2. The monopolist restricts his output with a higher price than in perfectly competitive conditions.

The economist's considerations of monopoly are supply-side rather than demand-side based. The demand-side argument about monopoly would be based on Levitt's views that all products compete if a broad enough view is taken.[6] In the final analysis all products are in competition for a larger share of consumers' limited budgets. In the short run consumers may have little choice in some circumstances, for example, having purchased an IBM computer, compatible peripherals and software must be purchased if the need arises. In the longer term wider choice may be feasible, replacing the whole computer system in the above example. It could be argued that the initial decision to purchase the computer would have included consideration of the inherent short-run restrictions on associated equipment purchasing.

It can be argued that in the longer term, British Telecom is in competition with the Post Office and even with British Rail, British Airways, car makers and oil companies, in the sense that consumers could decide to telephone or send a letter rather than make a personal visit. For example, a market research company may have to decide whether to use postal, telephone or personal interviews in a survey. This argument culminates in the assertion that there is no such thing as a monopolist when viewed from the consumer's perspective in the longer term.

To consider the role of the brand under these conditions with regard to the product, it may be feasible to differentiate the monopolist's product to add appeal to market segments based on usage characteristics. Off-peak electricity and telephone calls are examples of this strategy which can lead into a diversification policy designed to move the demand curve for the monopolist's product to the right. British Rail's move into the holiday market (based, of course, on rail travel) is an example of this diversification policy. Value could also be added by improved service aspects or by differential service levels associated with the monopolist's product. In some cases this leads to the basic product being fragmented into a range of brands each marketed to specific market segments based on usage characteristics, with the aim of increasing overall demand and/or sales revenue and profit performance.

With regard to promotion it could be argued that there is no need for it as consumers have to buy the brand anyway, although to follow Levitt's arguments, promotion is necessary to build the perceived benefits of the product and to thus shift the demand curve to the right at least in the long term. It is often difficult to persuade people to shift attitudes, for example to switch from gas to electric cooking would involve not only an attitude change for many consumers but also the cost of switching which could be high. Using MEAL data[7] for 1983 in the UK there were five monopolists amongst the top 30 advertisers, led by the British Telecommunications in 6th position overall (see Table 3.1, page 34), spending £24.4m on media advertising including 22.9 per cent on TV advertising.

Because of the high profile of many monopolists, public relations are often a very important part of a monopolist's marketing strategy. In early 1985 British Rail launched an advertising campaign which stressed the helpfulness of their staff to the public. Corporate image building which stresses efficiency and cost-effectiveness can often forestall public criticism in what can be a sensitive area.

If a market segmentation policy is adopted by the monopolist it is often the case that discrimination can be effectively used to reach more price-sensitive segments. In particular, if the organization uses a marginal cost basis for internal cost allocation then additional marginal revenue from low price sales often involves little or no marginal cost and is thus worth gaining. For example off-peak telephone calls at a low rate help to spread usage more evenly. Extra off-peak usage of existing equipment can have a very low marginal cost of provision, thus providing a significant profit contribution.

Thus, in summary, there is potential for the use of the brand with associated marketing activity in monopolistic market structures, in some instances.

3.4 BRAND POLICY UNDER CONDITIONS OF MONOPOLISTIC COMPETITION

It is perhaps worth noting that, in taking a practical approach to market structure, the distinction between types of structure become blurred. Thus, for example, some of the discussion in the above sections could have been included in this section on monopolistic competition. Oligopoly is included as a special case of monopolistic competition. Many of the features of this market structure are marketing related:

1. Product differentiation through branding is a common feature. Each company supplies brands which customers believe to be different from competitive brands. The basis for this perceived difference is the brand image created by the use of marketing methods. The aim of this branding can be to attempt a monopoly situation in which the brand is regarded as a product of which its supplier is the monopolist.
2. It is often difficult to define the industry because of the production of differentiated products.
3. There are few firms within the industry and they are interdependent. The decisions of one firm have effects on other firms in the industry.
4. Competition is not just based on price but on the use of promotion, innovation, the threat of new entry and on branding.

The role of brands in this market structure is of paramount importance. It can be considered by examining each of the major marketing variables in turn.

3.4.1 Price

Price competition is often avoided by tacit agreement in favour of non-price competition under conditions of monopolistic competition. Koutsoyiannis suggested a number of reasons for this:[8]

1. Price cuts can easily be matched by rivals quickly. This can lead to a ruinous price war. Brand and advertising changes take time to match.
2. Technological progress has provided opportunities for branding and product diversity as a form of competition.

3. Tastes have changed as income levels have risen, leading to a demand for increased quality and variety.
4. Firms can influence demand via advertising, sales efforts and new product development as well as by price.
5. Price reductions may be associated with real or perceived quality reductions.
6. To avoid time lags in matching rivals' actions, firms continually innovate, advertise and promote.
7. Brand changes are less obvious than price changes to buyers.
8. Price clusters tend to form and provide customary price levels which are often retained through time while brand quantity or quality is changed.
9. Price rises are often disguised by brand improvements or other promotions.
10. Brand differences make price discrimination more effective in various segments with different elasticities.

Thus in many circumstances price competition is not in the best interests of the firms in the industry. Occasionally price wars break out. A good example is the attempt by Laker Airways to undercut established airlines' prices on the North Atlantic run which sent shock waves through the industry. The subsequent collapse of Laker Airways has resulted in multimillion dollar lawsuits in the US emanating from the allegation that the major airlines colluded to drive Laker out of business, in breach of US anti-trust legislation. Another, less dramatic, example is the retail pricing of petrol in the UK. Price differences expressed in tenths of one pence are affecting consumer choice of petrol station, and extremely complex price structures have evolved as the oil companies assess the local area competition around each of their retail petrol stations. Daily price changes are not uncommon as the actions and reactions of competitors occur.

A price war occurred in the early 1980s in the pricing of cross-channel journeys between Sealink, European Ferries and P and O, probably due to excess capacity. This ended when British Rail divested and Sealink was sold off, and in early 1985 European Ferries took over the P and O cross-channel operation.

In theoretical terms, Sweezy[9] and Stigler[10] advanced the concept of the kinked demand curve to explain the observed lack of price competition. This assumes that prices change only to reflect cost differences as firms each assume that if they reduce price all competitors will follow and extra sales will not result (i.e., price-inelastic demand for price falls) and no competitor will follow an upward price rise not associated with an industry-wide cost rise (i.e., price-elastic demand for price rises). This approach does not explain how the initial price is formed, however.

3.4.2 Branding

The firm's strategy is to make its products different from its competitors' in such a way that customers can be convinced that they are superior. This can be done by making the physical product different or by making the way in which the customer perceives the product different, i.e., by psychological or emotional differences. These factors can be achieved by packaging differences, by having a range of sizes, shapes, qualities, etc., by gimmicks, by after-sales service provision or perhaps most importantly by promotional activity — usually linked to at least one of the other differences.

In monopolistic competition promotion is very often *the* main form of competition. The main aim of media advertising or 'above the line' promotion is to create a definite and distinct brand image. In 1983 the top 5 advertisers in the UK, and 17 of the top 20 in terms of media expenditure, were all oligopolists as shown in Table 3.1 below.

As TV is the major medium for brand image creation, as will be seen in Chapter 5, the figures in Table 3.1, showing the very high proportion of TV advertising,* reflects the statement above.

* Imperial Tobacco with only 30 per cent TV, reflects the fact that in the UK the TV advertising of cigarettes is banned (but cigar and tobacco advertising on TV is permitted).

Table 3.1 Top 10 advertisers in the UK 1983

Position	Company	Amount Spent (£)	% Spent on TV
1	Procter and Gamble	59.9	98.7
2	Mars Confectionery Division	39.9	99.7
3	Kelloggs	28.5	98.7
4	Imperial Tobacco (Imperial Group)	26.9	30.3
5	Rowntree Mackintosh	26.5	95.3
6	British Telecommunications	24.4	22.9
7	Pedigree Pet Foods (Mars)	26.3	98.8
8	Cadbury Schweppes Confectionery Division	23.5	98.7
9	Electricity Council	21.7	75.4
10	Gallaher	21.1	32.8

Source: MEAL[7]

Other forms of promotion — 'below the line' promotions such as money-off offers, free gifts and competitions — are used to make customers try the brand or switch brands and are often used to create extra short term interest in a brand in the mature stage of its life. Such promotions can be brand demeaning in that they encourage consumers to buy the brand not for its inherent qualities but for ephemeral reasons. Such converts are likely to be least brand loyal and most easily converted back to their original brand preferences by a subsequent promotion from competitors. This is further discussed in Chapter 5.

Successful branding creates a type of monopoly situation for the firm in which a higher price can be charged for the brand to reflect perceived extra value by brand-loyal consumers, while retaining their custom. Successful branding consists of convincing potential customers that that brand alone can satisfy the customers' needs in a valued way which competing brands cannot match. It involves personalizing the brand in a way with which customers can identify. Brand loyalty can also be obtained through customer inertia or habitual purchasing in situations where they are 'passive' rather than 'favourable' in their attitude towards the brand.

The sales and distribution function has a vital role in the branding process in this market structure. Distributors often adopt selective brand-stocking policies. This is typified in grocery retailing where an oligopsony exists in the UK, with the largest six retail chains accounting for over 50 per cent of grocery retail sales. This buying power is reflected via negotiating power in lower buying-in prices. Manufacturers compete for shelf space and for good display space. The retailer may have a policy of stocking his own brand, the leading brand and perhaps the second-to-leading brand. Thus the third and fourth brands in a market may find shelf space difficult to obtain which can lead to a downward spiral as lower distribution levels lead to falling sales. This point will be developed in Chapter 8.

The key to successful marketing is the integration of the various aspects to form a meaningful whole. This is centred around the brand. Increasingly, oligopolists recognize the value of brands which can be treated in a very similar way to other fixed assets. Advertising is used over time to build a successful brand image which accumulates in effectiveness. It is very common to find that the oligopolist's major brands are long established: the Mars Bar, for example, began life in the UK in the early 1930s.

This section should illustrate the vital significance of the brand in modern business. In later chapters the detail of branding will be examined. In the remaining part of this chapter the relationship between the brand and other aspects of market structure will be examined, beginning with barriers to entry.

3.5 THE BRAND AS A BARRIER TO ENTRY

The Economist's interest in barriers to new competition within an industry stems from the effect of the existence of such barriers on price levels and profitability of firms within the industry. The threat of new competition may cause firms to modify their behaviour to avoid new entry. Sources of barriers can include:

— tariff levels on imports.
— control of raw materials.
— patent protection.
— high initial investment levels.

In the context of this book, we are concerned with the brand as a barrier to entry. Oligopolists use the technique of brand proliferation as a form of protection in many industries. If each of three oligopolists produced only one brand each, a new entrant may aim at 25 per cent of the market as a reasonable target for the new brand. If each oligopolist produced 10 brands then the new entrant's brand would be 31st rather than 4th in the market with a market-share expectation of 3 or 4 per cent as a realistic target. Of course, the new entrant could produce 10 brands itself but the cost and risk of such a strategy would probably make this extremely unlikely.

As noted in the last section, brands can be regarded as a long term investment with advertising expenditure being equivalent to a capital injection aimed at boosting future potential and at protecting the brand from competition. Advertising expenditure on brand image creation and development can thus be seen as a cost of entering and remaining in a market.

The successful brand has the same effect as if it were a separate product. It provides a type of monopoly position in that consumers recognize that other brands are not, from their perspective, competitors of the successfully branded good or service.

As Bain has pointed out, in such circumstances a new entrant would have to incur heavy marketing costs in the form of extra advertising outlays, higher distributor margins, etc., in order to compete satisfactorily.[11] This process would also take time. Many markets are very well established and new entrants can only hope to make very slow progress in terms of brand share.

Obviously there must be exceptions to the above state of affairs, otherwise markets would be completely static. The chapter on new brand development, Chapter 7, will examine how existing firms innovate. New firms could enter a market with a brand which has been successful in other markets. This process could reduce risks both on the demand side and on the supply side. On the demand side, if the brand has been a success in another market then this could mean success in the new market but this is not automatic, owing to the possibility of cultural, social, taste and other differences between markets. On the supply side, the unit cost of production is likely to be low, as sales in the brand's existing market already exist. Adding extra units may reduce unit cost still further which could be beneficial to the firm in its existing market.

Technological advances in other markets could give rise to new product developments with advantages over brands in the protected market. If the advance leads to a new product which in effect creates a new market then the existing brands in the protected market may suffer. The critical factor is the degree of consumer-perceived brand enhancement caused by the technological advance. The new brand may be perceived as a new type of product rather than being similar to existing brands. This may create a monopoly position for the new brand until such time as imitations are launched. This in turn will depend on the degree of protection which the brand enjoys.

A new manufacturer's decision whether to attempt to enter a market or not will be strongly influenced by the existing brand's perceived strengths and profitability. There is an argument that the profitability of an existing brand should be limited so as not to attract new competition. The 'success' of an existing brand may be judged primarily by its price level compared with other brands, as this is the most visible evidence of the success of a branding policy. Thus if the manufacturer's brand sells at what is perceived as a high price compared to other brands, including own label brands, then this could attract new competition into the market. The opposite view could also be taken, that the 'high price' brand is too strong to be challenged. In other words it is acting as a barrier to entry rather than an inducement to enter. How the potential new competitor views this situation will depend on his views of his own strengths and weaknesses *vis-à-vis* the market especially in relation to financial resources.

If the price of the existing brand is perceived as too low this could be taken as a signal that its manufacturer is in financial difficulties which again may or may not induce new competition to enter the market, perhaps depending primarily on the perceived market development. Other clues to brand profitability — from annual reports, from trade press or trade gossip for example — can be an input to the decision on whether to enter the new market.

As already noted the main financial cost involved in creating a brand image, besides the production cost, is often advertising cost. The level of advertising expenditure, as shown in Table 3.1, supporting a brand is often very high and importantly accumulates over time in establishing a brand image.

Another increasingly important factor is distribution. The difficulty of gaining effective distribution for a new brand can be a barrier to entry in many markets. This factor, which is concerned with distributor stocking policies, is discussed in detail in Chapter 8 and is developed below when vertical integration is considered.

The brand and brand-proliferation can act as a barrier to entry. While it is possible for the threat of new competition to restrict marketing activities, in particular through price levels, the stronger argument seems to be that by increasing the strength of the brand, the difficulty of new entry is increased and this is the preferred strategy. If oligopolists are seen as frustrated monopolists then this argument is strengthened. The brand seen as a 'fixed asset' of the manufacturer is a cornerstone of company success and is thus likely to be protected and developed accordingly.

3.6 CONTESTABLE MARKETS AND THE BRAND

A recent development in this area is the concept of contestable markets. This has been developed by Baumol[12] and is discussed in detail by Baumol, Panzar and Willig.[13] Traditionally in industrial economics, the model used to explain competition is structure → conduct → performance. Indeed in this book this route is implied, since structure is being discussed before market conduct. Thus the brand-marketing strategy follows from the type of market structure which the industry sustains.

Baumol challenges this view. His alternative is that market structure depends on the conduct of firms within the industry rather than the reverse. A perfectly contestable market is defined as one

> that is accessible to potential entrants and has the following two properties: First the potential entrants can, without restriction, serve the same market demands and use the same productive techniques as those available to the incumbent firms. Thus, there are no entry barriers. Second, the potential entrants evaluate the profitability of entry at the incumbent firms' pre-entry prices. That is, although the potential entrants recognise that an expansion of industry outputs leads to lower prices — in accord with the market demand curves — the entrants nevertheless assume that if they undercut incumbents' prices they can sell as much of the corresponding good as the quantity demanded by the market at their own prices.[14]

Thus in this limiting case even a short-run profit could trigger off entry, as it is possible for the entrant to depart without cost if the incumbent firms react against the new entrant. A contestable market will attract entrants if prices are sufficiently high for attractive profits to be thought achievable.

Because of the threat of entry, the long-term equilibrium in the market must involve minimizing industry costs. Any excess profits would be competed away by new entrants and, in the case of a perfectly contestable market, equilibrium price with two or more suppliers would be equal to marginal cost.

Whatever market structure satisfies these equilibrium conditions, it is argued, will turn out to be the only consistent structure. This is determined within the industry along with prices and output.

One of the main attractions of this model is that it is concerned with the empirically observable situation of dynamic competition. It refers to action and reaction and threats of new competition as a constraint on incumbent firms' actions. Baumol argues that the model cuts across the traditional structural types. There is thus no reason why an oligopoly should not be a perfectly contestable market. Traditional oligopoly models on price-setting are constrained because of the need to assume the type of reaction by rivals to a firm's pricing decisions. This is avoided by the contestable markets model.

Baumol *et al*. do not apply this model to the role of brands. Indeed 'brand' does not even appear in the index to the book. The brand must act as a constraint to contestability. Successful brand-image creation, as already noted, helps to create brand loyalty which, through the role of habits, affects consumers' reactions to price and output changes by suppliers. Brand loyalty would thus lag reactions to lower priced brands from new entrants via the customer concern with perceived quality. Even if quality of brands were physically identical, unless Lancaster's objective and measurable characteristics approach applies (see Chapter 2), perceived quality of brands may differ between consumers. Their preferences will also differ, not necessarily for objective reasons. In practice this may limit the contestability of a market for branded goods or services.

In summary, although this model can be argued to improve the treatment of competition in the theoretical treatment of market structure and market conduct, the emphasis on supply-side decision-making does not include a treatment of the role of the brand. Demand influences, likely to limit contestability, are not considered in detail by Baumol through the medium of brand image and non-economic influences on demand. Nevertheless the model is very recent and no doubt further consideration will be given to these issues.

3.7 VERTICAL INTEGRATION AND THE BRAND

In brand terms, vertical integration can occur by distributors manufacturing their own brands or by manufacturers distributing their own brands. From the manufacturer's perspective such a move would give control of distribution channels making for easier co-ordination of brand-marketing activities. If the move does not lead to exclusive distribution then conflict with other distribution channels can be caused. Such a move could act as a barrier to new competition and is more likely where specialist distribution skills are limited. Similar arguments could be raised by distributors moving into manufacturing. The major problem in each case is the possible conflict with other distributors. This aspect is covered in Chapter 8.

Reasons for vertical integration could be based on increased power, cost savings, marketing opportunities, distribution problem solving or as a means of protecting a brand. Control over how the brand is presented to the consumer is increased via product quality control, price control and promotion presentation, and personal selling of the brand can also be more effectively controlled in a vertically integrated channel.

3.8 ECONOMIES OF SCALE AND SCOPE

Finally in this chapter the role of the brand in relation to economies of scale and scope will be considered. Economies of scale occur with larger-scale production giving rise to lower unit costs of production. Economies of scope are the advantages to the firm of producing similar products, e.g., applying expertise in marketing one brand to marketing another in a similar market. Studies have shown a positive relationship between brand share and profitability. Booz, Allen and Hamilton found that both small and large brand shares were associated with high profitability while medium shares had weak profitability.[15] The Strategic Planning Institute found a positive straight-line relationship between market share and profitability.[16] Thus a strong brand leads to gains in perceived value by consumers, leading to a higher price per unit, while increased sales also reduce unit costs through economies of scale.

Successfully creating a brand in one market may give a firm an increased chance of success in brand creation in similar markets due to accumulated marketing expertise. This is an economy of scope. Indeed, in their 1984 Annual Report, Saatchi and Saatchi Compton Worldwide argue that the search for economies of scale and scope is a major influence on the trend towards globalization of brands. This is discussed in Chapter 9.

In both cases strong brands have positive profitability and synergistic implications for firms, which re-emphasizes the points already made in this chapter.

3.9 THE BRAND AS A COMPETITIVE WEAPON

This Chapter has set the framework for the rest of the book in that the structures of markets have been examined from the point of view of their relationship with the brand. As the modern firm operates in a number of markets, the brand can be seen as a major competitive device which enables the firm to attempt to meet its objectives across markets.

Kotler has identified the strategy options within a market for market leaders, challengers, followers and nichers (firms strong in a particular small-market segment).[17] Within this analysis the brand plays an important role. The success of a firm within a market depends at least in part on its success in brand creation.

The chapters which follow examine elements of the marketing mix applied to the brand in a competitive environment. Taking the structure of the market as given, we assess how the firm should use marketing variables tactically and strategically to compete effectively.

To end the chapter two examples are given to illustrate the relevance of market structure.

3.9.1 The chocolate confectionery industry

The chocolate confectionery industry in the UK is dominated by three firms, Cadbury, Rowntree and Mars, which have about 85 per cent of the market, each having about the same share but each with strengths in particular market segments. Each firm has many brands, most being long established. Cadbury is strong in the solid chocolate-bar segment with the Cadbury's Dairy Milk (CDM) brand. In the mid-1970s the price of cocoa escalated rapidly and this percolated through the production process so that production costs rose sharply. The firms reacted by increasing price or reducing quantity or both. The CDM brand was made thinner.

Rowntree, who were using continuous market research to monitor the changes, detected a note of consumer dissatisfaction with the CDM brand. Amongst other factors this led them to develop a 'chunky' chocolate brand positioned as being energy-giving, long-lasting chocolate in 'bite size' pieces. Originally they intended to call this brand 'Rations' to evoke memories of the wartime use of chocolate for giving energy to soldiers as part of their rations. Indeed the same moulds were to be used in shaping the chocolate. However, market research showed that this image was too austere and after further consumer testing the brand was launched with the name 'Yorkie'.

The research proved to be correct and the brand was successful, taking sales from CDM and Galaxy (the Mars brand). Soon these brands were reshaped into chunky bite-sized pieces, also as a retaliation against Yorkie which has retained a high level of sales in a highly competitive market by expanding sales in a market segment in which it had been weak compared to the other two oligopolists.

There are a number of lessons here:

1. It is essential to protect valuable existing brands. Cadbury made a mistake at a time when change was forced on them by outside pressures. The importance of consumer perceptions is hard to overstate in this context.
2. Competition by innovation can be successful even when existing brands are well established.
3. Expect competitors to retaliate. Brands are too big an investment not to protect. Cadbury reformulated CDM in the short term, and in the longer term attacked a segment previously dominated by Rowntree by launching the brand Wispa to compete with Aero. The story of this launch is told in Chapter 6.
4. Even dominant firms can be attacked by successful branding in oligopolistic markets.

3.9.2 The washing powder industry

This industry is dominated by two firms in the UK: Unilever, and Procter and Gamble. Each offers a range of brands (brand proliferation) with a very high advertising expenditure (see Table 3.1). The industry was investigated by the Monopolies Commission which reported to Parliament in August 1966 that the two firms earned higher profits than was the average at the time for manufacturing industry. This, they found, was due to the use of non-price rather than price competition. The Commission recommended a reduction in selling expenses of 40 per cent and a reduction in the wholesale price by 20 per cent, as the two firms were not acting in the public interest.[18]

Since this time, the two firms have continued to dominate the industry with the use of non-price competition. Competition stresses product quality and branding. It can be argued that no amount of advertising will make housewives buy more washing powder than they need to do the weekly washing. Thus advertising is used in maintaining brand images and attempting to make consumers switch brands. Indeed, in a negative way, advertising can be seen as a cost of remaining in the market. If the brand is not advertised it will, after a time-lag from accumulated advertising, lose sales as consumers lose their brand image and begin to 'forget' the brand. Why not collude therefore to stop all advertising of brands? The answer to this is that advertising and brand proliferation act as a barrier to potential competitors and stop them entering the market. Stopping advertising would increase the chance of new competition and probably increase the share of the market taken by own-label brands.

This case study again illustrates the powerful role of brands in competitive markets and also points to the role of advertising in brand image creation. This will be developed in Chapter 5 on non-price competition after the role of pricing in relation to brands has been considered.

REFERENCES

1. Baumol, W. J. (1977) *Economic Theory and Operations Analysis*, 4th edn., Prentice-Hall, Englewood Cliffs, New Jersey, Ch. 16.
2. Pickering, J. F. (1974) *Industrial Structure and Market Conduct*, Martin Robertson, London.
3. Stigler, C. J. (1957) 'Perfect competition, historically contemplated', *Journal of Political Economy*, **65**, 1–17.
4. Lambin, J. J. (1976) *Advertising, Competition and Market Conduct in Oligopoly over Time*, North-Holland, Amsterdam.
5. Gorton, K. and I. Carr (1983) *Low-cost marketing research: a guide for small businesses*, Wiley, Chichester.
6. Levitt, T. (1960) 'Marketing myopia', *Harvard Business Review*, July–August, 45–56.

7. MEAL (1984) *Quarterly Digest of Advertising Expenditure*, Fourth Quarter Media Expenditure Analysis Ltd, London.

8. Koutsoyiannis, A. (1982) *Non-Price Decisions*, Macmillan, London, pp. 3–4.

9. Sweezy, P. M. (1939) 'Demand under conditions of oligopoly', *Journal of Political Economy*, 47, 568–73.

10. Stigler, C. J. (1947) 'The Kinked oligopoly demand curve and rigid prices', *Journal of Political Economy*, 55, 432–447.

11. Bain, J. S. (1954) *Barriers to New Competition*, Harvard University Press, Cambridge, Mass.

12. Baumol, W. J. (1982) 'Contestable Markets: an uprising in the theory of industrial structure', *American Economic Review*, 72, 1, 1–15.

13. Baumol, W. J., J. L. Panzar, and R. Willig (1982) *Contestable Markets and the Theory of Industry Structure*, Harcourt Brace Jovanovich, New York.

14. Ibid, p. 5.

15. Booz, Allen and Hamilton (1982) *New Products Management for the 1980s*, Booz, Allen and Hamilton, New York.

16. Strategic Planning Institute, *The PIMS programme*, Strategic Planning Institute, Cambridge, Mass.

17. Kotler, P. (1984) *Marketing Management*, 5th edn, Prentice-Hall International, London, Ch.12.

18. Monopolies Commission (1966) *Household Detergents*, HMSO, London.

MARKET CONDUCT (1): PRICE COMPETITION

4.1 INTRODUCTION

While much of the economic analysis of pricing assumes a single price within a market for a product, in practice the pricing variable is much more complex than this. Issues such as the balance between list and achieved prices, quantity discounts, credit, channel margins and the promotional role of price add to the complexity of pricing in practice. Thus we are concerned empirically with a pricing structure which allows for all sizes, shapes, colours and other product variants, besides the underlying determinants of the price level.

Pricing is made more complex in practice because of the number of parties involved in the process. The customer, in the real world of imperfect information, perceives price as one component of the rather nebulous concept of 'value for money'. The perceived price may be higher, lower or equal to the actual price and in the absence of other information will suggest a product quality to the consumer. 'Blind tests', in which respondents are given two samples of an identical physical product but told only that the price of one sample item is higher than the other, show that in this restricted environment respondents tend to assume that the higher priced item is of a higher quality than the lower priced item. The highly subjective value-for-money analysis of competing brands which consumers make in purchasing choices can lead to decisions which appear irrational to the outsider but, as argued in Chapter 2, rationality may be viewed from the consumer's subjective perspective.

Middlemen also take a perspective on price. Increasingly, the power of middlemen is reflected in the negotiation of price levels and distributor margins with manufacturers. The main weapon which the manufacturer holds in this bargaining process is the strength of the brand, which pressurizes the distributor to stock it. Potential and actual competitors also take a view on brand price. If they perceive the price as too high this may stimulate new entry into the market in search of above average returns on investment. On the other hand it may cause competitors to avoid the market because they perceive the high price as reflecting the strength of the brand. Similarly if they perceive the price as too low they may avoid competition because of low profit expectations; alternatively they may see the low price as a sign that the brand is weak or the company is experiencing financial problems and be attracted to the market.

Suppliers may try to negotiate higher raw material prices if they perceive a high price for the finished good, and trade unions may attempt to negotiate higher wage rates if they perceive prices as being high and a brand as being successful. Finally the Government may take an interest in a market if they perceive that higher than usual profits are being made through higher prices. Legal controls could also affect price levels.

Besides being complex, pricing is often a sensitive area especially for monopolists in high profile industries. In brand pricing this political dimension can be a major influence on pricing strategy.

This chapter will begin with a consideration of practical pricing objectives and continue with an examination of the underlying influences on price determination. Finally the issues of price elasticity, pricing research and price–quality interaction will be considered. All these factors will be examined within the framework of market conduct, using price competition within a marketing strategy.

4.2 PRACTICAL PRICING OBJECTIVES

It is often necessary to view the brand as part of the company product range for pricing purposes. Taking this broader view can give the firm more flexibility in the pricing of individual brands. Price has a major strategic and tactical importance in the marketing mix as, unlike other marketing variables, it is unidimensional, unambiguous and quantitative in nature. It has a direct impact on consumers through their limited budgets and their utility maximization deliberations. This sensitivity should be reflected in company pricing strategy. Possible alternative pricing strategies include the following:

4.2.1 Market penetration

This strategy involves setting a relatively low price in order to stimulate market growth and/or to obtain a large share of the market. An example occurred in the UK motorcycle market when low-priced Japanese imports took an increasingly large share of the market, causing the market exit of UK suppliers. The Japanese products were then gradually increased in price after they had dominated the market and the threat of new competition was very limited. To use this strategy, a firm would need to be convinced of the long-term viability of the market, of the high level of price sensitivity of the market and that low prices would discourage competition. In addition if unit costs fall with increased output due to economies of scale this would be a bonus to the supplier. This objective is not really consistent with a policy of branding. Price rather than non-price competition is made the focus of marketing strategy and the implication is that all brands in the market are similar. The success of a brand creation policy leads to the reduction of the price sensitivity in a market through brand differentiation and higher perceived brand values by consumers. As noted above, low prices may encourage competition if they are perceived as illustrating financial weaknesses. The concept of value for money may lead consumers to take a broader view of price which includes quality connotations. Other things being equal, they may equate a low price with low quality. Thus this pricing strategy holds potential pitfalls, in particular where successful branding is possible.

4.2.2 Market skimming

This strategy involves charging a relatively high price to take advantage of those consumers willing to buy at a premium price because the brand has a high present value to them. This is usually a short-term strategy often associated with new brands with a high novelty value. Over time the relatively high price is gradually reduced in real terms to make inroads into more price-elastic segments. This is equivalent to price discrimination over time. An obvious requirement is enough buyers with a relatively price-inelastic demand willing to pay the initial high price. This can be extremely difficult to forecast. Also if unit costs of production are high for small volumes then this could offset the advantage of charging a high price in profit contribution terms. The other main danger is that the high price will stimulate competition. Some protection can be afforded against this eventuality by high barriers to entry, for example through patent protection, high development costs or raw material control.

Two advantages of this approach are that it is usually easier to reduce price than to increase it if a mistake is made, and that a high price usually creates an impression of a high-quality product. This strategy may be consistent with branding although it is a dangerous strategy when concerned with a new brand aiming at long-term survival. A high initial price raises quality expectations amongst consumers; if the brand fails to live up to these expectations then its long-term viability could be put in doubt through adverse word-of-mouth comment and a rapid fall-off in repeat purchasing activity. Once disappointed in a brand's quality and performance, it may be very difficult to persuade consumers to try it again. Worse still, they may pass on negative views which dissuade others from trying the brand. This 'social connotation', so important in new brand success, is an important criterion in considering this pricing strategy.

4.2.3 Product-line promotion

This occurs where the price-setting for one brand is undertaken to attempt to maximize profits from the entire product range. Thus the brand-pricing strategy will be more flexible than if the profit from each brand separately is to be maximized. The cross-elasticities need to be considered, as discussed in Chapter 1. These involve the degree of complementarity or substitutability within the product range. Thus a razor may be sold at a cost-covering, or loss-making price (i.e., act as a 'loss leader') if this will commit buyers to repeat purchasing of replacement blades at a relatively high price. In this way the profit for the product range is increased even though one component brand makes a loss. Again, this strategy may have quality implications for individual brands, which should be considered in the pricing decision.

With regard to the pricing of new brands, a company will need to consider the 'cannibalization aspect'. This is the extent to which sales of a new brand are drawn from the company's own existing brands rather than from competitor's brands. If sales are, to a significant extent, drawn from the company's existing brands then this may be sufficient to halt a new brand development if the market research evidence is available early enough. However, if the profit margin on the new brand is greater than on existing company brands it may still be worth introducing the new brand with a high degree of company brand cannibalization. Further, if the profit margin is lower on the new brand, it may still be worth introducing the new brand if it is feared that a competitive new brand may cause the company to lose sales of its existing brands in any case.

Thus product line promotion can in practice be a complex matter, leading to pricing decisions which, taken at the brand level, seem illogical but when seen as part of the overall product-line pricing strategy have a rational explanation. This complexity is increased when the other elements of the marketing mix are considered. In economic theory the assumption of *ceteris paribus* leads to this important empirical factor being ignored. In practice, price changes are often accompanied by promotional offers which disguise the price change in the short term. This can be achieved by changing the product quality or quantity, packaging changes, 'money-off' coupons, competitions, free gifts or other promotional gimmicks. In particular, changes in product quantity per unit rather than price changes are common in some industries in some situations. Thus when the price of cocoa rose rapidly in the mid-1970s pushing up the cost of chocolate, the reaction of some chocolate bar suppliers was to reduce the weight of chocolate bars rather than to increase price. This reflects price expectations of consumers which tend to move more slowly than do actual price changes especially in times of rapid inflation. The suppliers argued that certain price levels were thought by consumers to be appropriate for the purchase of particular types of chocolate bar. For example, they use the concept of the 'one coin purchase' for purchases by children, leading to a number of brands being priced at 10p on the assumption that this will seem less to a child than having to part with a number of coins. Also, 10p is a common sum to give to a child as a small reward or gift.

The price level for a brand also needs to reflect the type of distribution outlet used. One would expect to pay a higher price for an item in Harrods than in Woolworth's and the degree of exclusivity of distribution outlets is likely to be reflected in price. This is particularly the case when the distributors' margins are considered where, as with most product groups, there is freedom of pricing at the retail level for the distributor.

Further, a relatively high brand price is likely to be accompanied by a media advertising campaign which aims to create a quality image for the brand to complement the 'high' price.

Thus the marketing mix interaction of the product line is another factor in the pricing strategy consideration. In deciding which pricing strategy to use, there are three major types of factor which have an influence: cost, competition and demand factors. Each of these will now be considered in turn.

4.3 INFLUENCES ON BRAND PRICING STRATEGY

4.3.1 Cost factors

The work of Hall and Hitch based on research interviews with businessmen indicated that costs are the predominant influences in price-setting in practice. Many firms were found to adopt simple cost-plus rules.[1] A study by Lanzilotti gave a number of reasons for this predominance.[2] These include:

1. Planning of investment — capital rationing is made easier.
2. Easier assessment of divisional performance.
3. Emulation of successful large companies.
4. Belief by management in a 'fair return' policy.
5. Fear of government action against 'excessive' profits.
6. Tradition of production orientation rather than marketing orientation.
7. Tacit collusion in industry to avoid competition (see discussion in Chapter 3).
8. Constraint of adequate profits for shareholders, giving no incentive to maximize profits.
9. Easier administration of cost-based pricing strategies based on internal data.
10. Stability of pricing, production and employment produced by cost-based pricing over time.
11. Social equability.

There are two main types of cost-based pricing: full-cost pricing and cost-plus pricing.

Full cost pricing This takes account of the full average cost of production of a brand including an allocation for overheads. A conventional profit margin is then added to determine the selling price. This is often used for non-routine jobs which are difficult to cost in advance, e.g., the work of solicitors and accountants where the price is often determined after the work has been performed.

To calculate the average cost of production involves an assumed production level. This is often done on the basis of a 'standard volume' and was used by Jaguar, as described in a most interesting case study.[3] In turn it is assumed that this 'standard volume' will be sold at the price which is set, although some allowance or safety margin can be built into this analysis.

Although this method is basically straightforward in principle, the allocation of overheads between brands in a multibrand company can be difficult, especially when joint- or by-products are involved.

Although superficially it would appear that demand factors are ignored in this analysis, in practice, especially in the longer term, this can be reflected through the level of the profit margin which is added. This is also likely to reflect the level of actual potential competition from firms in the industry or capable of entering it.

Cost-plus pricing Here only the more easily measurable cost components such as labour and raw material inputs, fuel and transport per unit are calculated in the unit cost. An additional margin incorporates an overhead charge and a residual profit element. This is used where the overhead allocation to unit costs is too complex or too time-consuming. A common example occurs with the use of mark-up pricing by retailers in which a fixed margin is added to the buying-in price of goods for resale. The fixed margin tends to be conventional within product classes. In the UK, for example, fast-moving items such as cigarettes carry a low 5—8 per cent margin (also because of tax factors), fast-moving but perishable items such as newspapers carry a 25 per cent margin, while slow-moving items which involve retailers in high stock-holding costs such as toys or jewellery carry 33 per cent, 50 per cent or even higher mark-up margins.

Again the margin may vary to reflect changes in demand or competition. The cost basis for calculations may be actual costs, expected costs or costs based on standard production levels. If all the firms in the industry use this pricing basis then prices will reflect efficiency.

The problems with this approach occur with the difficulties in defining direct costs and allocating overheads and with over- or underestimation of attainable production levels. Also price adjustments may cause high administrative costs because of the cost-based price-setting process used. This may lead to price stability and price changes which reflect cost changes, and can lead to a marketing strategy which is reactive rather than pro-active. The other problem is the very limited consideration of demand in cost-based pricing strategies. Although if all firms use this approach then allocative efficiency can occur, from a marketing perspective cost-based pricing can reflect missed opportunities, as little or no account is taken, particularly in the short run, of the price consumers are willing to pay for the brand which, as in the case of the Jaguar cars example, may prove to be higher than the cost-based price. In that example a resale market developed in which a new car could be immediately resold for a substantially increased price due to a shortage which Jaguar overcame by a waiting-list system rather than by increased prices.[3]

It must be stated that the attractions of cost-based pricing, as already noted, can easily lead companies to adopt this approach which provides a practical solution to the pricing problem. The traditional imperfect competition model is of limited practical value for a number of reasons:

1. It assumes that the demand curve can be identified with certainty.
2. It ignores the market research costs associated with acquiring the knowledge of demand.
3. It assumes the firm has no productive constraint which could mean that the equilibrium point cannot be reached.
4. It is a static analysis (i.e., concerned with only one point in time).

Finally, the use of cost-based pricing for a new brand can cause particular problems as the initial low production level could lead to a very high average unit cost. It may thus be necessary to take a longer-term view which accepts short-term losses until full production levels are attained. Also if the firm is using a product-line promotion strategy then there is likely to be added complexity in the pricing process as cross-subsidization needs to be taken account of.

4.3.2 Competition factors

This section is closely related to the discussion on market structure and marketing strategy in the last chapter and relates to conditions in which prices are set on the basis of what competitors are charging rather than on the basis of cost or demand. A theoretical justification of this phenomenon was presented by Sweezy as the kinked demand curve theory.[4] This is shown in Figure 4.1.

It is argued that price remains at OP even if marginal costs increase from MC_1 to MC_2. The justification is that firms assume that competitors would all follow a price decrease but that none would follow a price increase. Thus they assume that, for a price rise, demand is elastic but for a price fall it is inelastic. In each case a price change would reduce sales revenue.

This approach does not explain how the price is arrived at in the first place nor does it take account of branding which by differentiating one brand from others would have an effect on perceived price-elasticity expectations through brand loyalty.

In practice the kinked demand curve theory would lead to going-rate pricing in which some form

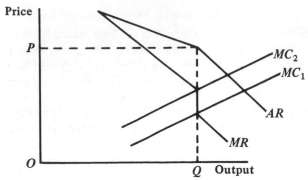

Fig. 4.1 The kinked demand curve

of average level of price becomes the norm, perhaps — in the case of a high level of branding in the market — including standard price differentials between brands.

As noted in the last chaper, in certain market structures price competition may be avoided by tacit agreement leading to concentration on non-price competition. In such cases price-setting is influenced by a need to avoid retaliatory responses by competitors which would lead to a break-down in the tacit agreement. Often price changes based on cost changes are led by a 'representative' firm in the industry and followed by the other firms. From time to time tacit agreements break down leading to a period of price competition which may be followed by a resumption of the tacit agreement. This is often the result of external factors affecting the industry. An example is the change in the basis of tax assessments in the UK to fit in with EEC regulations which had the effect of making 'king-size' cigarettes relatively less expensive compared with the then brand leaders, the medium-sized cigarette brands, such as Embassy. The pricing structure within the industry went through a period of turmoil before settling down again once the disturbances had worked their way through the firm's competitive strategies. Such industry-level agreements do not necessarily preclude short-term price competition for specific brands especially using sales promotion devices, such as 'money-off' coupons, which are discussed in the next chapter.

A special case of competitive-based pricing is competitive bidding. Many supply contracts especially concerning local and national government purchases involve would-be suppliers submitting a sealed bid tender. In such circumstances, the firm's submitted price needs to take account of expected competitor bid prices. In some cases firms will know the identity of competitors where a shortlisting procedure is used, in other cases they will be unaware of the identity of other bidders. It is often the case that past successful bids are published by purchasers and if this is the case it is possible to use these data to base a current bid price. It is possible to use Bayesian probability theory to maximize expected profit by making a probability estimate of winning the contract at each of a series of bid prices. This is discussed by Livesey[5] and by Fitzroy.[6] If the firm has the particular problem of bidding for a number of contracts before the results of any bid are known, then the productive (or supply) capacity may be important. The firm may need to win some contracts but not too few or too many. This is a further influence on the bid price. If past bid data is not published then there is very little objective basis for bid price-setting. The firm may have to rely on trade gossip, on conjecture or on an estimate of likely competitors' cost and profit requirements in price-setting.

The problem is exacerbated if the contract is not awarded purely on price (i.e., if the lowest bid is not automatically accepted). In the case of the supply of branded goods, the relative value of each brand must be considered on a value-for-money basis by the purchaser. It may be possible to use price-equivalents of extra features in a Bayesian model of the process but the bidder may have to rely on subjective 'feel of the market' analysis in determining bid prices. There are of course numerous instances where cases of actual and attempted bribery of officials have been uncovered in attempts by firms to use underhand means of winning contracts.

4.3.3 Demand-based factors

Rather than use cost and competition as prime determinants of price a firm can base pricing strategy for a brand on the intensity of demand, although of course cost and competitive factors remain influences or constraints on freedom to set price. Thus a strong intensity of demand may lead to a high price, and a weak intensity to a low price. Much depends on the ability of the firm to segment the market by price elasticity. Figure 4.2 shows a simple downward sloping demand curve in which there is one price (P_0) and the total quantity demanded is Q_0. The shaded area A represents consumer surplus, i.e., an area of extra benefit to the consumer. For example, a consumer may be willing to pay P_1 but only pays P_0, the market price, gaining a consumer surplus of $P_1 - P_0$. If the firm can increase prices to those willing to pay more then it could reduce this area of consumer surplus without necessarily causing the consumer not to buy.

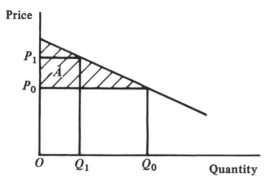

Fig. 4.2 Consumer surplus and price setting

Pigou identified three types of such price discrimination:[7]

First degree price discrimination Each customer is charged the highest price he is willing to pay. An example would be negotiated car prices, although this works in reverse since the actual purchase price (list price minus negotiated discount) is based on what the customer is willing to pay and what the salesman is willing to sell for. It can be argued that this is unfair as it depends on the negotiation skills of the buyer.

Second degree price discrimination The firm sets a large number of blocks of prices and the customer pays the highest possible. This increases the sales revenue to the firm as shown in Figure 4.3.

SR is the sales revenue and equals the area under the dotted line in this case where eight price levels $(P_0 - P_7)$ are set. P_0 would be the lowest price at which the firm is willing to supply, P_7 the highest price which a worthwhile number of buyers would be willing to pay.

Third degree price discrimination The firm divides the market into a small number of groups each having different elasticities at the same price. Price is set according to this price elasticity (higher price for more inelastic demand).

In practice, measurement of price elasticity can be very difficult. It is discussed below in the section on pricing research.

There are a number of ways in which discriminating prices can be set:

1. *By customer, or groups of customer.* A cross-channel ferry company would market its services at different prices in England, Belgium and France for example. Services such as cinemas and hairdressers are often available at lower prices to old age pensioners and/or juveniles.

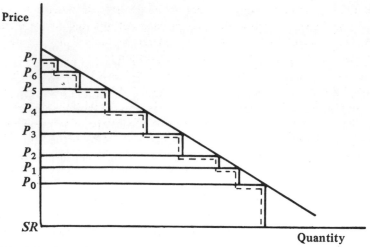

Fig. 4.3 2nd degree price discrimination

2. *By product version.* Many car models have 'add on' extras which enable one brand to appeal to a wider cross-section of customers. Indeed BMW used add-on-extras sales as a major part of their marketing strategy when faced with a limited supply of cars from Germany. The final price need not reflect the cost price of the add-on extras directly: usually the top-of-the-range model would carry a price much in excess of the cost of provision of the extras, as a prestige appeal.
3. *By place.* Theatre seats are usually sold according to their location so that patrons pay different prices for the same performance according to the seat type they occupy.
4. *By time.* Perhaps the most popular type of price discrimination. Off-peak travel bargains, hotel prices, telephone and electricity charges are all attempts to increase sales revenue by covering variable but not necessarily average cost of provision.

In each of these cases, some customers pay more than others for essentially the same product or service, reflecting different intensities of demand as expressed by different price elasticity values. There is an ethical dimension to this practice and firms need to consider their objectives carefully before using this approach. For instance, by taking advantage of a short-run shortage of a product and increasing price, a firm may harm long-run profit prospects through a resentment by customers of what they may interpret as exploitation. This is particularly the case as consumerism develops, since vociferous groups of consumers can create widespread publicity which can be adverse for the brand supplier in the short and/or longer term.

Price discrimination can only be effective if a number of conditions hold.

1. The market must be segmentable in price terms, and different sectors must show different intensities of demand. Each of these sectors must be identifiable, distinct and separate from the others and accessible to the firm's marketing communications.
2. There must be little or no chance of a 'black market' developing, i.e., that those in the lower price segment can resell to those in the higher priced segment.
3. There must be little chance that competitors can and will undercut the firm's prices in the higher priced (and/or most profitable) market segments.
4. The cost of segmenting and administering the arrangements should not exceed the extra revenue derived from the price discrimination strategy.

If the firm is to price at what the market will bear, whether or not this involves price discrimination, then some market intelligence about price elasticity is a necessary input to the pricing decision. It may be necessary to examine past price–quantity relationships in the market and project these to estimate future price-elasticity values. This is more likely to work at the industry or perhaps at the product level of analysis but at the brand level of analysis there are problems of isolating price effects from quantity-demanded changes. This is exacerbated by short-term marketing tactical changes such as sales promotions, advertising bursts and sales campaigns. Multiple regression techniques have been used to isolate price effects and an example is given by Fitzroy which illustrates this type of approach.[8]

The firm could use a market test to estimate the demand effect of a price change. This would involve a change of price in one region and a comparison of demand for the brand with past sales in the region and sales in similar regions at the old prices. This is a high-risk strategy: special circumstances may affect the test area (e.g., a competitor's advertising campaign) which could affect results. Also consumers may change allegiance from the test brand if a price rise is being considered and become brand loyal to a competitive brand and not switch back even if the price is subsequently lowered again.

The other alternative is to attempt a direct attitude survey with respondents. Pricing research is notoriously difficult especially if respondents try to appear rational to the interviewer or do not wish to offend the interviewer. Usually there is a lack of realism in such research, the respondent is not in an actual choice situation faced with having to pay out hard-earned income and may give a hypothetical answer which is not then translated into actual purchasing behaviour. Nevertheless, pricing research is increasingly common in practice as firms attempt to assess consumers' perceived brand value as an input to their pricing decisions.

4.4 PRICING RESEARCH FOR BRANDS

Early research on the price sensitivity of consumers in brand choice was initiated by Gabor and Granger at Nottingham University in the late 1950s and resulted in important publications in the 1960s[9] which are summarized by Gabor in his 1977 text.[10] The early findings based on interviews in 1958 with 428 housewives covering 5276 purchases of 15 commodities and other survey work indicated that:

1. Consumers have a concept of a 'just price' — a feel for what is about the right price to pay for a commodity.
2. Consumers search for price information before buying, becoming price-aware when wanting to buy but forgetting soon afterwards unless a regular purchase is involved.
3. Consumers will buy at what they consider to be a bargain price without full regard for need and actual price.
4. For consumer durables it is the down payment and instalment price rather than total price which is important.
5. Price consciousness is inversely related to social status as measured by price recall. However, in this period low inflation was the norm, resale price maintenance still existed in the UK (abolished in 1964) and there were few special offers on price, all of which are likely to explain the high recall of prices experienced (tea 94.7 per cent, eggs 93.4 per cent, soap 72.6 per cent, flour 62.7 per cent — average accurate price recall was 82.0 per cent). These conditions do not now hold in the UK (or in most Western economies). In addition, branding is much more prevalent and the Gabor—Granger research showed that price recall was lower with higher branding.
6. In times of rising prices the price image tends to lag behind the current price which indicates a resentment of the price increase. It is thus very important to relate consumers' image of price to the actual price as this will determine reactions to a price change. Kotler reports the case of Bell Telephones in the US.[11] The company was concerned about lack of sales of extension telephones. When, as part of a market research survey, consumers were asked to name the actual price of an extension telephone, most overestimated it. By keeping the existing price but running

an advertising campaign featuring the price, Bell were able to increase sales as consumers became aware of the lower-than-anticipated price.

Price perception is an important factor in the ways consumers react to prices. The economist's downward sloping demand curve may not hold at least in the short term. For example consumers may react to a price increase by buying more because:

1. They expect further price increases to follow.
2. They assume the quality has increased.
3. The brand takes on a 'snob appeal' because of the high price.

In retail selling the concept of a 'quantum point' is often referred to. When the price of an item is increased from, say, £9.65 to £9.95 sales may not be affected because consumers do not notice the price change. However if the price is increased from £9.95 to £10.05 a major fall in sales may occur, £10 acting as a quantum point which can be approached but not passed if the price is not to deter would-be purchasers.

As an interesting aside, the odd-number pricing syndrome, i.e., pricing at £1.99, £2.99, etc., rather than £2, £3, etc., is said to have originated not as a marketing concept but in department stores in order to ensure the honesty of their sales assistants. The customer has to wait for change from £1.95 when as is usual they offer, say, £2 in payment, so the assistant has to use the till. If the price was £2 and customer need not wait for change, there was thought to be a greater temptation to shop assistants to pocket the money and not enter it into the till.

As already described in Chapter 4 confectionery firms have used the psychologically based concept of a 'one-coin purchase' in pricing tactics. Rather than change price to reflect cost changes, such firms often alter the quantity in the unit of the product and keep the same price. This is a case of 'price minus' pricing in which the firm determines what the market will bear and works backwards, planning to produce and market a brand which will be profitable to them, selling at the nominated retail price. In some markets, groups of brands sell around a number of prices which seem to be acceptable to consumers. Ball-point pens may sell at around 12p, around 50p or around £1 or £2, each price level reflecting a particular type of purchase. Gift purchasing is often based on price which is taken to reflect quality. Thus if a gift is to be purchased in an unfamiliar product category a price level is often fixed by the buyer and a choice made from the brands available at that price. Cosmetics are often priced at £4.99 and £9.99 to appeal to gift purchasers at the £5 and £10 price levels. Importantly, packaging is a major part of the appeal and must reflect a quality brand image, an important part of the psychology of gift choice.

4.4.1 The buy-response method

The work of Gabor and Granger on pricing sensitivity led them to develop the buy-response method which is still a common means of practical pricing research. This method assumes the concept of an upper and lower price limit when a consumer approaches the market. Asking a direct question would suggest to the consumer that such limits exist. To avoid this the consumer is asked if she would buy the brand at each of a series of prices (up to 10 based on experience). A random order of presentation is used starting from the prevailing price, or close to it. This avoids an anchoring effect.

Using a hall method, a mock shopping display can be created with easily changeable prices to add realism to the respondent's task. The 'price last paid' is also determined from the respondent. This input is then used to assess brand preference and brand loyalty over a range of price ratios. A cumulative log normal distribution which empirical tests showed to be a good fit based on the buy-response curve is derived from the equation

$$L(P) + H(P) + B(P) = 1$$

where $L(P)$ = probability that a random member of a homogeneous population will find the product 'too cheap' at a price P;

$H(P)$ = probability that a member of the population will find the product 'too expensive' at a price P;

$B(P)$ = probability that a randomly selected consumer will not find price an obstacle to buying at a price P;

$B(P)$ is the buy-response curve.

In product fields where the consumer knows the brands, price does not act as an indicator of quality so much and $L(P)$ becomes very small. The research showed that $1 - L(P)$ and $H(P)$ are approximated by a cumulative log normal distribution. If $p = \log_n P$ then Figure 4.4 illustrates the shape of these curves.

This innovative research has much to offer in pricing research for branded convenience products. The problem of lack of realism is minimized although of course the respondent does not actually pay money. An approach which tried to take this into account was devised by Pessemier.[12]

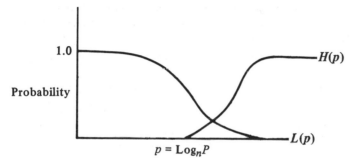

Fig. 4.4 The buy-response curve

4.4.2 Pessemier's approach

Using a random sample of 2–300 from 6000 students, subjects were asked which brands in a product field they normally purchased. Each was then given 'assortment sheets' on which the preferred brand was offered at a higher or lower price with the price of other brands unchanged. Each subject was invited to make a number of simulated shopping trips to the local store with enough money to buy the highest price good with some change. They were told to assume a need but could postpone purchase. The subjects knew there was a small chance of them retaining the chosen item. Samples were shown to the respondents before the shopping trip.

The data were then translated into a demand curve which not only showed brand-switching behaviour at each price but also the brands switched to or from. This would then given price-elasticity estimates by brand over a range of prices.

Essentially this approach attempts to hold other variables than price constant so that the price—quantity relationship can be investigated. Very little time elapses between the stimulus of the price change and the consumer's choice. The external validity of this method and the buy-response method must be questioned. In both cases the option of the consumer shopping around and buying the same brand at a lower price elsewhere is not incorporated into the model. A controlled marketing experiment may ensure internal validity but may at the same time be staged so artificially that relevance to real world marketing conditions is limited. However, experimentation in these 'laboratory' settings may be preferable to real market tests even though it is difficult to assess longer-term effects of price changes.

4.4.3 Conjoint measurement

Introduction In contrast to these direct methods of pricing research, an indirect approach has been developed and has been growing in importance over the past 10 years especially in the US but increasingly in the UK. The underlying principle of conjoint measurement is that consumers 'trade off' features between brands in the choice process because no one brand represents an ideal combination of features (or attributes or characteristics) from their perspectives. The approach taken here is concentrated towards marketing practice rather than towards a mathematical exposition of the theoretical underpinnings of the technique, and realistic examples are given to illustrate practical applications.

What is conjoint measurement? The method is based on a monotonic analysis of variance using a computer algorithm which essentially breaks down products into their attributes and measures the value of each of these component parts based on consumer judgemental input. As Johnson notes,[13]

> The basic idea is that by providing consumers with stimuli from among which to choose, we can make inferences about their value systems based on behaviour rather than upon self reports. The word conjoint has to do with the fact that we measure relative values of things considered jointly which might be unmeasurable taken one at a time.

Thus in deciding which model of car to buy a consumer may consider such attributes as seating capacity, price, top speed, rate of acceleration, name, and so on. While the consumer may not put a value on any one of these attributes in isolation, they are considered in combination as constituent parts of the total product offering. Because it is unlikely that the consumer will find an ideal combination of attribute levels in any one product offering, the technique is based on the assumption that a trade-off between attribute levels will occur, based on the consumer's value system for the attributes. Thus it is likely that no available alternative will appear to the consumer to be clearly better on every dimension of interest.

As with many multivariate techniques applied in marketing, conjoint measurement was developed in another social science discipline and transferred across. Thus early work by Debreu in 1960[14] and by Luce and Tukey in 1964[15] on psychological issues led to the publication by Kruskal in 1965[16] of a technique for measurement based on a simple method of data collection known as MONANOVA. The first marketing application was published by Green and Rao in 1971.[17] Subsequently further advances were made leading to the development of other computer algorithms for conjoint measurement using either 'pair-wise' comparison of attributes or 'full-model' comparison (see below). Various approaches are compared by Jain, Acito, Malhotra and Mahajan in 1978.[18] The major UK applications of the techniques, of which there are few, feature in publications by Westwood, Lunn and Beazley in 1974[19] and by Blamires in 1981.[20]

How does the technique work? Data are collected from the respondents in the form of ranking judgements about a range of possible attribute levels of products or services. For example, suppose a pricing decision has to be made for a new chocolate confectionery brand which could have one of two fillings (nut or caramel), one of two chocolate types (milk or dark) and one of three prices. This gives rise to $2 \times 2 \times 3 = 12$ possibilities. The consumers are asked to rank these 12 possible products in order of preference usually using a matrix structure of the type shown in Table 4.1.

Rankings are shown within the matrix with most preferred combination = 12, least preferred = 1. It follows that a milk chocolate bar with caramel filling offered at a retail price of 10p promises to be the most successful of the alternatives considered.

It should be noted that this is a simplified example. In most cases more attributes and/or attribute levels would be necessary. In this case it is possible to use a pair-wise comparison[13] in which each possible pair of attributes is considered by consumers at each attribute level (i.e., in this example, chocolate type vs. filling, chocolate type vs. price, filling vs. price). The consumers' ranking task is

Table 4.1 Hypothetical preference price rankings for a new chocolate confectionery brand

	P_1	P_2	P_3
Milk chocolate, nut filling	4	8	2
Milk chocolate, caramel filling	10	12	7
Dark chocolate, nut filling	3	6	1
Dark chocolate, caramel filling	9	11	5

e.g. $P_1 = 9p$, $P_2 = 10p$, $P_3 = 11p$.

simplified under conditions where the process could be absurdly complex. For example in the above case, five names, six designs and four price levels would mean 5 x 6 x 4 = 120 rankings in the full model which is clearly unrealistic and would lead to respondent fatigue. In the literature the term 'trade-off models' tends to be applied to the pair-wise comparison method. The full model can employ a fractional factorial design to make the respondents' task easier.[21]

Before the ranking data can be analysed, the basic form of the relationship between product attributes and preference rankings must be specified. In most applications the simplest approach, that of an additive relationship, is used although Johnson describes an application in which a multiplicative model provided a better fit.[13] The linear additive model assumes that total utility to the consumer is simply the sum of the utility of the parts, the attribute levels.

A computer-based algorithm, such as MONANOVA, is then used to attempt to place utility values of each attribute level so as to 'explain' the consumer preference rankings. Thus ordinarily scaled input is converted into interval-scaled output. This forms a major attraction of the technique as it is argued that the consumers' judgemental input is more realistic, in that they are likely to decide only that one brand is preferred to another at a particular price rather than specifying by how much it is preferred.

Kruskal developed a 'goodness of fit' measure to assess the success of the data transformation. This he defined as:

$$\text{Stress} = S = \sqrt{\sum \frac{(Ri - \widehat{Ri})^2}{\widehat{\Sigma}(\widehat{Ri} - R)^2}}$$

where Ri is the actual monotonic transformation of the rank of version i ($i = 1 \ldots n$ versions, in this case 12),

$\widehat{Ri}$ is the predicted rank from the calculated scale values,

R is the mean of the estimated rankings.

Thus the numerator is an expression of the closeness of fit of the predicted and the actual rankings and the denominator is a scale factor. This approach is not dissimilar to standard deviation calculations in simple statistics and is indeed close to Kruskal's measure of stress applied in the closely related technique of non-metric multidimensional scaling.[22] Clearly, a better fit is achieved when S is smaller because the numerator approaches 0 as the predicted and actual ranks are closer. Thus $S = 0$ is a perfect match between the predicted and actual values.

In general the algorithm in MONANOVA will find a solution so as to maximize the goodness of fit (minimize S) between the two rank orders. A starting solution is generated and the algorithm then uses an iterative process to improve the solution (reduce the value of S) until a stop criterion is reached. This may be in terms of a maximum number of iterations or a minimum stated improvement in the value of S for example.

Thus, although the goodness of fit (stress) measure concerns the two rank orders, the partial

Table 4.2 Derived utility scales in chocolate example

Attribute level	Estimated utility value
Milk chocolate	0.2
Dark chocolate	−0.2
Nut filling	−1.4
Caramel filling	1.2
Price level 1	0.1
Price level 2	1.3
Price level 3	−1.3

utility values associated with the predicted ranks can also be used in marketing planning. In the simple example given in Table 4.1, the utility scales values calculated by the MONANOVA programmes were as in Table 4.2.

These data can be interpreted for marketing decision-making. Thus for example a switch from nut to caramel filling (gain of 2.6 units of utility) is equal for this consumer to a price increase from P_2 to P_3 (loss of 2.6 units of utility) and could be used to justify a higher price for this new product on this evidence. Using the additive model assumed, these utility values can be summed for each of the 12 versions which the hypothetical consumer ranked, and the fit compared as in Table 4.3.

In practical terms P_2 (10p) is the most preferred price (other things being equal) with P_1 (9p)

Table 4.3 Total utilities predicted and actual rankings in chocolate example

Product version	Predicted total utility	Predicted rank	Actual rank
MNP_1	−1.1	4	4
MNP_2	0.1	7.5	8
MNP_3	−2.5	2	2
DNP_1	−1.5	3	3
DNP_2	−0.3	5.5	6
DNP_3	−2.9	1	1
MCP_1	1.5	10	10
MCP_2	2.7	12	12
MCP_3	0.1	7.5	7
DCP_1	1.1	9	9
DCP_2	2.3	11	11
DCP_3	−0.3	5.5	5

Key   M = milk chocolate
D = plain chocolate
N = nut filling
C = caramel filling
P_1–P_3 = price levels
(In the case of a tie, the mean position is taken)

being an alternative. P_3 (11p) has a strong negative effect and should not on this evidence be considered. The brand manager should use P_2 as the price on this evidence if it is at all possible.

Table 4.3 shows a very close fit which is almost exact apart from two tied rankings. Such ties are much more likely to occur in simple examples than they are in more complex attribute level combinations.

Applying Kruskal's stress formula to these data:

$$S \sqrt{\frac{1}{140}} = 0.0845$$

which is a very low value illustrating a very close fit of the actual and predicted ranks. Because the data are ordinal it is not possible to apply the usual statistical significance tests such as t-tests which only apply to normally distributed data although some non-parametric tests have been applied (see below). Also the estimated interval scale for the partial utilities is of arbitrary origin and unit and may be transformed for convenience by arithmetic operations.

Before examining practical pricing applications for the technique it is necessary to examine briefly the advantages and disadvantages of the process.

Advantages of conjoint measurement The major advantage is the data collection method. It would appear to be more realistic to get the respondent to consider a complete brand with specific attribute levels than to try to question the respondent directly on individual elements (such as price) of the brand. Moreover it is possible to use visual aids to enhance realism — dummy packs, advertisements or even product samples can be used in the data collection process. Ranking can also be argued to be more realistic and more akin to how consumers choose between alternative brands. They are likely to decide if one brand is better than another overall, not necessarily by *how much* it is better, i.e., they make ordinal-scaled not interval-scaled judgements in making purchasing decisions.

The output from the analysis offers a manager valuable insights into consumer choice. As Green and Wind postulate, 'Being able to separate overall judgements into psychological components in this manner can provide a manager with valuable information about the relative importance of various attributes of a product. It can also provide information about the value of various levels of a single attribute.'[23] Thus pricing decisions can be considered in the light of consumer utility judgements and compensating changes could be introduced for a price change.

If the conjoint analysis is repeated across a representative sample of a target market then, in conjunction with other data on consumer characteristics, the output can be used as a basis for market segmentation. The technique could identify the most (and the least) price-sensitive segments, which could then be used to guide marketing action. This will be illustrated by the example which follows later in this section.

Because the respondents' trade-offs between attributes are explicitly taken into account, the problems involved in asking questions about 'ideal' combinations of attributes, which are essentially unrealistic, are avoided. Bias in response, such as rationalizing, halo-effects and 'more is always better' thinking, is avoided. For instance in the above example price level 2 is most preferred rather than the cheapest price (P_1). The technique also means that both metric attributes (e.g., price) and non-metric attributes (brand name, pack design) can be compared together even when they are considerably different.

Disadvantages of conjoint measurement It is necessary to define the brand attributes and their particular levels before the data collection commences. Consumer responses are made to specific attribute combinations. If these attributes are not all the relevant ones for the consumer then, although the method will still operate, the obtained results will be misleading. It is thus necessary to undertake preliminary research with a pilot group of consumers to ensure that the criteria for the research are identified exactly and correctly.

As already noted, the complexity of the task for respondents increases rapidly as more attributes and/or levels are added. For a realistic assessment an upper limit of perhaps 25–30 rankings by a single respondent seems feasible. This may involve a more complex design and/or an elimination of some of the interaction effects.

The model specification must also be identified at the outset of the research. In the above example an additive model is used; it would have been possible to multiply rather than add the calculated utility values, for example. Unfortunately the wrong model specification is not necessarily signalled by a high value of S. An assumption of the technique is that the attributes are independent of each other. Thus there is no interaction between variables, i.e., the degree of our hypothetical respondents' liking for nut filling does not vary according to price or type of chocolate. If such interaction does occur it can be detected by using Kendall's *tau* statistic which can be used as an alternative to Kruskal's stress measure.[24] As already noted significance testing of the goodness of fit criterion is not possible and the results should be validated outside the method before use.

Finally, some attributes may have a threshold level below which there can be no trade-off for other attributes by consumers. Again, this should be identified by preliminary research so that all attribute levels included in the research are above this threshold level. An example might be a car which must be capable of at least 20 miles per gallon before a consumer would even consider buying it, whatever the price or other relevant attributes. Thus the levels of this attribute in the conjoint analysis must be greater than 20.

On balance the technique has limitations which can be overcome and potential marketing applications which seem to offer a significant advance in practical pricing research. Fenwick concludes his assessment of the technique with a word of warning:

> Despite . . . dangers conjoint measurement promises to be a powerful analytical tool. . . . Nonetheless, conjoint analysis is no panacea and the pitfalls for the unwary are severe. In particular, the technique is such that goodness of fit provided little indication of the appropriateness of the underlying model, or of the trade-off scales obtained. Consequently analysis results should never be applied without substantial validation.[25]

Blamires has criticized the conjoint analysis data collection approach because the alternatives presented to the respondent are not necessarily the ones which the respondent would consider in making a real purchasing decision.[20] Also he argues that a high price may in practice make the respondent buy the same brand but at another store (i.e., shop around for the lowest price of that preferred brand). This option he argues is not available (but presumably could be incorporated into the research design). Respondents may also wish to appear rational to the interviewer which may affect the rankings selected. This is a major problem for any form of pricing research.

Blamires suggests a hybrid model which he claims is a bridge between Gabor and Granger's buy-response method and trade-off analysis. However, the technique is retail orientated and relates to fast-moving consumer goods only. It disaggregates demand curves by price levels to assess price sensitivity by collecting data in a 'simulated-store' testing procedure for added realism. It does not seem to be a new method, but rather a special case of the buy-response method from individualizing the approach according to respondent's next most preferred brand or brand repertoire and by offering the choice to shop elsewhere.

An application of conjoint measurement in pricing research: Colour TV choice Anttila, van den Heuvel and Moller report an application of conjoint measurement in segmenting the market for colour TVs.[26] They used four price levels, three brand names, three screen sizes, three levels of colour reproduction, two designs and absence of, or one year's, guarantee (determined in a pre-study). Using a fractional factorial design in which each of 200 respondents ranked 26 product compilations, data were collected in personal interviews. By carrying out an individual respondent conjoint analysis and then aggregating across respondents, they were able to isolate particular market segments on the basis

Table 4.4 Relative attribute importance for three utility segments

Attribute	N = 200 Total response	N = 59 Price-sensitive segment	N = 71 Quality-prone segment	N = 35 Design-size-conscious segment
	%	%	%	%
Price	17	44	9	5
Screen size	14	15	12	24
Brand name	22	14	24	12
Colour reproduction	31	20	38	25
Guarantee	11	5	16	4
Design	5	2	1	30

Source: Adapted from Anttila *et al.*[26]

of relative attribute importance by using a cluster analysis. These are shown in Table 4.4 on the basis of these aggregated data.

Thus the price-sensitive segment was less concerned about colour reproduction than respondents as a whole, whereas the largest quality-prone segment was price-insensitive but highly influenced by colour reproduction, brand name and the availability of a one-year guarantee. The third segment shows above-average concern with screen size and design. As they report:

> the results were used for an evaluation of the competitiveness of the company's colour TV models within the segments. This evaluation showed a good coverage of the segments by the current product line except for the design-size conscious segment. After a follow-up research project designated to have a better estimate of the total size of this segment . . . a new model specially designed for this segment was added to the product line.[27]

Summary of conjoint measurement in pricing research This type of model applies in a situation where products are sold as a basic unit with various add-on optional extras. It is a complex procedure. In the UK context it is suggested that the development of applications of this technique are constrained by the rate of acceptance by marketing managers. Although there is evidence of a number of applications of the technique and of a number of market research agencies offering models based on conjoint analysis, they are relatively limited and credibility needs to be developed. This can only occur when managers are convinced that the technique can make a cost-effective contribution to their pricing decisions. This will occur over time as a successful 'track record' for the application of the technique develops.

Future prospects for the use of conjoint measurement are bright it it is used with care and common sense. It has valuable diagnostic power and can give very useful indications of the likely effects of alternative strategies. It is flexible and versatile and, on balance, shows great promise in consumer pricing assessments which is a difficult research area.

4.5 SPECIAL CASES IN THE PRICING OF BRANDS

Finally in this chapter a number of special cases in the pricing of brands are discussed.

4.5.1 The Pricing of new brands

This is a particularly difficult problem for firms because of a lack of market reference points. A new product has a perishable distinctiveness which the firm may be able to capitalize on in the short term by a skimming pricing strategy. Alternatively price may be set at an initially low price to stimulate the market. These strategies have already been discussed.

4.5.2 Transfer pricing

In vertically integrated firms, particularly multinationals, internal pricing may be necessary as a brand is moved from one stage to the next in its movement towards the market. If reference points are available, such as competitive market rates, then this can be used to fix the internal transfer price. In the case of multinationals it may be necessary or desirable to weight the transfer price so as to locate the profit in a particular country for tax or other reasons.

4.5.3 Price-quality interaction

The interaction between price and quality is implicitly considered in the sections above on pricing research and on demand-orientated pricing approaches. An approach which straddles the two is product analysis pricing.[28] This approach is usable by industrial firms where each order may be slightly different but is in essence based on the same product. The essence of the approach is to calculate the perceived value (by the consumer) of all the attributes of the product and sum these to produce a selling price.

In practice this could be done by taking a sample of products with known selling prices and values on each of the attributes. This is feasible where the attributes are objective rather than subjective and where it is possible to ignore interaction effects. Regression techniques can be used to derive a formula for pricing of the form

$$P = aX_1 + bX_2 + cX_3 + dX_4 \text{ etc.}$$

where P is the selling price

a,b,c,d etc. are parameters estimated by regression

$X_1 \ldots X_n$ are product attributes.

This formula can then be applied to further pricing decisions.

In a similar vein Cowling and Rayner[29] devised a technique for assessing quality effects of price. Essentially this adds a disturbance term U to a linear regression equation of the type above. It represents, for a sample of brands in a market, that part of the price which cannot be explained by objective attributes of the brand.

Thus, in a study of the UK tractor market they found that

$$P = 223.5 + 8.12h_p + 85.5D + \mu$$

where P = price of the tractor, h_p is the horse power and D is a dummy variable (= 1 if the model had a diesel engine). μ is the residual, an estimate of the difference between the actual market price of a tractor and its price estimated from its features. Thus if μ is positive, the tractor has a higher price than the attributes would suggest which indicates a high quality tractor. This technique could be of use in pricing a new brand in a market which has a number of existing brands and the brand positioning is aimed at a quality segment. This approach could then indicate the price that could be charged for a brand of the quality intended.

4.5.4 Promotional aspects of price

Price can be used as a form of sales promotion by spending promotional money on price discounts. This is very common for grocery products. A well-established brand may generate additional short-term consumer interest by price promotions. 'Special offer' packs can be used although this can raise distribution problems. For example, retailers could be left holding normal stock they cannot sell because of the lower price special offer. This would cause ill will unless remedied. A more substantive criticism is that the price discount is given to all customers when some would presumably have been perfectly willing to buy at the old price. This can be avoided by using a 'money-off next purchase' label to encourage brand loyalty or by using money-off coupons in press advertisements or mail shots to consumers' homes. Here, only the more price-conscious consumers will be likely to be influenced by the promotion.

At the retail level, price promotions may be initiated to increase store loyalty. The use of 'loss-leader' pricing where deep cuts in price are made in selected but basic items' prices to encourage shoppers to use a particular store is made on the assumption that these deep-cut items will not be the only items bought and the overall store profit will be increased.

Such price promotions can be viewed by consumers as being product-demeaning in the sense that they may be perceived as reducing the inherent attractiveness of the brand and may have quality and/or brand image connotations. They are likely to attract price-conscious consumers who may easily and quickly be attracted to a competitive product by a rival price-promotional tactic.

The whole issue of promotion, the major part of non-price competition, is discussed in the next chapter.

REFERENCES

1. Hall, R. L. and C. J. Hitch (1939) *Price Theory and Business Behaviour*, Oxford Economic Papers, 2.
2. Lanzilloti, R. F. (1958) 'Pricing Objectives in large companies', *American Economic Review*, 48, 921–41.
3. Harrison, R. and F. M. Wilkes (1983) 'A note on Jaguar's pricing policy', *European Journal of Marketing*, 7, 3, 242–6.
4. Sweezy, P. M. (1939) 'Demand under conditions of oligopoly', *Journal of Political Economy*, 47, 568–73.
5. Livesey, F. (1976) *Pricing*, Macmillan, London, Ch. 10.
6. Fitzroy, P. T. (1976) *Analytical Methods for Marketing Management*, McGraw-Hill, Maidenhead, pp. 238–42.
7. Pigou, A. (1938) *The Economics of Welfare*, 4th edn, Macmillan, London.
8. Fitzroy, op. cit., pp. 17–25.
9. Gabor, A. and C. W. J. Granger (1966) 'Price as an indicator of quality: report on an enquiry', *Economica*, 33, 43–70.
10. Gabor, A. (1977) *Pricing Principles and Practices*, Heinemann, London.
11. Kotler, P. (1980) *Marketing Management*, 4th Edn, Prentice-Hall, Englewood Cliffs, New Jersey, pp. 399–400.
12. Pessemier, E. A. (1960) 'An experimental method for estimating demand', *Journal of Business*, October, 373–83.
13. Johnson, R. M. (1974) 'Trade-off analysis of consumer values', *Journal of Marketing Research*, 11, May, 121.
14. Debreu, G. (1960) 'Topological methods in cardinal utility theory', in *Mathematical Models in the Social Sciences*, K. J. Arrow, J. Karlins and P. Suppes (eds), Stanford University Press, Stanford.
15. Luce, R. D. and J. W. Tukey (1964) 'Simultaneous conjoint measurement: a new type of fundamental measurement', *Journal of Mathematical Psychology*, 1, February, 1–27.
16. Kruskal, J. B. (1965) 'Analysis of factorial experiments by estimating monotone transformation of the data', *Journal of Royal Statistical Society*, Series B, 27, 2, 251–63.
17. Green, P. E. and V. R. Rao (1971) 'Conjoint measurement for quantifying judgemental data', *Journal of Marketing Research*, 8, August, 355–63.
18. Jain, J. K., F. Acito, N. K. Malhotra and V. Mahajan (1979) 'A comparison of the internal validity of alternative parameter estimation methods in decompositional multiattribute preference models', *Journal of Marketing Research*, 16, August, 313–22.
19. Westwood, D., J. A. Lunn and D. Beazley, (1974) 'The trade-off model and its extensions', *Journal of the Market Research Society*, 16, 3, 227–41.
20. Blamires, C. (1981) 'Pricing research techniques: a preview and a new approach', *Journal of the Market Research Society*, 23, 3, 103–27.
21. Green, P. E., J. D. Carroll and F. J. Carmone (1978) 'Some new types of fractional factorial designs for marketing experiments', in *Research in Marketing*, Vol. 1, J. N. Sheth (ed.), JAI Press, Greenwich C.T., pp. 99–112.

22. Kruskal, J. B. (1964) 'Non metric multi-dimensional scaling: a numerical method', *Psychometrika*, **29**, 115–29.
23. Green, P. E. and Y. Wind (1975) 'New ways to measure consumers' judgements', *Harvard Business Review*, July–August, 108.
24. Johnson, op. cit., 125.
25. Fenwick, I. (1978) 'A user's guide to conjoint measurement in marketing', *European Journal of Marketing*, **12**, 2, 210–11.
26. Anttila, M., R. R. van den Heuval, and K. Moller, (1980) 'Conjoint measurement for marketing management', *European Journal of Marketing*, **14**, 7, 397–408.
27. Ibid., p. 406.
27. Brown, G., T. Copeland and M. Millward (1973) 'Monadic Testing of New Products – an old problem and some partial solutions', *Journal of the Market Research Society*, **15**, 2, 112–31.
28. Brown, W. and E. Jacques (1964) *Product Analysis Pricing*, Heinemann, London.
29. Cowling, K. and A. J. Rayner (1969) *Price quality and market share*, Economic Research Paper No. 7, University of Warwick.

MARKET CONDUCT (2): NON-PRICE COMPETITION

5.1 THE BRAND IMAGE

Branding has grown so strong that today hardly anything goes unbranded. Salt is packaged in distinctive manufacturers' containers, oranges are stamped with growers' names, common nuts and bolts are packaged in cellophane with a distributor's label and automobile components — spark plugs, tyres, filters — bear separate brand names from the auto makers.[1]

Consumers buy brands (not products or services) and by developing a personality for the brand (as opposed to attaching a proposition to it) the brand is made more meaningful to the consumer and this added value strengthens loyalty.[2]

In Chapter 2 Lancaster's characteristics approach was analysed. This assumes that a brand consists of objective characteristics which are perceived objectively by potential consumers in their choice process. Preferences are then expressed by consumer choice from the different combinations of (objective) characteristics offered by competing brands. In practice, much marketing expenditure concentrates on creating a subjective 'personality' for brands in the minds of potential consumers. The primary process for achieving this objective is media advertising, but many other forms of promotion are also used. This objective is really a means to an end: that of increased sales and profits. Individual promotional campaigns can have a number of alternative objectives which can be identified by examining the 'hierarchy of effects' models of advertising.

A number of writers have postulated that advertising can be used to move consumers along a continuum from unawareness of the brand to brand loyalty revealed through repeat buying of the brand. Strong, writing in 1925, suggested a four-stage process for consumer choice:[3]

$$\text{Awareness} \rightarrow \text{Interest} \rightarrow \text{Desire} \rightarrow \text{Action}$$

while this was extended by Lavidge and Steiner[4] in 1961 to:

$$\text{Awareness} \rightarrow \text{Knowledge} \rightarrow \text{Liking} \rightarrow \text{Preference} \rightarrow \text{Conviction} \rightarrow \text{Purchase}$$

and further by Engel, Blackwell and Kollat[5] in 1978 to:

$$\text{Perceived information} \rightarrow \text{Problem recognition} \rightarrow \text{Search} \rightarrow$$
$$\text{Evaluation of alternatives} \rightarrow \text{Beliefs} \rightarrow \text{Attitudes} \rightarrow \text{Intentions} \rightarrow \text{Choice}$$

In these cases the assumption is that consumers formulate a behavioural intention which then leads to actual behaviour (i.e., attitude change → purchasing, in the case of brands). Advertising, in these models, aims at moving consumers along this continuum by first informing them of the brand's existence, qualities (objectively and/or subjectively assessed), price and availability and then by persuading them to change existing attitudes and behaviour and buy the brand. Naturally, one advertising campaign would not move all consumers from unawareness to regular brand purchasing, but specific objectives of a campaign could be expressed in communication goals such as:

— To increase brand awareness to w per cent of the target population.
— To increase preference for the brand over competitive brands X, Y and Z by x per cent.

or by sales goals such as:

— To achieve brand trial of y per cent.
— To increase repurchase rates by z per cent.

Campaigns can be tailored to a target audience's needs by considering their position on this continuum. Message content and channels of communication should also reflect these needs. Thus to inform consumers of a new brand of chocolate confectionery may involve prime-time TV advertising, stressing the novelty of the new brand. To increase preference for a hi-fi brand, however, may involve a detailed technical product description in an enthusiasts' magazine.

Advertising-effects models of this type imply a strong role of advertising in brand image creation in order to inform and persuade consumers of the value of the brand to them. The time element is also stressed. Over time, consumers can be moved along the continuum towards regular purchasing of the brand as shown in Table 5.1.

Table 5.1 The 'strong' role of advertising in brand creating

Unawareness → Awareness → Knowledge of brand features →

Brand preference (if rival brands) → Brand trial →

Brand repurchase → Regular repeat purchasing

Thus, advertising can be used at any stage, under this model, to change consumers' behavioural intentions or behaviour in a positive way towards the brand. An alternative, 'weak', theory of the role of advertising has been proposed by Ehrenberg and Goodhardt[6] developing earlier work by Ehrenberg.[7] They assume a three-stage process in consumer adoption of brands:

Awareness → Trial → Reinforcement

This is justified as follows:

Awareness Advertisements use repetition and obtrusive effects to overcome consumers' perceptual selectivity (i.e., avoidance of advertisements). Awareness is created only with difficulty as there is intensive competition for consumers' attention from a vast array of advertisements. The impact of advertising is informative rather than persuasive at this inaugural phase. What is all-important is brand trial.

Trial Brand trial occurs in an atmosphere of ignorance and uncertainty. The trialist may have been informed about the brand by advertising but could also have found out about it from other sources, especially word of mouth or point-of-sale display (for convenience products).

The key role of advertising is the reinforcement of whatever satisfaction the customer feels as a result of buying and using the brand.

Reinforcement If advertising has raised expectations from produce use which the brand does not deliver then repurchase is unlikely. The user's direct comparative observation is most important in determining consumers' attitudes to the brand. The major function of advertising at this stage is to remind consumers of the benefits of the brand, but they will not be persuaded to buy again after a negative use experience as this is likely to override advertising claims.

This 'weak' model of advertising effectiveness perhaps underplays the role of advertising in brand image creation. Brand usage leads to image creation in this model. In sharp contrast to the hierarchy of effects models discussed above, the 'weak' theory emphasizes behaviour as preceding behavioural intention. Thus it is the usage experience which leads to the formation of attitudes about the brand and future behavioural intentions (purchasing intentions): brand image is created primarily from product use experience.

Expanding this argument to a broader scale, Ehrenberg and Goodhardt argue that the primary role of competitive brand advertising is not to increase market share but to prevent the erosion of sales levels. They argue that there is no evidence of the sales effectiveness of advertising for established brands. This is discussed later in the chapter. Thus in terms of market structure as discussed in Chapter 3, this is a defensive strategy – a negative role for advertising as a part of marketing strategy. 'Advertising helps to keep one's satisfied customers by reinforcing their existing habits and attitudes. It is the price to pay for staying in the market.'[8]

Economists' views of advertising have tended to concentrate on industry-level effects rather than individual brand effects, and the concept of the brand image has therefore tended to be undervalued in economics. An exception to this is found in the work of Nerlove and Arrow.[9] They utilize the concept of advertising goodwill and assume that advertising does not influence sales directly but acts to increase the level of goodwill. Sales are influenced by the level of goodwill (in addition to price and/or environmental variable), not by advertising per se. If advertising is stopped they assume that goodwill declines at a constant rate, reflecting the behavioural phenomenon of forgetting. This is a similar view to that of Ehrenberg and Goodhardt, above. Also the intermediate stage 'goodwill' is a parallel concept to the use of 'characteristics' between 'goods' and 'utility' in Lancaster's work discussed in Chapter 2.

The concept of goodwill in this sense is not far from the concept of the brand image, especially in the long-run sense. Taking a long-run view, advertising expenditure in this 'stock of goodwill' approach can be seen as being similar to any other fixed asset investment. The brand is then viewed as a fixed asset of the company and advertising expenditure can be seen as additions to this fixed asset. A lack of advertising is equivalent to a lack of provision for depreciation: the brand loses value due to memory lapse over time.

In their 1984 Annual Report, Review of Advertising Operations, Saatchi and Saatchi Compton Worldwide assert that 'in the more sophisticated economies advertising has come to be regarded as a protection for the largest single asset of major companies (except that it does not appear on balance sheets) – the brand franchise.'

This 'investment' view of advertising can explain why companies continue to spend money on brands. Mars have spent a consistently high amount on advertising, using the same slogan 'A Mars a day helps you work rest and play', for the past 25 years. This can also act as a barrier to entry in a market as it can increase brand loyalty to existing products. So brand image can be viewed as the result of an accumulated investment in advertising expenditure over time.

Brand loyalty, a predisposition to buy the same brand on consecutive purchasing occasions, can be seen in these terms also. Use experience which is satisfactory, as reinforced by advertising, leads consumers to avoid the risk of trying a new brand and therefore to buy the same brand again. Experience accumulates over use occasions. A number of writers have investigated the features and correlates of brand loyalty, particularly Jacoby and Chestnut[10] and Carman[11] in the US and Charlton, Ehrenberg and Pymont in the UK.[12,13,14] Generally results have been inconclusive. Engel and Blackwell[15] summarize the major findings as follows:

1. Socio-economic, demographic, and psychological variables generally do not distinguish brand-loyal consumers from other consumers when traditional definitions of brand loyalty are used.
2. When extended definitions of brand loyalty are used, some socio-economic, demographic, and psychological variables are related to loyalty. However, these relationships tend to be product-specific rather than ubiquitous across product categories.
3. There is limited evidence that the loyalty behaviour of an informal group leader affects the behaviour of other group members.
4. Store loyalty is commonly associated with brand loyalty. Moreover, store loyalty appears to be an intervening variable between certain consumer characteristics and brand loyalty. In other words, certain consumer characteristics are related to store loyalty, which in turn is related to brand loyalty.
5. There is some evidence that brand loyalty is inversely related to the number of stores shopped.
6. The relationship between amount purchased and brand loyalty is uncertain because of contradictory findings.
7. The relationship between interpurchase time and brand loyalty is uncertain because of contradictory findings.
8. There is limited evidence that perceived risk is positively related to brand loyalty.
9. Market-structure variables, including the extensiveness of distribution and the market share of the leading brand, exert a positive influence on brand loyalty.
10. The effects of the number of alternative brands, special deals, and price activity are uncertain due to contradictory findings.

Although there are these measurement difficulties related to the concept of brand loyalty, it nevertheless does imply that success in brand image creation can, at least in theory, be assessed in loyalty terms.

We now briefly consider the economic aspects of advertising as they relate to brand-level analysis.

5.2 ECONOMICS OF ADVERTISING

Much has been written by economists on the subject of advertising. The primary level of concern is the industry, especially advertising effectiveness measurement and the impact of advertising on the structure-conduct performance debate. The detail of this debate is summarized by Chiplin and Sturgess[16] and by Reekie.[17]

The main elements of the debate as they relate to the brand include:

5.2.1 Advertising and concentration

Greer[18] argued that advertising intensity varies with concentration as shown in Figure 5.1 where the four-firm concentration ratio is used. This is the share of the output of the industry accounted for by the largest four firms.

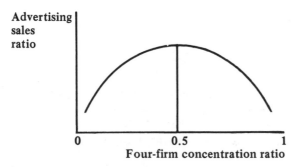

Fig. 5.1 Advertising intensity and concentration

The maximum advertising:sales ratio occurs with a four-firm concentration ratio of 0.5, according to this model, again fitting with the argument in the last section that advertising is defensive or self-cancelling rather than aggressive. This is likely to lead to a higher level than the profit-maximizing level for the industry as a whole. Greer argued that tacit agreements between oligopolists reduce the intensity at higher levels of concentration, but this is not borne out by other studies. There is a further problem of two-way causation. While advertising could lead to an increase in concentration, this in turn could lead to an increase in advertising expenditure. It thus becomes extremely difficult to disentangle the effects. As noted in Chapter 3, advertising is the focus of competition in many oligopolists' marketing strategies but it is difficult to disentangle cause and effect. The brand is very often the centre of the oligopolists' advertising strategy.

5.2.2 Advertising and profitability

Advertising can help to create brand loyalty and this in turn, by differentiation from other brands, enables a brand to become more like a product, i.e., in effect creating a monopoly for the company as the 'prize' for successful brand image creation. Higher profitability is associated with higher market share, although it can become increasingly difficult (and expensive) to attract the more inert and (other) brand-loyal consumers to further increase market share.

There can be scale effects in advertising, although this again is debated. It can be argued that (a) diminishing returns set in immediately. That is, the first advertising pound is spent more effectively, etc. Alternatively, (b) there may be a threshold effect. Below the threshold level, advertisements have little effect but once it is passed, increasing returns occur, at least for some higher expenditures, before diminishing returns set in again. These two cases are illustrated in Figure 5.2.

The advertising elasticity of demand is generally held to be less than 1 over most levels of expenditure, i.e., a company needs to spend more than in proportion on advertising to increase sales. Advertising expenditure is wasted on the disinterested and the already committed. It is however difficult to measure the profit implications of advertising expenditure because of the lagged effects of advertising and because profits are also influenced by other variables, as noted in Chapter 1 in the discussion on the complexity of marketing practice.

5.2.3 Advertising and prices

Again, there is no agreement about the relationship between advertising and prices. One argument is that if advertisements inform, then informed consumers are likely to buy at the lowest available prices, thus advertising lower prices. The value of advertising to consumers is in reducing consumers'

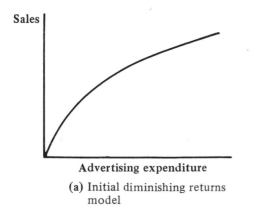

(a) Initial diminishing returns model

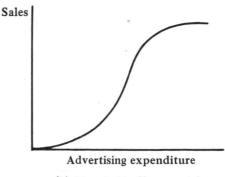

(b) Threshold-effect model

Fig. 5.2 Advertising returns

search costs for information about available brands. If search costs are included as part of the overall price which the consumer pays, then advertising reduces price in this argument. The main element to search costs is time, so the value of time to consumers is an important input to this model. If consumers put a very low price on their search time then the time-saving nature of advertising is of little value to them. This would seem to be the practical position, as discussed in Chapter 8; increasingly consumers seem to be regarding shopping as a leisure activity undertaken as a family unit which implies a low time-value. The more common view is opposite to this, that advertising decreases price elasticity of demand (see Chapter 1) and increases barriers to entry (as discussed in Chapter 3): both conditions are likely to lead to price increases.

It has also been argued that advertising, by increasing demand, can lead to increased economies of scale in production and marketing leading to a fall in the selling price. The advertising element of price is present for all buyers whether or not they need it. More controversially it has been argued that advertisements convey misinformation which leads to the misallocation of scarce resources which tends to increase prices. This is moving towards the Galbraithian view that wants are shaped by the advertising and salesmanship of firms, which reduces consumer sovereignty.[40] But are consumers fooled by advertisements? This ethical debate emanates from the persuasive intentions of most brand advertising and from consumers' responses to such persuasion. While much of this debate is beyond the scope of this book, two areas of analysis can shed some light: the campaign planning aspect of brand advertising, and the measurement of advertising effectiveness. In other words we can examine how firms set out to use brand advertising and how they try to measure their success in achieving advertising aims.

5.3 CAMPAIGN PLANNING FOR BRANDS

There can be many specific objectives for an advertising campaign for a brand. In practice the particular objective will be related to a marketing problem or opportunity identified by market research. In their 1984 Annual Report, Review of Advertising Operations, Saatchi and Saatchi Compton Worldwide identify a number of reasons why the advertising of brands is growing in importance:

1. Battles for market shares.
2. Importance of brand ranks – any brand below third in a market has potential profitability problems as it is trapped in the middle ground: it cannot keep up with the brand leader on advertising, nor can it match the own-brand manufacturer on price.
3. Self-service retailing. This concept is developed in Chapter 8.
4. Media complexity enables advertising to be used as a rifle rather than a shotgun.

Whatever the advertising objective, the campaign will need to consider a number of factors in the planning procedure.

5.3.1 Factors influencing brand advertising campaigns

Product type Whether the product is new or established will be an important influence on the campaign. In terms of the hierarchy of effects model, the content of the advertising message will vary in each case. Also important is the frequency of use and range of usage of the brand. A frequently purchased brand may need to be supported by a regular flow of 'reminder' advertising. The unique selling proposition of the brand, the major differentiating feature from competing brands, is also important in campaign planning. If, for example, a brand of perfume has a particular psychological appeal then the use of TV advertising to create an appealing mood and atmosphere to creatively dramatize the brand's appeal may be obligatory. An appeal based on a high rate of return for a brand life insurance cover on the other hand, may require a press campaign to put across the financial details of the claim in a retainable form, perhaps with a returnable coupon for use as a proposal form. The product range can also be important in this context as a decision has to be made as to whether the whole range or particular constituent brands are to be featured in the advertisement.

There are two other associated factors. The first is the packaging of the brand. As we shall see in Chapter 8 on distribution, self-selection has to a very large extent replaced counter service for a wide range of consumer (and some service and industrial) suppliers. In the case of groceries, adjacent displays of competing brands is the norm. The would-be purchaser has to take the positive step of choosing from this array. In this context the packaging takes on a particular marketing significance, moving beyond the original primary function of protection during transit. The use of colour, lettering style and wording are used to attempt to make brands stand out from the competition. Promotion, especially advertising, will tend to emphasize the appearance of the package to try to pre-sell the brand to the potential purchaser. At the point of sale the pack should then remind the shopper of the advertising claims. In short, the pack becomes the focus of an advertising message in the self-selection process.

In many mature markets, packaging is often used to try to rejuvenate brands and improve or extend their appeal. In the 1960s Pepsi-Cola based their attack on Coca-Cola's dominant market position on a development of the packaging of the soft drinks. Over a period of time the product was made available in different sizes of plastic bottle and in cans as well as the traditional small glass bottle container. This widened the appeal of the brands. Rather than being bought only for immediate consumption (in cans), the larger size bottles were stocked in supermarkets, appealing to housewives for family use on a number of usage occasions. The use of 'bubble packs' for nails, screws, nuts and bolts and so on has increased the ease of display for these products in self-service situations, broadening their distribution outlet range.

The second associated factor is the brand name. The brand name can have a very positive effect on sales prospects. It can be viewed as an investment just as much as fixed assets can be for a firm. In marketing terms, the brand name should encapsulate the appeal of the brand by suggesting the brand's benefits to consumers. It should be simple to pronounce, free of unpleasant associations in any language and ideally have promotional possibilities. Associated trade marks, symbols and logos can also be used promotionally. In the UK, Midland Bank advertisements focus on a cartoon version of a griffin which has appeared as a Midland Bank logo for many years. The distinctive Coca-Cola trade mark 'Coke' has been promoted heavily worldwide to make it a universal symbol of the brand.

In many cases, company or brand names are long established and their promotional possibilities are a matter of historical accident. Increasingly firms spend heavily to ensure that a new brand name has strong brand-image-enhancing qualities. Companies can feature their own name as part of the brand name to suggest quality. The 'family name' image is used by IBM, Kelloggs, Heinz for example. The disadvantage is that the brand name choice is limited. More importantly, the company name is inextricably linked to every brand. A brand failure may have negative repercussions on the sales of the rest of the 'family range'. The alternative approach is not to associate the company name with that of the brand. This approach is used by Proctor and Gamble and Unilever for example. Their washing powder brands such as Persil, Bold, Omo and Daz are long established in their own right. These and similar well established names and their associated connotations are recognized as very valuable assets by the companies that own them. They convey immediate quality expectations about the brand which can add to the price which purchasers are willing to pay.

In introducing new brands, the use of an established name can be used to confer legitimacy on the new name. In terms of the hierarchy of effects model, the easier recognition of the new brand is made possible if potential consumers are already familiar with, and respect, the name from an existing company or brand.

The establishment of a valuable brand name is usually a long-term process and is a costly process in that advertisement content is often centred on the name. The benefits from successful establishment are that consumer awareness of, interest in, and expectations from, the brand are quickly communicated because of favourable predispositions. In summary, the product type in all its myriad aspects has a major impact on campaign planning, determining — at least in part — the medium to be used, the message content and the target audience.

The market Many of the other elements of a campaign plan follow from the definition of the target audience and the competition for their attention from rival brands. It follows from the hierarchy of effects models that the target audience can in part be defined according to their position on the continuum in Table 5.1. However, there are many other dimensions for categorizing audiences, although of course these are not all relevant in each case.

Socio-economic variables, along with the demographic features of the market, can specify an audience for consumer goods by cross-tabulating such factors as:

— Sex.
— Age-group.
— Marital status.
— Number and ages of children.
— Social group.
— ACORN group*.
— Location.
— Income levels.
— Social group membership (e.g., sports, hobbies, professional).
— Stage in life cycle.
— Buying roles within the family (purchaser, user, influencer).
— Ownership of particular consumer durables.

In addition to these basic factors, personality and attitudinal variables can be added to give a more detailed insight into the life-style of the audience. This psychographics approach enables campaigns to be planned which emphasize how the brand has relevance for the style of living of the target audience. Creativity is used to emphasize mood, atmosphere and environment for brand usage, usually relying on non-verbal communication such as the background setting for an advertisement (indoor/outdoor, relaxed or tense environment, type of music, style of furniture, use of colour schemes, appearance of the models, etc.).

These factors are particularly relevant when the aim of the campaign involves persuasion of the audience. Various research projects have been conducted which have attempted to identify relevant correlates of persuasibility. Although on balance the evidence is not conclusive, Karlins and Abelson conclude their studies by stating that 'In our society, women are more persuasible than men.'[19] Other studies, summarized by Delozier have shown that 'in general a person low in self esteem is more persuasible than someone high in self esteem, especially when social approval is involved' and that 'no consistent relationship exists between general intelligence and persuasibility'.[20]

For industrial goods the social and socio-psychological variables are still valid but perhaps not as important as are economic factors in the audience dimension definition process. Factors such as:

— Size of company (turnover, number of employees, profit levels).
— Production process used.
— Type of business activity.
— Location.
— Centralization of buying.

* ACORN (A Classification of Residential Neighbourhood) is a system based in the UK devised by CACI which classifies housing types into 11 major groups which have been identified. These classifications are linked with social groups and can be cross-tabulated with postcodes and 1981 Census returns to qualify and quantify the groups (see also Chapter 8).

— Buying process (individual, committee).
— Inter-departmental rivalries and other organizational issues.

If a specialist purchasing officer is involved then expert knowledge, objective comparison of competing brand features (as in Lancaster's model) and other 'rational' factors are relevant, along with the individual idiosyncrasies of the buyer/user and influences in the buying process which can be a time-consuming, complex process.

One would expect advertisements for industrial goods to be in the specialist press, stressing performance, cost and technical brand features rather than using mood, style and other psychological appeals in a TV campaign. Exceptions to this exist, especially for new brands from market leaders. Recent examples include a new Rank Xerox photocopier and the IBM personal computer.

For both goods and services it is also relevant to consider competitive brand promotional activity. Various strategies exist, for example to try to dominate one medium, to make directly comparable claims for the brand *vis-à-vis* competitive brands. Whatever the response is to be, the use of promotion by rivals is a relevant consideration.

Once the relevant dimensions and segments of the market have been determined for a specific campaign, these can be quantified and compared against audience characteristics of the available media.

Media choice In this section the advertising media will be briefly considered while other forms of promotion will be considered later in the chapter. Although it is extremely difficult to compare costs between media, media buying being a specialist and complex business, the concept of 'cost per thousand opportunities to see' is used in the industry. In practice, although the cost per thousand will vary between media, the total cost will depend on the total audience size and the 'quality' of the 'opportunity to see'. Thus, a fleeting glimpse of a billboard while passing in a car is of limited quality when compared to viewing a 30-second commercial in the comfort of one's home. The available media will be considered in terms of their features from the point of view of brand advertising.

Available Media

TV Because TV appeals to more than one sense (sight and sound) and employs colour and movement, the scope for creatively dramatizing a brand is greater than for most other media. It is easier to gain and retain attention and prolong memory than with other media. In the UK TV-am and Channel 4 extended supply of advertising air-time by 90 per cent in the early 1980s and extended the types of audience profile which can be reached.

Detailed audience measurement in the UK, by BARB (Broadcasters Audience Research Board) using a sample of 3000 households whose TV viewing is monitored automatically, provides advertisers with a rapid indication of the size and constitution of the audience reached by the transmission of any particular advertisment.

Net annual TV advertising expenditure rose from £109 million in 1971 to £697 million in 1982 and was more than £1000 million in 1984. Recent technological developments have led to concern about the quality of advertisement viewing. For example, remote control devices enable viewers to 'channel-hop' easily during the transmission of advertisements. The use of video recorders enable 'time-shift viewing' to occur. If the timing of the brand advertisement during the day (or day of the week) is important then time shifting (i.e., viewing at a different time of day and/or day of the week) can reduce the 'quality' of the opportunity to see the commercial. The availability and use of a (remote control) fast-forward switch on a video can mean that the recorded commercial is not viewed at all, but could also mean that the commercial is viewed in detail (repeatedly).

TV advertising is particularly useful for brand image creation, the qualities of the brand can be communicated persuasively and informatively, forming lasting impressions. The use of humour, fear, glamour, style, mood, drama, sound, cartoons, and colours are but examples of the many dimensions which advertisers can creatively draw upon to personalize their brands.

It is not surprising that TV is the leading medium for brand creation. When used, TV is almost always the prime medium, though a campaign may perhaps use other media for cost reasons to extend a campaign initiated on TV.

Newspapers Unlike TV, newspapers can be used to pass on detailed information in a retainable form, if necessary in a regular flow, drawing on topical events. However, only appealing to one sense (sight) limits the memory factor. Many readers may scan an advertisement (or ignore it) rather than reading it in detail, thus only low depth of content is possible. The quality of the opportunity to see a brand advertisement is limited.

Local newspapers (including free sheets) in particular can develop strong reader identification and involvement through letters pages, crosswords and other competitions, the chance of reading about someone known to the reader, and so on, which leads to added credibility. Retail advertising predominates but may be based on price competition for manufacturers' brands. The trade press form a particularly important medium for industrial and some consumer brand advertising. These can be used to attempt to influence distributors and to emphasize brand features. It is common to draw distributors' attention to forthcoming promotions, consumer advertisement campaigns or recent brand successes by using the trade press.

Brands can be advertised in newspapers but this is less common than is the use of TV. There are exceptions to this contention. In the UK, cigarette advertising is often newspaper-based as it is banned from TV. When colour is available in the newspaper, then its use to advertise brands is more common. Brands of financial services are often promoted in newspapers, especially when financial advice or business news sections are published. Coupons for direct response are a particular feature of this sector's brand advertising. Finally, the publication of colour magazines along with newspapers (especially on Sundays) has broadened the appeal of the medium for brand advertising. The use of high quality production in colour enhances brand image creation. This is particularly the case when the readership profile of the newspaper closely matches that of the target audience.

Magazines Unlike newspapers, magazines are often elective rather than being regarded as necessities. This leads to stronger reader-identification and more detailed reading of the contents (including the advertisements) and longer retention of the copy. The trust of the medium is likely to spill over to the advertisement content as a form of 'halo' effect. The availability of colour and good quality printing enables brand image advertising to use this medium. Inserts and 'scratch and sniff' patches can be used to give product samples to readers especially for shampoo and cosmetic brands.

The particular appeal of magazines in brand advertising is due to audience definition. A vast array of magazines are available for advertising, covering many specific market segments defined by factors such as:

— Sex (*Woman's Own, Men Only*).
— Age-group (*16*).
— Interest/hobby (*Popular Gardening, Personal Computing, DIY*).
— Consumer-durable ownership (*Car, Hi-Fi News, Caravanning* — the arrival on the scene of 'The Toaster-Owners Gazette' is awaited with interest!).
— Professional (*Accountancy, Bankers' World, Marketing Week*).

Thus campaigns can if necessary be targeted on specific segments of the market quite cost-effectively. While TV and national newspapers are often compared with a 'shotgun' approach, blasting a wide range of the audience with the message, special interest magazines take a 'rifle' approach, pinpointing a particular market group accurately.

Radio In the UK, radio retains a 'pop' image but in the 1980s has broadened its appeal. While the audience can be reached in a variety of locations (e.g., car, place of work), the medium involves low information and a low memory factor. In brand advertising terms, radio can be used to remind consumers of a brand name or of a TV campaign rather than being the primary medium in a campaign.

Outdoor media Billboards are often used to repeat the copy line of a TV brand campaign which extends the life of a campaign at a low cost. Sites for billboards are static and limited in location and gain little attention and retention of advertising content, although novel appeals can develop the potential of billboards. Recently a car was stuck to a billboard site to advertise a brand of (strong) glue, adding an extra dimension to the medium.

Other outdoor media include bus shelters, bus and lorry sides (which by movement gain more attention) sports grounds, parking meters, taxis, car-parking tickets and telephone kiosks.

The major brand advertising use is to remind consumers of a recent TV or press campaign copy line or of the brand name in a location which is, perhaps because it may be unexpected, likely to gain more attention than otherwise. Taking advertising campaigns into the High Street means that would-be buyers are reminded of a brand and its qualities closer to the point of sale than is possible by any other advertising medium. Costs are relatively low but so is the quality of the opportunity to see.

Electronic Finally, there is likely to be a growth in new, electronic media usage. In early 1985 there were 53 000 Prestel sets installed in the UK. Among other things these can be used for in-home shopping (Nottingham Building Society's 'Home-Link') or banking (Royal Bank of Scotland). Once the growth of this type of service is more widespread it may become attractive as an advertising medium with the possibility of instant consumer response (Prestel links a telephone line with a TV set to give a two-way communication capability). This could be used to access a database of product information to help with a purchasing choice or to actually purchase brands from an electronic 'catalogue'.

The proposed EFTPOS service (Electronic Funds Transfer at the Point of Sale) is a further indication of the growth of instant-response cashless electronic systems growth. Cable TV which offers a plethora of channels covering specific subjects (films, cartoons, sport, etc.) again has advertising opportunities when the service is more widely available.

Choice of Media The choice of media will be influenced in part by these features but also by factors such as:

The size of the media budget Most brand image TV campaigns are costed in hundreds of thousands (if not millions) of pounds. Unless the budget is large enough, TV is not an option.

The frequency of advertising exposure That is, how often a target audience member should see the advertisement. The value of repetition is linked to the learning process in psychological terms. An assessment needs to be made of the number of times an average consumer in the target audience sees the advertisement before becoming bored with it, while still gaining the intended message from it.

Flexibility To a large extent this depends on supply and demand factors. The supply of advertising space/time is limited: with high demand, rationing is by price; with limited demand, more flexibility is available to advertisers who may wish to change a schedule at short notice.

Medium effectiveness The effective cost of a medium is determined by the cost per thousand actually seeing the advertisement (rather than having opportunities to see the advert) and by the effectiveness of the advertising message (which medium puts the message across most effectively?) Both these factors need to be considered alongside the viewing/readership patterns for each possible medium. It is clear that measurement of advertising effectiveness is a complex issue and we shall return to it later in this chapter.

Actual media usage In 1984 in the UK actual expenditure on advertising was split between the media as shown in Table 5.2.

Table 5.2 UK advertising expenditure by medium, 1984

	Amount (£m)	% share
Press	2558	63
TV	1245	30.7
Posters	150	4
Radio	86	2
Cinema	16	0.3
Total	4055	100

Source: Adapted from Advertising Association data.

The press share of total advertising expenditure rose for the first time since 1973 (except for the abnormal year of 1979 when a 13-week ITV strike severely distorted the figures) and was expected to grow at 8 per cent for 1985 while TV was expected to have an expenditure growth of 7 per cent.

Part of this expansion in press advertising results from the growth of 'free-sheets' which are delivered free to all households in an area on a regular basis (usually weekly, although 1985 saw the first daily version in the UK). Advertising expenditure in free-sheets rose from £2 million in 1970 to £220 million in 1984.

Consumer magazines also grew in importance, moving from 1152 titles in 1975 to 1624 titles in 1984 giving a wider range of opportunities for advertisers to target particular market segments effectively.

The effect of introducing VAT on advertising in the 1985 Budget remains to be seen. Although of course most businesses would simply claim back this tax payment, cash flow would be adversely affected in the short term. Private advertisers almost always use the press and this could reduce the use of classified advertising by private advertisers and small (non-VAT registered) business advertisers.

The advertising budget In theory, the size of the budget should follow from the advertising task which has to be performed. An estimate should be made of the cost of meeting the advertising objective, thus setting the budget. In practice this is very uncommon. Most commonly the budget is set according to what can be afforded after other costs have been met. Very often the budget is linked to sales by:

— A percentage of last period sales.
— A percentage of expected sales.
— A percentage of past (or expected) profit.

This is somewhat perplexing as the level of advertising depends on sales rather than the reverse. Thus if sales (and/or profits) fall, advertising will be cut. It can be argued that an increase would be more appropriate.

The alternative approach is to match (or to outspend) major rivals' expenditures. Again there is little theoretical justification for this approach.

The major problems in setting the advertising budget include, as mentioned, the measurement of likely effects of advertising, and the prediction of competitive reaction to the instigation of a new campaign. The additional complexity is caused by different levels of creative effectiveness between agencies. The lagged effects of advertising make measurement more difficult. There are a number of delays between an advertisement being planned and a purchase resulting from it. These include:

— The execution lag between placing the advertisement and its appearance.
— The viewing lag between the appearance of the advertisement and the content being read by the audience member (print ads only).
— The action lag between seeing the advertisement and acting on it (buying the product).

When brand image creation is the main aim of a campaign then the lagged effects may be more long term, current advertising adding to an accumulation of image effects over time. If advertising can be seen as an investment then it may be possible to use discounted cash-flow methods to assess the value of an image campaign.

In summary the optimum size of the advertising budget will depend on:

1. The ease of moving potential consumers along the hierarchy of effects continuum (Table 5.1).
2. The number, dispersion and media accessibility of potential customers.
3. The relative effectiveness of other promotion variables.
4. The strength of countervailing forces — the sales decay rate, the rate at which sales fall without advertising support.

The message As advertising is aimed at persuasion, creating more favourable attitudes to the brand, then the starting point in the determination of message content and structure is to identify existing attitudes and the reasons why they are held. This is frequently done using qualitative market research in which small groups of consumers discuss in detail the brand and its meaning to them *vis-à-vis* competitive brands. The discussion is led by a moderator, usually a trained psychologist. For sensitive issues individual depth interviews may be used. An example of an application of this approach is provided by Dickens.[21] Chisnall[22] gives details of other motivational research methods which can be used in this context. The dangers in message determination are primarily psychological: the message received is not necessarily the same as that which is intended by the advertiser.

People are selective about advertisements to which they pay attention. They are likely to have the opportunity to see hundreds of advertisements each day. This selectivity reflects their needs, value systems and past experience, and means that advertisements must engage the consumer psychologically to gain his or her attention. Consumers are not uncritical receivers of advertising messages: they will distort or disbelieve a message if it is not credible to them from their past experience of the product group or their predispositions towards a brand. Also memory is selective and consumers are more likely to remember an advertising message if they perceive that it has relevance to them.[23] These factors, outside the scope of this book, are discussed by Schramm[23] and summarized by Delozier.[20]

Much research work has been conducted on various aspects of message appeals such as:

— Fear appeals (Janis and Feshbach,[24] and Ray and Wilkie[25]).
— One sided vs. two sided messages (Lumsdaine and Janis,[26] McGinnies[27]).
— Message ordering: climax vs. anticlimax (Hovland, Janis and Kelley[28]).
— Recency vs. primacy (Cromwell[29]).
— Emotional appeals (Bettinghaus[30]).
— Source credibility (Hovland and Weiss[31]).

Again the evidence is not conclusive in most cases but illustrates the need for great care in the construction of advertising copy which is to achieve the desired effects on recipients.

Other marketing variables Finally in this section it is important to note that, although attention has been focused specifically on advertising, the planning of a campaign must take into account the rest of the marketing mix. The campaign must match the overall brand objectives and be consonant with the other strategic elements in a co-ordinated plan. Important elements include:

Price The message content must reflect the absolute and relative price of the brand. A relatively highly priced brand should use advertising campaigns in up-market media, using quality settings for the brand in terms of both verbal and non-verbal appeals.

Distributors The number and types of distributors should be considered along with their locations. The degree of co-operation is important if the maximum impact of a campaign is to be achieved with high levels of distribution. The use of co-operative advertising may be possible. For example, lists of local stockists can be included in national brand advertising, local newspaper advertisements may centre on the brand but give the local dealer's address within the copy. Unless the brand is available to those consumers who wish to buy it because of the campaign, i.e., unless distributors have it in stock, prominently displayed, the effect of the campaign will be reduced. Co-operation is thus essential.

Sales Force Distributor co-operation can be attained by a well co-ordinated selling-in effort in which the forthcoming campaign is used by the sales force as an inducement to distributors to stock and display the brand and to use point-of-sale display material to remind consumers of the campaign. Where personal selling is used as with many industrial goods, consumer durables and services, training courses (technical and sales) may be provided to ensure that key points in the sales presentation to clients are emphasized. The merchandising function at the retail level must reflect the advertising campaign and be co-ordinated with it.

5.4 OTHER FORMS OF BRAND PROMOTION

Besides the use of media advertising, brands can be promoted in many ways. The main types only are considered here.

5.4.1 Sales promotion

Sales promotions include all paid-for non-media promotional activity aimed at stimulating brand sales. They can be aimed at dealers ('into the pipeline' promotions) or at consumers ('out of the pipe-line' promotions). Whereas media advertising often has longer-term strategic marketing aims for brands, sales promotions are usually tactical devices for gaining attention for a new brand or an established brand which is 'in the doldrums' of static sales and is in need of a short-term boost to stimulate consumer interest. The overriding danger with sales promotions is that they can appear to be brand-demeaning, aiming to make consumers buy, not for the inherent qualities of the brand itself but for some other, ephemeral, reason. Examples of each type of sales promotion include:

Trade promotions

Same Product Give-away If the dealer buys a specified minimum quantity, a unit of the product is given to him for his personal use. This is aimed at stimulating personal recommendations to consumers of the 'I use it myself' type. It is obviously limited to personal service situations and runs the danger that the dealer will simply sell the extra unit which reduces the effect of the promotion.

Bonus Offer Here, extra units (or an extra cash discount) of the brand are given if the dealer buys a specified minimum quantity. The aim is to simulate price cuts in the 'off' season or to reduce stock levels in the manufacturers' stores.

Trade Competitions These can be linked to retailer co-operation, e.g., by in-store or window display of the brand which can then be judged. This can be aimed at improving display at the retail level. It can be linked to public relations coverage locally and in the trade press which broadens the effect (e.g., announcement of competition, presentation of prizes, photographs of displays).

Consumer promotions

Special Offer Packs Special price offer packs can be used either to introduce a new brand version or stimulate interest in a mature brand to increase short-term sales without making a permanent price reduction. A number of dangers exist. One is that of retailer conflict. The logistics of introducing a lower price special pack on a co-ordinated basis can be complex. Also retailers holding stocks of the normal (higher price) pack will be disgruntled unless they are compensated by a rebate as the old pack may not sell when the new lower price pack is available. Another problem is that the discount is given to all consumers when presumably most of them would have been willing to pay the 'full price' for the brand. In other words, the promotion is not selective in identifying the most price-sensitive purchasers.

Coupons One way of introducing selectivity is by the use of coupons. On the assumption that the most price-sensitive consumers will take the trouble to use the coupon and others may not, the proffered discount is taken up by 'marginal' customers. Coupons can be on-pack, offering discounts off the next purchase, or can be delivered by print advertisement or by direct mail. Alternatively, to encourage brand loyalty, the collection of a number of coupons can lead to a cash refund from the manufacturer as a coupon promotion. This avoids the practical difficulty of retailer co-operation. Some supermarkets may give the coupon discount off *any* brand purchased rather than the specified brand in the knowledge that the manufacturer will refund the cost anyway and that consumers also gain. The only loser is the manufacturer who could be giving a discount off a competitive brand! Coupons are low cost but relatively low in effectiveness even though they can be attractively selective.

Free Gifts Consumer gratitude can be stimulated by free gifts. These can be off-, on-, or in-pack. However with the increasing use of self-selection and supermarket-type display, often only in-pack gifts are feasible as on-pack offers may limit stacking capability and off-pack offers (i.e., the gift is given at the check-out) is not encouraged by retailers because of the need to speed up customer flows and minimize queue lengths and waiting times. In-pack offers mean that consumers do not see the gift before the purchase (this can be an advantage) which reduces impact. This type of offer is becoming less popular.

Self-Liquidating Offers This refers to an offer in which the consumer has to send a number of 'proof of purchase' coupons plus an amount of money to purchase a reduced price, brand related, item at well-below-usual retail price levels (usually about 65–70 per cent of normal retail price). The aim is to stimulate sales and brand loyalty at a low cost. The term 'self-liquidating' refers to the aim of the promotion to be self-supporting in that the price paid by the consumer should cover the cost of the offer in full, thus providing a highly cost-effective promotion. The danger to the manufacturer is in under- or overestimating demand for the offer. Underestimating leads to delays in fulfilling customer orders and a consequent loss of goodwill. Overestimating leads to a stock of unsold offer items. Selling these off cheaply can have adverse effects on any goodwill created by the offer. The choice of offer item should be made taking into account the type of customer for the brand, how often purchases are made, the type of product concerned. The promotion should have some link with the brand.

Consumer Competitions These can generate brand loyalty if 'proof of purchase' label collection is required. In addition, public relations coverage can be obtained. The Lotteries Act requires some element of skill to be involved if consumers have to pay to enter the competition, although random chance competitions with free access to entry are allowable. The popular type of competition involving the arrangement of a number of brand features into an order of importance can provide useful market intelligence to the company as a spin-off benefit. The glamour of the first prize can add to the perceived company or brand image. Advertising support can be used to maximize interest in and entry to the competition.

The difficulties involved with these promotions emanate from the short-term and product-demeaning aspects of their use. Sales gains are likely to be short-term as a popular promotion can be copied by competitors. Those attracted to a brand by these gimmicks are probably the type of consumers most easily persuaded to re-switch by a competitive promotion. Nevertheless, they provide a means of quickly reviving flagging consumer interest in a brand.

5.4.2 Trade fairs and exhibitions

Manufacturers can use trade fairs and exhibitions for a number of purposes:

1. To launch a new brand to distributors or the public.
2. To enter a new market with a new or existing brand, especially an overseas market.
3. As a form of sales promotion.
4. To launch a rejuvenated version of an existing product.
5. To provide a convenient forum for discussions with distributors in a socially acceptable setting.
6. To provide a physical demonstration of a brand, especially a complex or technologically advanced product.
7. To provide an economical means of meeting sales prospects quickly especially when entering a new market overseas.
8. To test a market and gain market reactions quickly and cheaply.
9. As a public relations exercise for long-run brand image purposes.
10. To obtain competitor information.

The problems with the use of exhibitions include:

1. The close proximity of competitors, enabling customers to make direct comparisons easily. This may mean that a firm has to spend heavily to ensure that their stand is at least as good as competitors and that sufficient hospitality is extended to important visitors.
2. The need to deal with time-wasting enquiries.
3. The high redundancy of many contacts made.
4. The high cost involved, including the time of the salespeople staffing the stand, the rent and cost of equipping the stand.

Despite these problems exhibitions form a valuable forum for manufacturers, especially of industrial goods and services, to obtain face to face contact with clients at a convenient location in a setting which can be controlled by the manufacturer to maximize the appeal of the brand.

5.4.3 Sponsorship

It is becoming increasingly difficult to undertake any sporting activity which is not sponsored. Sponsorship has grown very rapidly in the last ten years, and this growth rate shows no signs of falling off. Insurance companies and tobacco companies have been at the forefront of this booming industry, covering cricket, swimming, table tennis, horse-racing and a host of other sports, and indeed arts events.

In marketing terms, sponsorship can be seen as a form of marketing communication. It stands alongside media advertising, personal selling, public relations and other forms of sales promotions as a method by which companies can 'speak' to potential customers. As an example the role of sponsorship for insurance companies will be examined in more detail.

To very many of the public, insurance companies are anonymous monolithic giants who communicate only through masses of unfathomable small print. The limited contact points between the public and the insurance company (such as visits to brokers, calls by representatives, telephone or postal communications, etc.) may or may not clear up this anonymous image which insurance companies can have. It is a function of effective marketing communications to create an attractive, appealing, sales-enhancing image. It is this image which recent marketing communications from insurance companies have sought to change. TV advertising campaigns, for example, have tended to stress features such as 'strength', 'protection', 'investment value' to try to change people's attitudes to insurance and insurance companies. The overall requirements of marketing communications should be to meet specific communications objectives of the insurance companies in moving prospects towards a purchase.

In terms of Table 5.1 the role of sponsorship would presumably be in creating awareness and interest in an insurance company (and perhaps its services) rather than, say, in persuading the prospect to choose one company's policy rather than a competitor's policy — which would require a more careful analysis of costs and benefits by the prospect.

Where then does sponsorship fit into the marketing communication process? Certainly sponsorship can help an insurance company reach a wider audience. Cornhill Assurance found that name awareness rose from 2 per cent in 1977 to 21 per cent in 1982, primarily as a result of their sponsorship of English test cricket. It can be argued that consumers might resist buying insurance from a company they had not previously heard of, and therefore that awareness is a prerequisite to an eventual purchase by the consumer. However, a major reason that Gillette ended sponsorship of cricket in the UK was that their market research found that, over time, respondents had stopped associating the name 'Gillette' with shaving products when used in the cricket 'Gillette Cup' context. This is a potential danger in the longer term, not only for Cornhill but for other companies with names which could become disassociated with their insurance services, such as 'Refuge', 'Prudential', 'Provincial', 'Royal London', for example.

It seems unlikely that there is a direct link between sponsorship and increased sales. It can be argued that the objectives of sponsorship should be communication goals if sponsorship is seen as one form of marketing communication. There are many other influences on sales, and it is extremely difficult to isolate the effects of a specific marketing activity on sales. There are, however, several other potential advantages of sponsorship, as well as awareness creation in a wider audience than could be reached cost-effectively by other forms of advertising and the media coverage generated by the sponsored events.

One advantage is in distributor and customer relations. Hospitality facilities at sponsored events can be used with effect to create and maintain positive attitudes to the company by middlemen, such as insurance brokers, and of course by important customers.

Further, the impact of sponsoring 'worthy' events can have a wider positive effect on potential customers. If the insurance company is seen as a benefactor of the sport or arts event it sponsors, these apparently altruistic motives might positively incline the potential customers towards the company's services. It should then be easier for the company's insurance salespeople to convert these prospects into sales.

Also sponsorship has wider implications in public relations terms. It demonstrates good corporate citizenship and it may also have a positive impact on the company's employees. This would seem to be more likely, the more the sponsored event fits in with the desired image of the insurance company. The image of 'solid dependability' and 'protectiveness' and 'traditional British values' which might be thought to be likely to appeal to those seeking insurance policies should fit with the type of events which the insurance company sponsors. Cricket, tennis, golf and athletics as well as national orchestras and other arts events are likely to provide such image links for example.

In summary, sponsorship seems to have two major advantages for insurance companies – creating awareness, and creating an acceptable image with potential customers at a relatively low cost compared with media advertising. The media coverage of sponsored events should ensure that an even wider audience is reached. Importantly, this coverage will be in editorial rather than advertising space (or time), which is far more potent in its effect on readers (or viewers).

A possible limitation of sponsorship for insurance companies is that those who receive communication from the sponsoring organization may not be potential customers. Only a small proportion will be likely to be taking out insurance policies in the near future. It could be argued that the communication is wasted on those who are not potential clients. Further, some of the small proportion of potential clients may already know of the company and its services from other sources. Thus in sales enhancement terms in the short term, the effect of a sponsorship may be very limited, although the longer-term effects and the rather nebulous 'goodwill' effects remain.

Overall the major problem in assessing the value of sponsorship to insurance companies, at least in marketing terms, is that of measuring the effectiveness of sponsorship. It is notoriously difficult to isolate the effects of individual marketing variables on consumer reaction, and we are left with a general difficulty in assessing marketing communication effectiveness – that of measuring attitude change. In theory, communication goals can be set and measured using before and after surveys, but there are practical measurement difficulties, as are noted later in this chapter.

In conclusion the following practical sponsorship-decision guidelines are offered:

1. What are the overall marketing communication goals of the company?
2. What is the role of sponsorship within the overall marketing communication strategy to be? How will this role relate to other parts of the strategy?
3. What are the specific communication objectives for the sponsorship programme?
4. Can these objectives be met using other marketing tools more cost-effectively?
5. How is the effectiveness of the sponsorship programme to be measured?

With the experience that is available within companies, sponsorship proposals should be subjected to a careful objective analysis and should, if accepted, be comprehensively monitored. Sponsorships should neither be rushed into nor undertaken because competitors have done so, but should be evaluated as a promotional tool as an integral part of a comprehensive marketing strategy.

5.4.4 The promotional mix

It is clear that a company has to make allocation decisions with regard to the overall mix of promotions to be used. Not only has the company to decide how much to spend on marketing overall, but also has to allocate these funds between the various marketing activities such as price cuts, quality enhancements, new product development, promotions and distribution. This is discussed in Chapter 9.

Within the promotional budget, funds have then to be allocated between the various options – media vs. non-media for example. These decisions need to be made taking into account the overall brand profitability and image requirements and with careful consideration of all the variables discussed in this chapter, especially:

— Is the product new or established?
— What are competitors doing with regard to promotion?
— Are target audience members easily accessible and persuasible?
— What unique benefits does the brand possess?
— How best can these benefits be communicated to consumers?
— Is there a conflict between short- and longer-term needs?

It is clear that a major input to these decisions is the complex task of measuring the effectiveness of different forms of promotion. The next section explores the complexities of this issue.

5.5 MEASURING PROMOTIONAL EFFECTIVENESS

Perhaps the most common quote about advertising, which has been attributed to several people (including Henry Ford), is 'I know half of my advertising budget is wasted — but I don't know which half!' This statement sums up the state of the art in advertising-effects measurement in an exaggerated but incisive way. The major problem appears to stem from the need to isolate the promotional effects from other factors which 'cause' sales to occur. There are two major types of approach: the 'sales' approach or 'direct' method which attempts to formulate a cause and effect relationship between advertising and sales, and the 'communications' approach or 'indirect' method. This latter approach follows from the premise that advertising (and other forms of promotion) is a form of communication and thus should have communication goals specified which can then be measured. An example would be 'to increase brand awareness by 20 per cent of the target population'. In the final analysis communication goals are sales-related, i.e., are means to an end. Certainly most organizations are interested in relating advertising expenditure to sales, whatever the problems, as this relates most closely to their decison-making process.

5.5.1. Relating advertising to sales

Economists have examined this relationship at various levels of aggregation, from economy-level studies of aggregate advertising expenditure and aggregate consumption, to industry, product group and brand-level analyses. At the brand level the great difficulty is to obtain a sufficiently long time series of data from which the advertising effects can be isolated. The rapid tactical changes in marketing variables as a form of competition exacerbate this problem. Even if such trend data exist, high correlation between advertising expenditure and sales of the brand is no guarantee of causality. Indeed, in referring to budget-setting above, it was noted that advertising budgets can be determined by sales levels, achieved or expected. If this is the case even the direction of causality is in doubt. As discussed in Chapter 2, Palda's use of a single equation model to estimate the impact of advertising on sales of Lydia Pinkham's Vegetable Compound is the most famous application.[32] The two-way causation problem affects Palda's model, and the lack of a price-based independent variable is unusual and surprising. The brand is highly unusual in that it enjoyed an almost monopoly position and was on the market for a long period of time (Palda's data related to a 53-year time span). However, it is interesting to note that the log of advertising expenditure is used in the model, indicating that, to increase sales, advertising expenditure would need to be increased much more than in proportion even though Palda postulated no independent variable for competitors' advertising expenditure.

Roberts examined the advertising—sales relationship for two drug products using data from a cross-section study of 1504 families.[33] He related total sales of brands A and B to advertising, city size, age of head of household, size of family, economic class, education, occupation and region. However, with regard to advertising, expenditure on A was strongly correlated ($r = 0.84$) with expenditure on B. It was not possible to give a reliable indication of overall advertising impact on sales because of this multicollinearity problem.

With regard to product type, Doyle found that advertising is heavier for low-priced commodities as, for expensive products, buyers would rely on direct search for information rather than on advertising.[34] This also applied to durable consumer goods compared to non-durables. He also found that advertising expenditure is lower for frequently purchased products since buyers are more likely to choose through habit or inertia with little thought being given to purchases.

In summary, there is great difficulty in isolating the sales effects of advertising from the impact of price, brand image, perceived brand quality, distribution variables (availability, store loyalty, stockouts, etc.) and other variables. In particular the lagged effects of advertising and the two-way causation difficulty exacerbate the problem.

In reality if marketing executives find that sales increase when advertising expenditure has been raised they may be unworried by the cause and effect issues discussed here but may simply accept the relationship, especially when their advertising agency is likely to claim a causal link!

5.2.2 Measuring communication effectiveness

Here the major issues are:

1. Forecasting how many of the target population will have access to the advertising message.
2. Forecasting how many of (1) will actually take in the advertising message.

The first issue relates to audience measurement and the second to advertising content research.

Media research

TV In the UK, TV Audience Research is conducted for BARB (Broadcasters Audience Research Board) by AGB. A major establishment survey of 20000 personal interviews annually provides information on the size and characteristics of the population in each of the 13 ITV regions. This determines the size of the potential audience and their characteristics (age, sex, social group, ownership of video-recorders and remote control devices, possession of teletext, number of sets per household, etc.). From this survey, the structure of the viewing panel in each region is determined. The national panel size is 3000 households (varying from 100—400 in each region, according to size). A monitoring device is attached to the TV which records when the set is switched on and to which channel it is tuned. Each member of the household is allocated a one-digit number (with spares for guests). When the member begins to view the relevant number is pressed on a control pad handset. When the family member ends the viewing spell, the number is depressed again. This information is also recorded and stored. Each night the central computer dials the home and the stored data is automatically transmitted down the telephone line. This overnight data collection enables the previous evening's viewing rates to be quickly established and made available to subscribers.

The audience figures, broken down by various consumer characteristics, can then be used to assess the 'opportunities to see' of the target audience. The TV companies use the audience figures to refine their rate cards for advertisers. The brand manager can use the data to assess the effectiveness with which the media schedule has been constructed and the TVRs* achieved. The problems in TV audience assessment were discussed earlier in the chapter in the section on media.

JICCAR, the Joint Industry Committee for Cable Audience Research, has recently been established in anticipation of growth in this form of TV viewing.

Press JICNARS, the Joint Industry Committee for National Readership Surveys, commissions the National Readership Survey (NRS) on behalf of the industry and advertisers. The mechanics of NRS are described by Chisnall.[22] Essentially, 30000 adult interviews are conducted in a continuous survey over the period of each year, using a stratified random-sample research design. The results are published twice yearly and cover major publications read, cross-tabulated by demographic characteristics, regional variations, TV viewing habits, cinema, commercial radio and special interests. Duplication of readership (cross-readership patterns) is also described.

Other Media Research In a similar although smaller-scale way, the other media use research to establish their audience sizes and characteristics in order to set advertising rates and to attract advertising revenue under the aegis of the relevant joint industry committee.

In addition BRAD (British Rate and Data) is published, giving current details of advertising rates

---

* TVRs or TV ratings measure success in reaching the target audience. For a detailed account of schedules and media planning, see Adams.[35]

for most UK media. The Audit Bureau of Circulations (ABC) measures net distribution of publications (as opposed to readership) on a twice-yearly basis. MEAL (Media Expenditure Analyses Ltd) publish estimates of advertising expenditures by brand in most consumer goods and services fields in the UK. The estimates are derived from published rate-card prices and do not take account of any unpublished discounts received or premiums paid.

The brand manager (or his advertising representative) is in a position to obtain detailed cost and efficiency data on advertising expenditures made and planned at least in terms of opportunities. The second part of the question is how to measure whether target-market consumers actually take up these opportunities to see, i.e., measurement of the quality of the advertising exposure.

Measuring the quality of opportunities to see This can be attempted by measuring recall of advertisement content. One system is the Gallup–Robinson impact test.[36] In this approach, which is for press advertising, the respondent is shown the cover of the issue and asked if he has read that issue. If he claims to have done so he is asked to describe anything he remembers having seen in the issue. If this substantiates his claim, for example, if he recalls at least one article, then he is considered a 'qualified issue reader'. He is then given a list of the brands/advertisers appearing in the issue each on a separate card. When he is then asked to sort according to recalled appearance in the issue. He is then questioned about the content of the advertisements he recalls seeing. This measures accuracy of recall and level of impact. He is then shown each advertisement recalled to check consistency. The measurement concept of 'proved name registration' is employed to measure those attaining this 'quality' of advertisement-content recall in a comparative context.

The Gallup–Robinson approach contrasts with the Starch recognition method[37] which uses three measures of the quality of readership:

1. Noted — a person who remembers having seen the advertisement in the issue under review.
2. Seen-associated — a person who not only noted the advertisement but also saw or read some part of it (which identified the advertiser).
3. Read-most — a person who read half or more of the written material in the advertisement.

For a particular issue these measures are computed into useful qualitative scores for advertisers:

1. Readers per pound (£) — by dividing the cost of the advertisement into each of the three readership measures.
2. Cost ratio — a ratio of (1) to the median score for all advertisements (half page or larger) in the issue, indexed to 100.
3. Ranks — the ordering of (2) for all advertisements in the issue.

While both these measures give useful quantification of advertisement effectiveness, they do not provide a complete answer. The comparative nature of these measures may lead advertisers to stress initial impact rather than lasting impression in advertising content. In general these types of measure vary in the amount of aid they give to the recall process by stimulus material (or the lack of it).

Direct response advertising is more easily measured by pre-coding the response coupons. While this measure is not exact it does give an insight into the impact of specific appearances of advertisements. This can be linked to sales for mail-order advertising and to take-up rate for brochure offers.

The major drawback in all the cases so far considered is that they are post-advertisement measures. While they can provide insights for any future advertisements which are being planned, they only measure after the event. Ideally advertisers would like to predict response to specific advertisements in particular issues (or at particular times on TV or radio).

Pre-testing of advertisements can be done in a number of ways. Perhaps the most popular is to use qualitative group discussions. Here a carefully selected group or groups, drawn from the target population, are invited into a comfortable environment (someone's home for a product aimed at housewives for example) and a discussion led by a trained moderator (usually a psychologist) explores the proposed advertisement and its impact on the group. This enables the advertiser to measure whether or not the message received is the same as that sent. An example of this approach is given for advertising planning for fresh cream cakes by Dickens.[21]

Other methods which have been popular include the use of physiological measuring equipment such as:

A Tachiostoscope This is a device for presenting a visual field (in this case the proposed advertisement) to the subject (the respondent) for a carefully controlled length of time (from 1 millisecond upwards). This enables measurement of the length of time necessary for the message of the advertisement to be understood by the recipient. This is particularly useful because most advertisements appear in a competitive context, i.e., they are competing for readers' (viewers') attention. The ability to transmit the main impact quickly in this context is a major consideration in advertising planning.

A Polygraph This is a device for recording physiological reactions to stimuli (again in this case the advertisement) and displaying them in graphical form. Thus pulse rate and breathing rate changes can be measured, as can heart beats (electro-cardiograms) and brainwaves (electro-encephalograms) and galvanic skin response (sweating).

The problems with this approach are that a laboratory setting is required which reduces realism and increases the testing effect (i.e., respondents know they are in a test situation which causes them to react abnormally). Also the measurement process seems rather dramatic for the context. The premise behind the approach is that emotional reaction to advertisements can be assessed by this device in a non-verbal way. In other words, if respondents are embarrassed or cannot express their feelings in words, this device can provide insights into their emotional response. Of course, the question can be raised, does this emotional response influence sales?

An Eye Camera This device is used to observe and record eye movement, blinking and pupil dilation which again is a non-verbal attempt to measure emotional response to the advertisement as a stimulus. To avoid respondent discomfort a system known as DEMOS (Direct Eye Movement Observation System) was devised. This allows the subject's eye movement to be recorded without his knowledge. Again the laboratory setting reduces realism. The method can be used to assess the way in which the respondent scans an advertisement (or a package or label). This enables the design of the copy to be laid out to give maximum initial impact. The emotional impact of the advertisement can be measured.

These methods are not now as popular as they have been, perhaps mainly because of cost but also because of the tenuous link between physiological reaction and emotional response and sales.

Finally there is the option of using both pre- and post-measurement of advertising effectiveness. For example, with a campaign aimed at changing consumer attitudes, the process would be:

1. Measure existing attitudes.
2. Run the advertising campaign.
3. Re-measure attitudes.

Of course, there are major measurement problems with attitudes and in particular, attitude change. The major attitude-measurement scale, the Likert scale[38] is a unidimensional attempt to measure a multidimensional concept. Nevertheless, at least in theory, this approach would give a comprehensive assessment of a particular campaign.

For campaigns with awareness, level of interest, or product-trial and repurchase-rate objectives then the trend data during the campaign may be valuable. In marketing practice these measures are obtained by tracking studies. An example of this approach is given by Sampson and Marshall for advertising for the Tea Council in the UK.[39] In these studies data can be obtained from an established continuous panel over time or by having statistically matched samples. In the former case, individual-level data can be analysed over time, whereas with the latter case the danger of preconditioning respondents exists. Tracking studies, as the name suggests, enable the time impact of advertising to be assessed and can be combined with pretesting techniques to enable a before-and-after study. The time impact of advertising on attitudes can, as with the tea application, be compared with the time impact on sales over the same period.

5.6 Summary

This chapter has, of necessity, strayed from a purely economics approach to advertising, to incorporate some of the practical considerations and issues in the use of promotion as a competitive device. The wider context of the ethics of advertising has been hinted at but not covered in detail.

The controversy centres on the subjective persuasion in advertising objectives and achievements. The Galbraithian argument noted above, that producers determine consumers' needs, may overstate the persuasive effects of advertising but nevertheless is one line of argument which can be taken.[40]

An interesting development of Lancaster's characteristics approach discussed in Chapter 2 provides a novel input to the arguments on advertising and consumer sovereignty. Much of the debate centres on the use of emotional appeals rather than appeals based on objective product qualities. If Lancaster's objective characteristics approach were used as a criterion to control advertising content then it could be argued that there would be more objectivity in advertising claims. Thus advertisements for cars could make claims based only on such factors as miles per gallon, performance (e.g., acceleration), seating and luggage capacity and other objectively measurable characteristics.

The comparison between models could then be made on the objective characteristics basis. Indeed some car advertising is on the direct comparison basis, relying on selective but objective characteristic comparisons with other brands. This practice is known as 'knocking copy' in the UK and 'ashcanning' in the US because it shows the advertised brand in the most favourable light by careful selection of the compared characteristics.

This approach could place a 'positive' requirement on advertisers to show that their proposed advertisement is based on objective rather than emotional claims. At present advertising control is based on advertisers not infringing published codes of practice (e.g., Advertising Standards Authority in the UK) which is a 'negative' control.

If this approach were to be adopted then the arguments against advertising in allocative efficiency terms (as referred to earlier in the chapter) are much less persuasive. Advertising would be much closer to the economic 'ideal' of providing objective information to potential consumers and leaving them to make a rational evaluation in their choice to maximize utility. The further issue, of whether advertising is the most efficient way of transmitting objective product information, is still open. The price paid for the brand would still include the advertising component for all buyers. If the objective advertising claims were available separately at a cost to those consumers willing to pay for the information then this controversy could be avoided. This would involve a similar system to 'Which?' reports which attempt objective evaluations of competing brands in a succession of product fields.

It is clear that this argument is complex with a wide range of dimensions, many not economic ones. In this chapter the many marketing aspects of promotion have been considered from economic and empirical viewpoints and discussion of relevant factors in some areas of business practice has been undertaken. This is a major part of the brand image creation process. However, it is not possible to see the promotion of a brand separately from the issues concerning the brand itself. In the next chapter the brand policy dimension is discussed in detail, and the role of the brand in the product mix of the firm. This is followed by a consideration of the role of new brand development in Chapter 7.

REFERENCES

1. Kotler, P. (1984) *Marketing Management*, 5th edn, Prentice-Hall, Englewood Cliffs, New Jersey, p. 482.
2. Crimp, M. (1981) *The Market Research Process*, Prentice-Hall, London, p. 150.
3. Strong, U. K. (1925) *Principles of Advertising*, A. W. Shaw, New York.
4. Lavidge, R. J. and G. A. Steiner (1961) 'A model for predictive measurement of advertising effectiveness', *Journal of Marketing*, **25**, 4, 59–62.
5. Engel, J. F., R. D. Blackwell and D. T. Kollat (1978) *Consumer Behaviour*, 3rd edn, Dryden, Hindsdale, Illinois.
6. Ehrenberg, A. S. C. and G. J. Goodhardt (1979) *Models of Change*, J. Walter Thompson Market Research Corp. of America, New York, pp. 12–14.
7. Ehrenberg, A. S. C. (1974) 'Repetitive advertising and the consumer', *Journal of Advertising Research*, **14**, 2, 25–34.
8. Ehrenberg, A. S. C. and G. J. Goodhardt (1980) *Consumer Attitudes*, J. Walter Thompson/Market Research Corp. of America, New York, p. 6.
9. Nerlove, M. and K. J. Arrow (1962) 'Optimal advertising policy under dynamic conditions', *Economica*, **29**, 129–42.
10. Jacoby, J. and R. W. Chestnut (1978) *Brand Loyalty, Measurement and Management*, Wiley, New York.
11. Carman, J. M. (1970) 'Correlates of brand loyalty: some positive results', *Journal of Marketing Research*, 7, February, 67–76.
12. Ehrenberg, A. S. C. and P. Charlton (1973) 'An analysis of simulated brand choice', *Journal of Advertising Research*, **13**, 1, 000.
13. Charlton, P., A. S. C. Ehrenberg and B. Pymont (1972) 'Buyer behaviour under mini-test conditions', *Journal of the Market Research Society*, **14**, 3, 171–83.
14. Charlton, P. and A. S. C. Ehrenberg (1976) 'An experiment in brand choice', *Journal of Marketing Research*, **13**, (May) 152–60.
15. Engel, J. F. and R. D. Blackwell (1982) *Consumer Behaviour*, 4th edn, Dryden, Hindsdale, Illinois.
16. Chiplin, B. and B. T. Sturgess (1981) *Economics of Advertising*, Holt Rinehart and Winston, London.
17. Reekie, W. D. (1981) *The Economics of Advertising*, Macmillan, London.
18. Greer, D. F. (1971) 'Advertising and market concentration', *Southern Economic Journal*, **38**, 19–32.
19. Karlins, M. and H. I. Abelson (1970) *Persuasion*, 2nd edn, Springer Publishing Co., New York, p. 89.
20. Delozier, M. W. (1976) *The Marketing Communications Process*, McGraw-Hill, Kogakusha, Tokyo, p. 124.
21. Dickens, J. (1982) 'The fresh cream cakes market: the use of qualitative research as part of a consumer research programme', in *Applied Marketing and Social Research*, U. Bradley (ed.), Van Nostrand Reinhold, Wokingham, pp. 4–43.
22. Chisnall, P. M. (1981) *Marketing Research*, 2nd edn, McGraw-Hill, Maidenhead, Ch. 8.
23. Schramm, W. (1971) 'How communication works', in *The Process and Effects of Mass Communication*, W. Schramm and D. F. Roberts (eds), University of Illinois Press, Urbana.
24. Janis, I. and S. Feshbach (1953) 'Effects of fear-arousing communications', *Journal of Abnormal and Social Psychology*, **48**, 78–92
25. Ray, M. L. and W. L. Wilkie (1970) 'Fear: the potential of an appeal neglected by marketing', *Journal of Marketing*, **34**, January, p. 57.
26. Lumsdaine, A. and I. Janis, (1953) 'Resistance to "counter propaganda", produced by one-sided versus two-sided "propaganda" presentation', *Public Opinion Quarterly*, **17**, 311–18.
27. McGinnies, E. (1966) 'Studies in persuasion III: Reactions of Japanese students to one-sided and two-sided communications', *Journal of Social Psychology*, **70**, 87–93.
28. Hovland, C. I., I. L. Janis, and H. H. Kelley, (1953) *Communication and Persuasion*, Yale University Press, New Haven.
29. Cromwell, H. (1950) 'The relative effect on attitude of the first versus second argumentative speech of a series', *Speech Monographs*, **17**, 105–22.
30. Bettinghaus, E. P. (1973) *Persuasive Communications*, Holt, Rinehart and Winston, New York.
31. Hovland, C. l. and W. Weiss (1951) 'The influence of source credibility on communication effectiveness', *Public Opinion Quarterly*, **15**, 635–50.
32. Palda, K. S. (1969) *Economic Analysis for Marketing Decision*, Prentice-Hall, Englewood Cliffs, New Jersey.
33. Roberts, H. V. (1947) 'The measurement of advertising results', *Journal of Business*, January, 131–45.
34. Doyle, P. (1968) *Advertising Expenditure and Consumer Demand*, Oxford Economic Papers, **30**, 394–416.
35. Adams, I. R. (1977) *Media Planning*, 2nd edn, Business Books, London.
36. Sandage, C. H. and V. Fryburger (1971) *Advertising Theory and Practice*, Irwin, Homewood, Illinois, p. 587.
37. Boyd, H. W. and R. Westfall (1972) *Marketing Research, Text and Cases*, Irwin, Homewood, Illinois.

38. Likert, R. (1932) *A Technique for the Measurement of Attitudes*, Archives of Psychology, No. 140.
39. Sampson, P. and K. Marshall (1982) 'Improving the efficiency of research methods used in advertising tracking studies', in *Applied Marketing and Social Research*, U. Bradley (ed.), Van Nostrand Reinhold, Wokingham, pp. 233–65.
40. Galbraith, J. K. (1958) *The Affluent Society*, Houghton Mifflin, New York.

BRAND POLICY

In this chapter the brand will be considered as an integral part of a firm's product strategy. This approach makes the empirically relevant assumption that the firm is a multibrand multimarket concern and decisions are taken to meet objectives which span this range of products and markets. The starting point for this discussion is the concept of the product life cycle as it is applied to brand policy. This leads to a discussion of product range considerations and then in the next chapter to new brand development as perhaps the most potent concern for firms in modern business when competition between firms often takes the form of increased new brand innovation.

6.1 THE BRAND AND ITS LIFE CYCLE

The concept of the product life cycle (PLC) is based on the argument that there is a sales cycle over time for all brands which is consistent at least in shape to that shown in Figure 6.1 and can be described in terms of the four stages categorized in this diagram.

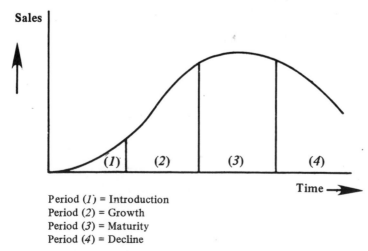

Period (*1*) = Introduction
Period (*2*) = Growth
Period (*3*) = Maturity
Period (*4*) = Decline

Fig. 6.1 The product life cycle

6.1.1 Introduction

When a new brand is launched on the market, sales initially grow slowly as purchasing a new brand involves risk for the buyer compared with repeat buying of an established brand. If this procedure is viewed from the buyer's perspective then it is feasible to consider the role of innovators in new brand purchasing. Innovators are those who try a new brand as soon as it becomes available. It has been postulated that consumers and brands vary in their innovativeness and that this is an important distinction for marketing managers. It is important to identify innovators because they will often give word-of-mouth reports to friends, colleagues and acquaintances which are potent persuasive forces. These reports can be positive or negative and, as they lack persuasive motive, are highly credible to the recipients. Research has been conducted to try and identify important correlates of consumer innovativeness and of innovations which are most likely to be adopted.

One of the earliest categorization schemes of consumer innovativeness was proposed by Rogers in 1962.[1] He assumed a normal distribution of innovativeness amongst potential consumers. This has useful statistical properties — the highest rate of adoption occurs at the mean time of adoption which divides the distribution into equal halves. He also makes use of standard deviation properties in devising categories of innovators as shown in Figure 6.2.

Rogers and Shoemaker discussed the five categories in depth and combined 'innovators' and 'early adopters' into 'earlier adopters'.[2] One reason for this is that marketing effort or marketing research would be difficult to focus cost-effectively on the 2.5 per cent innovators who are so important to the marketing process. Robertson[3] has suggested 10 per cent as the practical proportion of target populations who are innovators, and Midgley[4] suggests 16 per cent (1 standard deviation away from the mean of the normal distribution as a break point). Midgley argues that there is a need for only two categories using this division (innovators and the rest) rather than more complex schemes such as that suggested by Peterson based on cluster analysis.[5]

Moving on to examine the characteristics of these innovators, the early work by Bell in 1963, investigating consumer durables using the '10 per cent' definition of innovativeness, should be noted.[6]

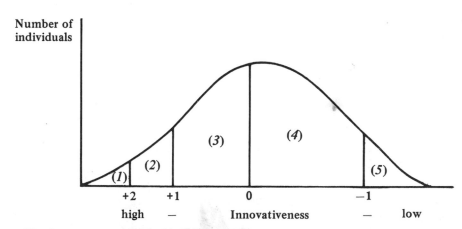

(1) = Innovators   = 2.5% of individuals
(2) = Early adopters = 13.5% of individuals
(3) = Early majority = 34% of individuals
(4) = Late majority = 34% of individuals
(5) = Laggards   = 16% of individuals
Source: Adapted from Rogers[1]

Fig. 6.2 Categories of innovators

He found that innovators thus defined tended to be younger, more educated and to possess higher incomes. They also were more likely to belong to AB social groups and to have greater exposure to the mass media. Out of the total, 75 per cent of them did not consult anyone outside their family regarding their decision to purchase. It was also found that the more radical the innovation, the more educated the innovators were and the greater their income.

In 1968 Robertson and Kennedy [7] found that, using multiple discriminant analysis on a sample size of 100 (60 adopters, 40 non-adopters) purchasing a small home appliance, the important characteristics of innovativeness were:

1. Venturesomeness — willingness to take risks in purchasing.
2. Social mobility   — degree of upward movement in the social scale.
3. Social integration — participation in the community.
4. Privilegedness   — financial standing relative to the community.

Uhl, Andrus and Poulsen studying low-cost grocery items in 1970 found that laggards had lower incomes than earlier adopters. This suggests: 'that laggards appear to cling to proven products. It may be that they are repelled by those products which appear to them to be too new, unproven and risky.' [8]

In studying clothing innovations Baumgarten found that innovators were more willing to take risks and had a more favourable attitude to change, were more socially integrated and had greater exposure to the mass media. [9]

In terms of psychological characteristics, Robertson [10] found that the innovators of a consumer appliance were significantly more impulsive, active and dominant than other individuals, but Pizam in 1972 argued that results in this area are inconclusive overall. [11] Donnelly and Ivancevich [12] found that earlier purchasers of a new brand of car were predominantly inner-directed when compared with later purchasers; this, it can be argued, means that the social character of the product is less important to the innovators.

For products such as consumer durables Rogers and Shoemaker generalized the following characteristics of innovators: they are more educated, intelligent, rational, cosmopolitan, socially integrated and able to deal with abstractions. [2] Robertson suggested a relationship between innovativeness and product category usage rate, i.e., that heavy users of similar products are more likely to be innovators. [3] No direct evidence on this point has been found for packaged consumer-convenience products.

Relatively few studies have been carried out for minor innovations with low-risk new products in the consumer convenience-good market compared to major innovations in the consumer-durable field. Midgley suggested reasons why the two areas could be expected to be different:

> The adoption of a major innovation such as a consumer durable requires adequate finance, and entails considerable perceived and actual risk, while the adoption of a new grocery product raises no such problems. Not only is the outlay involved minimal but if the product proves unsatisfactory then it need not be purchased again the next week . . . we might well expect that when studying low cost innovations most of the demographic and socio-economic variables would be of little relevance to the situation. [4]

Robertson found for grocery products that innovators were more socially mobile, had more favourable attitudes to risk and change, and had higher product-category usage rates. [3] He also found that innovators perceived less risk in adopting than later adopters. In addition, for grocery products, Donnelly [13] found a relationship between innovativeness and inner-directedness, and Summers [14] between innovativeness and exposure to the mass media.

Belk has investigated individual situational effects which are defined as the situations individuals encounter in the course of their everyday lives which have a pronounced effect on their purchase behaviour but which could not be predicted from their personal characteristics. [15] For snack foods he was able to show that these effects could explain a large percentage of observed purchase behaviour for established brands. This does not appear to have been investigated for new brands. This work emphasizes the importance of point-of-sale display and stresses the necessity for a manufacturer's strategy to be successful in gaining high levels of distribution and attractive display positions.

6.1.2 Characteristics of the innovation

Intuitively it would appear that the characteristics of the innovation are an additional factor to consider. If, for example, the taste of a new brand of confectionery is not expected to be liked then the brand may well not be tried at all for this reason alone, whatever the individual characteristics. The major characteristic which has been investigated is the degree of newness, i.e. whether the product is 'genuinely' new or 'artifically' new (a me-too product), which affects the perceived risk. Rogers and Shoemaker suggested five attributes which affect how an individual perceives an innovation:[2]

1. Relative advantage — how much better the new brand is than the existing ones.
2. Compatibility   — how well it fits the needs and values of the consumer.
3. Complexity   — how difficult it is to use.
4. Trialability   — the degree to which it can be used on a trial basis.
5. Observability   — how visible it is to others.

However for convenience brands these five attributes have limited applicability. Ostlund applied the attributes to new low-cost supermarket brands and, using multiple discriminant analysis, correctly classified 70 per cent of the innovators.[16] Adding personal characteristics made little difference to this percentage. In a later study using a consumer panel he identified 77 per cent of the innovators.[17] In rank order of importance the attributes found to be most important in the discriminant function were:

1. Relative advantage.
2. Perceived risk (an extra variable which Ostlund added).
3. Complexity.
4. Compatibility.
5. Observability.
6. Trialability.

Given the type of products tested, the low importance rankings are not surprising. A further complication is the interrelationships between the dimensions for a new brand.

Based on the Ostlund work, Midgley suggested that for low-cost new consumer products these five attributes are in themselves functions of:[4]

1. Product knowledge — the perceived characteristics of the innovation
2. Situational effects
3. Attitude to change
4. Attitude to risk
5. Product category usage rate
6. Other-directedness
7. Social mobility

in varying combinations and intensities. Ostlund concluded that 'perceptions of innovations by potential adopters can be very effective predictors of innovativeness'.[18]

A final point relating to both consumer and innovation characteristics and adoption is communication. The information flows between innovators and others are of vital significance to the marketing man and are well documented in terms of the two-step flow of communications developed by Katz and Lazarsfeld.[19]

Summers studied innovativeness and opinon leadership in 972 individuals and found that, depending on the product category, between 26 per cent and 52 per cent of product-category innovators were also opinion leaders (the highest figure being for women's fashion products). He also found that innovators were more exposed to media with a content relevant to the product category.[14]

The marketing implications of innovativeness are discussed later in the chapter.

6.1.3 Growth

In the growth stage of the product life cycle, sales increase at a rapid rate as the followers rather than the leaders (innovators and early adopters) buy the brand for the first time. It is during this phase that the likelihood of success of the brand is determined. Midgley has related consumer reaction to the new brand to success by using three categories of response:

1. Favourable (likely to repurchase).
2. Passive (may or may not repurchase).
3. Rejector (unlikely to repurchase).

The numbers in each category then determine success or failure.

If the new brand is perceived by competitors as being destined for success, then this is likely to attract competitive brands into the market which are similar to the first brand but perhaps have one unique characteristic.

6.1.4 Maturity

In the maturity stage, the brand and its competitors are well established, most of the consumers in the market have tried and/or rejected the brands in the market, and sales are at a repeat purchase rate although there is a level of brand-switching by consumers in most markets. At some point in the maturity stage, the brand is rejected by leaders who begin to move to more innovative products. In many markets the maturity stage can be extremely long.

6.1.5 Decline

In the decline stage, sales fall as followers begin to switch to more innovative products and the brand image becomes outmoded; remaining buyers are the laggards who buy out of habit. In general the brand is seen as old-fashioned but can still be profitable.

6.2 BRAND MARKETING STRATEGY AND THE LIFE CYCLE

To follow the above description of the major stages in the life cycle process it is appropriate to examine the marketing implications of each stage for brand-competitive strategy.

6.2.1 Introduction

The development of a new brand pre-launch will be dealt with in the next chapter. At the time of the launch, there is a high level of activity involved in the co-ordination and control. There are many launch activities such as selling-in to distributors and promotional expenditure to create awareness and interest in the new brand by both distributors and consumers, usually taking many different but linked forms. This often involves the use of free samples or free trials of the new brand to give consumers usage experience of the brand to reduce their perceived risk in trying the new brand. Promotion emphasizes product differences as the novelty of the new brand is greatest at this time. The aim is to let potential customers, especially early adopters, know about the new brand and to attempt to stimulate brand trial.

As noted above in the discussion on innovativeness, promotion should be aimed at innovative consumers and early adopters. If these consumers can be cost-effectively identified and reached by a promotional campaign, they may be persuaded to try the new brand. Perhaps more importantly, they may pass on their views of the new brand by word of mouth to acquaintances who may well respect their views on the product type. Of course these views may be positive or negative but they are likely to be highly potent as the early adopter is likely to be perceived as an independent and respected source of objective product information by other consumers who are considering (later) purchase of the product group. Initially distribution is likely to be limited until enough distributors can be persuaded to stock the new brand. As with consumers, distributors may vary according to their willingness to stock a new brand immediately it becomes available, with some preferring to wait and see if it is successful before risking their capital and display space by stocking the new brand.

As noted in Chapter 4 on price competition, the initial pricing decision is influenced by a number of factors and may be relatively high (skimming) or low (penetration). Other things being equal, there may well be a tendency to charge a higher price initially because:

1. The 'novelty effect' is at its greatest.
2. Higher margins may be necessary to entice dealers to stock the new brand.
3. Low initial output and sales usually mean higher unit costs.
4. It is often more acceptable to reduce rather than increase price. In times of inflation real price can be reduced while money price remains unchanged as costs rise. This may mean that consumers are less overtly aware of the real reduction, which could be beneficial to the supplier as it avoids adverse quality connotations.

It is usual for the brand to be launched in few varieties (or colours, shapes, sizes, etc.) initially, both to cut down on the planning task but also in order that initial consumer reaction can be used as an input to the range of varieties to be offered. Because novelty should be greatest at this stage, competition should be less important than later in the process.

6.2.2 Growth

Distribution should become more established and, if the brand begins to sell well, easier to obtain for suppliers. A particular feature of this stage is that new suppliers are attracted into the market if the initial brand appears to be destined for success. During the growth phase a battle for distribution can develop as dealers stock selectively from the available, competing brands. The first brand into the market should have advantages in this respect, but this will depend on the relationship which competitors have (or can develop) with relevant distributors. A scramble may develop to link with the few remaining distributors in the market.

The speed at which competition increases will depend on the ease with which the brand can be copied, whether mistakes have been made in the marketing strategy of the original brand which can be solved in competitive brands, and the market prospects as assessed by potential competitors.

The key to the marketing implications is thus the amount of competition attracted into the market. This will influence a number of marketing variables. Price, for example, may fall because of increased competition and reduced brand-novelty; it may be lowered to stimulate sales levels, brand share and output in order to gain lower unit costs through increased economies of scale. Promotion begins to emphasize brand advantages rather than product-type advantages which is more common in the introductory stage. Competition can also lead to new promotional vehicles being tested and also an increase in the varieties (flavours, sizes, shapes, colours or other conspicuous features) of the brands in the market. Penetration of other market segments which perhaps seemed less attractive initially becomes a competition-induced strategy for sales enhancement.

6.2.3 Maturity

By this stage in the life of the brand the market is both well established and well defined. Most potential customers have tried (or decided never to try) each of the competing brands in the market. Each has an established repertoire of brands. This is a shortlist of brands which are considered in a purchasing decision. It can range from 1 (i.e., complete loyalty to one brand) upwards. Market segments are well defined with consumer benefits from the product-type being well known to suppliers. Sales tend to be at the repurchase rate.

Competitive strategies are well established in the industry. As discussed in Chapter 3 on market structure there may be tacit agreement not to compete on price. Alternatively there may be pressure for price reductions as a form of competition, as there is less danger than earlier in the life cycle that consumers will suspect the quality of the brand.

Promotion and use experience should have led to the establishment and maintenance of a distinct brand image which is not easily changeable. Thus, promotion is used to reinforce the brand image and to remind consumers of the brand name. Sales promotions are frequently used to generate temporary interest in the brand as discussed in the last chapter.

Distribution is also stable, with the brand providing a 'normal' rate of return to suppliers. Relatively little brand-switching is likely by distributors, and good working relationships (both formal and informal) should have been developed between manufacturers and distributors.

Competitive attempts to stimulate the market are often focused on brand rejuvenation. By adding new features to the brand, it may be possible to open up new users for, more users of, or more usage of, the brand. The types of new features are manifold. Examples include:

— New formulations of washing powder, or new ingredients for good products.
— New flavours of ice cream or yoghurt.
— New styling of a car model.
— New packaging.
— New sizes/shapes of the brand — multipacks of beer or chocolate biscuits.

The aim of such rejuvenation is to extend the life cycle of the brand. Ford undertook this manoeuvre successfully four times in the UK in developing the Cortina from Mark 1 through to Mark 5.

This strategy may be pro-active, to take an initiative in order to gain market share from competitors, or reactive, to compete with innovative brands appearing in the market or to halt the decline in sales of the brand.

6.2.4 Decline

Joel Dean identified the major influences on the length of the life cycle as being:

1. The rate of technical change.
2. The rate of market acceptance.
3. The ease of competitive entry, i.e., the barriers to entry in the industry.[20]

For whatever reason, sales of the brand will eventually decline and the decline stage is reached. Those who still buy the brand can be characterized as traditionalists, since other users will have switched to innovative products which can make the brand appear outmoded. Sales to these habitual buyers can be achieved relatively easily although new customers are likely to be extremely uncommon.

A downward spiral of distribution can occur. As sales begin to fall, more and more distributors, faced with pressure on display space and the need to keep up profit per square metre, will drop the brand. In turn this will reduce overall sales, making the brand less deserving of advertising support by the supplier which will cause other distributors to stop taking the brand. Habitual buyers may switch brands rather than seek alternative stockists as the brand's distribution share falls.

The brand can still be profitable in the decline stage as demand may not be price sensitive, so that advertising and other promotional support can be withdrawn without unduly affecting demand. However, the brand will eventually be unprofitable as demand gradually declines, and the supplier is faced with the decision of when to withdraw the brand from sale. There is often an aversion to this decision in companies. Executives may feel that a stigma or failure may be attached to those making the decision. This can be overcome by a regular periodic review procedure.

The cost of weak brands is often not fully considered or even calculated by firms. There are a number of elements to this cost:

1. The trading cost, low output and high unit costs being set against low and falling sales levels.
2. Overhead charges are levied on less units of output.
3. Short production runs can lead to high changeover costs.
4. There are high levels of executive involvement generally and in relation to frequent marketing-mix changes, which involve costs of implementation, in an attempt to stimulate sales.

Eventually these costs will be too serious to ignore and the brand will be withdrawn. Of course with many industrial goods and consumer durables there will continue to be a need to supply spare parts for servicing and maintenance in order that after-sales service can continue to be available. To fail to do this may adversely affect company image although it may be feasible to sub-contract such work to other, perhaps smaller, suppliers.

6.3 CRITICISMS OF THE PRODUCT LIFE CYCLE CONCEPT

While the product life cycle concept is undoubtedly valuable in enabling a logical description and analysis to be given of the life of a product or a brand, there is some debate about the value of the concept in marketing practice. Essentially this criticism hinges on the empirical need to predict rather than simply to describe. If the concept is to be of real practical value, the turning points between the following stages:

— Introduction and growth
— Growth and maturity
— Maturity and decline

need to be predicted in both time and sales terms. This prediction of the time of occurrence and of the sales volume (or value) would enable marketing strategy to be adapted pro-actively. However, this could lead to a self-fulfilling situation. For instance, withdrawing advertising support from a brand because it has been forecast that it is about to move into the decline stage may *cause* a decline in sales.

It is difficult to identify any evidence within the life cycle concept itself which could enable fore-casting of turning-points to occur.

Polli and Cook defined the stages in the life cycle in terms of percentage changes in annual sales. In the food class they defined the changes as:

$> +5\%$ = Growth.

$> +1\%, < +5\%$ = Sustained maturity.

$> -1\%, < +1\%$ = Maturity.

$> -5\%, < -1\%$ = Declining maturity.

$< -5\%$ = Decline.

They reported considerable support for the life cycle in practice but found that sales decline is often followed by a period of maturity. They also found that the maturity stage for a product group could be made up of some brands in the growth stage, some in the maturity stage and some in the decline stage. Individual brand shares could vary widely over time while sales of the product group remain constant.[21]

Dhalla and Yuspeh criticize the concept as it applies both to products and, more particularly, to brands:

> ... when it comes to brands, the PLC model has even less validity. Many potentially useful offerings die in the introductory stage because of inadequate product development or unwise market planning, or both. The much-expected ebullient growth phase never arrives. Even when a brand survives the introductory stage, the model in most cases cannot be used as a planning or a predictive tool.[22]

They go on to argue that sales curves shed no light on expected sales levels and conclude that:

> ... clearly, the PLC is a *dependent* variable which is determined by marketing actions; it is not an *independent* variable to which companies should adapt their marketing programs. Marketing management itself can alter the shape and duration of a brand's life cycle.[23]

A further criticism is that the PLC focuses attention on new product development to an exaggerated extent. Companies may be better employed in rejuvenating existing brands in the late maturity/decline stage rather than in withdrawing marketing support and concentrating on new product development. This can be viewed as the PLC causing blinkered thinking.

On a more positive note, Doyle argues that empirical evidence shows that most products broadly follow a PLC pattern and that the average length is shortening due to economic, technological and social change rate changes.[24] He identifies turning point indices including:

— Market saturation.
— Competition (is there overcapacity?).
— Alternative products and technologies.

Cox[25] identifies six PLC curves from the basis of a study of 258 ethical drug brands, half of which follow a cycle—recycle format rather than the traditionally-shaped life cycle shown in Figure 6.1.

Doyle concludes his study by stating that 'used in conjunction with effective forecasts and with an understanding of the competitive dynamics of the market, the PLC offers valuable insights into allocating resources and into analysing future problems and opportunities.'[26]

There are obviously disagreements about the exact value of the PLC concept, in particular about the practical use of the technique. The predictive rather than the descriptive role of the technique must be open to question. The strategic value of the technique is difficult to assess from the evidence but the PLC concept must be treated with care.

In the next chapter, the emphasis moves to new product development and to the role of market research in this process. If new brands fail, it is very often because of a lack of demand; this should presumably be forecast from market research for the new brand, so what goes wrong? The next chapter examines this problem area which is of vital importance for most companies. The rest of this chapter examines the product-range aspects of the brand policy and is closely linked to the discussion in Chapter 4 on the pricing implications of product policy.

6.4   PRODUCT RANGE CONSIDERATIONS

In modern business, unlike the classical economic assumption of the single-product firm, firms are multibrand conglomerates, in most cases offering a combination of physical product and services to an identified series of target audiences. It is clear from the discussion of the product life cycle that a firm needs a mix of brands. It must avoid having too many in the introduction or decline stage at the same time, as these can be a drain on resources. Equally it must not complacently expect current cash flow from maturity-stage brands to continue indefinitely. The firm must have a clear policy of review and development for the existing brand range. This policy should be linked to the top management strategies to meet company objectives. If the firm expects to grow then new opportunities in product and/or market terms must be identified.

The dimensions of the product range include:

1. Width   — the number of types of brands.
2. Depth   — the number of variants of each brand in the range.
3. Consistency — how closely related the brands are.
4. Length   — the total number of brands in the range.

The top management objective may well be to maximize profits across the whole range of brands. This may involve each brand making a contribution to profits but a loss-making brand may be carried for other reasons such as prestige, or as a loss leader for related company brands, or to complete a full range of brands to cover the market as a defence against competitors.

In strategic terms, top management may wish to develop a new brand or retain existing, declining brands as a defensive or offensive strategy which can override purely economic considerations. Modernization of the range can be undertaken but timing is usually of great importance and should involve careful research.

Any change to an existing brand should be made only after very careful consideration, as the brand is a major asset for companies. For example, Rowntree spent three months researching the decision to add a red line to the Black Magic box! This may seem excessive but the brand has been highly successful in the UK for over 50 years and the original utility image of the black and white box, intended to focus attention on the value of the contents, had not previously been changed in such a drastic way.

Vacuum cleaners, which have a basic unchanging operation, have been constantly rejuvenated by changing the style of the existing brands, which has involved more gadgets being added, and colour, shape and size changes.

To meet a strategic need for diversification, a firm may develop or acquire (by merger, take-over, etc.) brands to increase the width of the product range. To increase market segmentation, the depth of the product range can be increased. It can also be necessary to reposition existing brands to take account of increased competition or changes in consumer tastes.

Most products have at least some service aspect. This can be in terms of one or several of the following:

- Delivery speed.
- Prompt quotation.
- Technical advice.
- Discount structure.
- After-sales service.
- Ease of personal contact.
- Guarantee availability.
- Credit availability.
- Complaints handling procedures.

The service aspect is an essential part of the product range, consideration being different in many respects from the physical product considerations. For example, services are intangible and inseparable from their source. They can vary in quality and are perishable (for example, guarantees eventually lapse). Nevertheless, service aspects of a brand may be the major reason for a purchase choice. Brands can also represent services rather than physical products. For example, Royal Insurance markets a 'Car Shield' motor insurance policy. The essential principles of branding, however, remain the same.

6.5 SUMMARY

In summary, brand policy decisions involve many considerations, not all of them economic in nature. They relate to corporate strategy as the means of achieving company objectives. While it is necessary to be aware of these broader issues it is not feasible in this context to take the discussion further along these lines. Specialist texts by Foxall[27] and Weitz and Wensley[28] are examples of work in the strategic marketing area.

In the next chapter the marketing research aspects of new brand development are considered (primarily for consumer goods although in most circumstances the principles apply to service and industrial goods) by taking account of essential brand differences. The concentration on market responses reflects the author's conviction that new brand failures are primarily caused by a failure to realistically and accurately assess demand for a proposed new brand.

REFERENCES

1. Rogers, E. M. (1962) *Diffusion of Innovations*, Free Press, New York.
2. Rogers, E. M. and F. F. Shoemaker (1971) *Communication of Innovations*, Free Press, New York.
3. Robertson, T. S. (1971) *Innovative Behavior and Communication*, Holt, Rinehart and Winston, New York.
4. Midgley, D. F. (1977) *Innovation and New Product Marketing*, Croom Helm, London.
5. Peterson, R. A. (1973) 'A note on optimal adopter category determination', *Journal of Marketing Research*, **10**, 325−9.
6. Bell, W. E. (1963) 'Consumer innovators: A unique market for newness', in *Proceedings of the Marketing Association*, A.M.A., Chicago.
7. Robertson, T. S. and J. N. Kennedy (1968) 'Prediction of consumer innovators: Application of multiple discriminant analysis', *Journal of Marketing Research*, **5**, February, 64−9.
8. Uhl, K., R. Andrus, and L. Poulsen (1970) 'How are laggards different? An empirical enquiry', *Journal of Marketing Research*, **7**, February, 51−4.
9. Baumgarten, S. A. (1974) 'The diffusion of fashion innovations among U.S. college students', *Proceedings ESOMAR Conference, December 1974*, ESOMAR, Amsterdam.
10. Robertson, T. S. (1967) 'Determinants of innovative behaviour', *Proceedings of the American Marketing Association*, A.M.A., Chicago.
11. Pizam, A. (1972) 'Psychological characteristics of innovators' *European Journal of Marketing*, **6**, 3, 203−10.
12. Donnelly, J. H. and J. M. Ivancevich, (1974) 'A methodology for identifying innovator characteristics of new brand purchasers', *Journal of Marketing Research*, **11**, August, 331−4.
13. Donnelly, J. H. (1970) 'Social Character and Acceptance of New Products', *Journal of Marketing Research*, **7**, February, 111−13.
14. Summers, J. O. (1970) 'The identity of women's clothing fashion opinion leaders', *Journal of Marketing Research*, **7**, 178−85.
15. Belk, R. W. (1974) 'An exploratory assessment of situational effects in buyer behaviour', *Journal of Marketing Research*, **11**, May, 156−63.
16. Ostlund, L. E. (1974) 'Perceived innovation attributes as predictors of innovativeness', *Journal of Consumer Research*, **1**, September, 23−9.
17. Ibid., p. 26.
18. Ostlund, L. E. Op. cit., p. 28.
19. Katz, E. and P. F. Lazarsfeld, (1955) *Personal Influence*, Free Press, New York.
20. Dean, J. (1950) 'Pricing policies for new products', *Harvard Business Review*, November−December, 28.
21. Polli, R. and W. J. Cook (1969) 'Validity of the product life cycle', *Journal of Business*, October, 385−400.
22. Dhalla, N. K. and S. Yuspeh, (1976) 'Forget the product life cycle concept', *Harvard Business Review*, January−February, 102−12.
23. Ibid., p. 107.
24. Doyle, P. (1976) 'The realities of the product life cycle', *Quarterly Review of Marketing*, Summer, 1−6.
25. Cox, W. E. (1967) 'Product life cycles as marketing models', *Journal of Business*, October, 375.
26. Doyle, op. cit., p. 6.
27. Foxall, G. R. (1981) *Strategic Marketing Management*, Croom Helm, London.
28. Weitz, B. A. and R. Wensley (1983) *Strategic Marketing*, Kent, Boston, Mass.

NEW BRAND DEVELOPMENT

This chapter concentrates on the marketing research aspects of new brand development. The last chapter examined how existing brands are marketed and fit into a product range; here potential additions to this range are considered from a consumer viewpoint.

7.1 NEW BRAND DEVELOPMENT

A company, to guarantee survival and/or growth, needs to maintain a range of products of differing maturity. In cash flow terms, profits developed from the late growth and maturity product life cycle stages can be used to finance new brands which are eventually intended to generate positive cash flow. There can be many reasons for introducing new brands:

1. To generate temporary interest in a staid product line.
2. To copy competitors.
3. To forestall expected competition.
4. To counteract falling sales from existing products.
5. To take advantage of researched market opportunity.
6. To use by-products from an existing product production process.
7. To complement existing brands.
8. To move into new markets as a form of diversification.

The reason for a particular development can often be a complex combination of various endogenous and exogenous variables.

The definition of a new brand used here will be 'a product with a new name'. This simple practical definition implies that a new brand is a major investment for the company. It is not a rejuvenation (e.g., Cortina Mark 4) nor a minor addition to an existing range (e.g., Sainsbury's Apple and Pear Yoghourt). There are doubtless marginal cases but as a workable definition this approach seems to be feasible.

The definition of 'success' or 'failure' in new product development is much more difficult as it can vary from company to company. In some cases a brand may enter a market, be successful briefly and then be withdrawn and be judged a 'success' or 'failure' according to criteria which vary between companies.

There are also organizational implications of new product development. It is not intended to examine the literature but the work of Burns and Stalker[1] has implications for the innovation process within companies of various sizes which are concerned with the development of new brands.

Assessing the failure rate in new product development is extremely difficult. As noted above it is very difficult to define 'success' or 'failure' and very difficult to compare between companies. Just because a brand is quickly withdrawn from the market does not mean it is necessarily a failure and any 'counting' methods of measurement need to be done in conjunction with company assessments. Obviously in many cases the definition will be clear-cut.

What is clear from examining specific cases, is that both large and small companies have product failures. Spectacular failures can occur, as with the launch of NSM cigarette brands by the major tobacco companies in the late 1970s. It is necessary to have company-specific definitions of success against which to compare predicted performance before launch. Some evidence is provided by the consultancy firm of Booz, Allen and Hamilton, who in 1968 produced the study of new product development referred to later. In 1982 they updated this study and published the following findings:

1. Management reported an average new product success rate of 65 per cent.
2. Companies were able to develop one successful product out of each seven they researched. In 1968 the rate was one from 58 ideas!
3. Only 10 per cent of new products were 'new to the world' and 20 per cent were 'new product lines' but these highest-risk products represented about 60 per cent of the most successful new products.
4. Successful new product companies do not spend more on research and development and marketing as a percentage of sales than unsuccessful ones.
5. The median number of new products introduced between 1976 and 1981 was five – this was expected to double in the next five years.
6. Managers expect new products to increase company sales growth by one-third over the next five years, while the position of total company profits generated by new products is expected to be 40 per cent.

These results were from a mail survey of 700 companies in the US, combined with depth interviews of 150 new product executives.[2]

Further information was provided by the retail audit firm A. C. Nielsen who found that from a sample of 228 frequently purchased consumer products test-marketed in the US in 1977 only 35.5 per cent were launched nationally.[3]

It is clear from this that there is still cause for concern and much room for improvement in the success rate of new product development and that even at the test market stage a high proportion of new products are withdrawn.

There can be many reasons for failure. Although some are 'supply-side' problems such as failure to maintain quality standards or raw material supplies, or to have a sufficiently long shelf-life, most reasons are 'demand-side' problems. Essentially a lack of demand is the reason why products fail. The rest of this section examines what may lie behind the success or failure of market research techniques in predicting such a lack of demand before the company has made a heavy investment in marketing and production planning.

What is clearly important is the number of individual adopters. Midgley splits adoption into 'favourables' and 'passives'.[4] Favourables have positive attitudes to the new brand and buy it more frequently whereas passives are neutral about the brand but may buy it occasionally. In this book this definition will be followed: adoption will be taken to include both the brand loyal and those who are likely to buy the brand occasionally. Non-adopters will be others, those who are unlikely at this stage to buy the brand (but whose attitudes may change in the future, causing purchasing to occur). It is important not to confuse this with individual innovativeness which has been discussed

3. Advertising campaigns do not logically begin with the concepts, but rather with the target market. Breaking down a campaign to cover only the basic concept is not realistic.
4. Propositions may be associated differentially with brands already on the market which may bias the results.[6]

Overall, King attacks the lack of realism from the position of the respondent housewife who cannot identify with the concepts being tested in any realistic way.

This section has been concerned with some of the issues involved in practical approaches to concept testing using market research. It has highlighted some of the limited published evidence on concept testing. The overall success of concept testing seems to be very limited. Pessimistic attitudes have been recorded. The area seems to be beset with practical problems concerned with realism of the testing procedure. The lamentable dearth of published material on the accuracy of empirical concept tests makes for difficulty in assessing current techniques and approaches. The fact remains that many companies are using various forms of concept testing in practice.

This chapter will now progress to the third stage of marketing research involvement with new brand development, that of product testing.

7.2.5 Product testing

By this stage in the development process, the product concept has been tested, proved worthy of further development and has passed successfully through a form of business analysis. Prototype versions of the proposed brand have been produced. The market research function at this stage involves the provision of information as an input to the decision of whether or not to produce the brand in quantity for a (test) market launch. It is necessary, as is apparent from the discussion on validity in the previous section, for the company to be developing the whole of the market strategy to be applied to the new brand, besides the physical product.

Because of the existence of the physical product and at least an outline marketing strategy, it becomes possible to assess consumer response on a wider basis and in more realistic situations. It is often the case that more than one prototype brand has been formulated at this stage, with each being a variation on a theme rather than being substantially different product types.

Greenhalgh suggested that there are five basic questions to be answered by market research data at this stage:

1. Does the brand live up to its concept in terms of saleability?
2. Does the brand warrant further investment of time and money?
3. Which of the alternatives are likely to be most successful?
4. In what ways can the brand be further improved?
5. Which are the most promising market segments?[37]

Most commentators are agreed that the primary requisite is to expose the product to the respondent under conditions which as closely resemble reality as is possible. As with Section 7.2.4 on concept testing, with which this section has considerable potential overlap, a number of contentious issues will be considered in relation to brand testing.

Firstly, there is the question of sample selection. It is obvious that any sample used should be representative, but representative of what? Greenhalgh argued that the representative sample should not be too restrictive and suggests that users rather than purchasers should be sampled, if these can be identified at this stage. Midgley argued that:

> the only sensible procedure is to elicit responses that are indicative of future behaviour from potential innovators. The attitudes, opinions and expectations of the rest of the population will largely be formed by the reactions of these innovators to the product's performance, and in actual usage, not laboratory conditions.[44]

The problem with this approach lies in the difficulties inherent in the identification of potential innovators. The techniques suggested by Midgley for overcoming this problem[45] are likely to prove highly expensive for market researchers in 'high risk' product markets. One method of identifying new brand innovators would be in terms of the characteristics of innovators of previous new brands. These identified characteristics would then be used in sample selection for current brand tests. However, as Midgeley pointed out:

> the main difficulty is that there has been relatively little work done on these characteristics as they affect new product introductions and it would therefore be unwise for a company to rely on the characteristics listed in the literature without any empirical confirmation.[46]

Ostlund has tested a method based on an assessment of how a sample of the target population perceives the new brand, using dimensions of relative advantage, comparability, complexity, trialability, observability and perceived risk.[47] Based on these responses, categories of innovators and later adopters are established. In tests Ostlund correctly identified 77 per cent of innovators on the basis of prior measurements. To apply this technique to new brand testing would involve the assignment of cut-off points on each dimension in order to establish categories of innovativeness in respondents.

A further problem with this approach is that innovators may have quite different buying habits from other consumers. A brand which scores highly with innovators (who typically would form a small proportion of the total market) may be rejected by other consumers. This possibility would also need to be researched if such an approach was to be made.

Batsell and Wind suggested the use of a probability sample and 'if certain characteristics of the target market are known to affect product preferences, taking a stratified random sample may greatly increase the precision of the sample estimates'.[48] In addition to ethnic, demographic, and other personal characteristics, a sample might also be stratified by usage, brand loyalty, media habits, etc.

Penny, Hunt and Twyman reported on an experiment designed to compare results for:

1. Panel members responding to self-completed postal questionnaires (600 members).
2. Newly recruited housewives responding by self-completed postal questionnaires (300 housewives).
3. Newly recruited housewives responding to a face to face interview (300 housewives).

Two types of products were used (washing powder and margarine). There were no differences in results between the groups for either of the product groups.[29]

Intuitively, the ideas of Midgley appeal in situations where:

1. There is little difference in buyer behaviour (apart from when the brand is first bought) between innovators and later adopters. Although it could be argued that if there is little difference the sample need not be solely composed of innovators, it is more realistic to use innovators as these are the early actual consumers of the new brand.
2. Innovators can easily (inexpensively and accurately) be identified.

A second issue relates to the use of blind tests. Greenhalgh intimated that the use of brand names is not necessary at this stage unless it is an important part of the package design or is a direct extension of an existing brand. He suggests that competitors' products can be repackaged to provide comparisons under blind test conditions.[37] Batsell and Wind stated that 'although most product tests are blind, since real work product choice is not based on physical product features alone, the question is under what conditions should the stimulus be restricted to a blind test of physical product features vs. a more complete (and realistic) product test – which includes a package and brand name'.[49]

In a study by Allison and Uhl, beer drinkers rated six different unlabelled brands of beer and, one week later, the same six labelled. Brand knowledge clearly affected the ratings by biasing the ratings of the drinker's favourite brand in a positive manner.[50] This was confirmed in studies by Beckwith and Lehmann in 1975[51] and by Beckwith and Kubilius in 1977.[52] Respondents tend to respond more favourably to a product labelled as 'their' brand. Penny, Hunt and Twyman showed results for a food product where labelling by brand had no effect on product evaluation.[29]

Batsell and Wind recommended that if 'the study objectives require assessment of consumers' likely purchase behaviour in the marketplace where brand information is provided, a task in which the respondents evaluate labelled stimuli should be considered'.[53] Green and Wind showed an example of a conjoint analysis design which specified the brand name as a factor from which the effects can be explicitly assessed. This is one approach which can overcome the problem of halo effects in branded tests.[54]

Brown, Copeland and Millward reported their attempt to overcome halo effects in monadic testing by using a strong appeal to respondents at the beginning of the interview for frank opinions, using a videotape including the message 'it is just as important to know what is wrong with it (the new brand being tested) as it is to know whether you like anything about it'. Their assessment of the use of this strong appeal concluded that 'it did not appear to have helped although we cannot discount the possibility that it may have contributed in some degree to the success of our other devices.'[55]

The need to avoid halo effects caused by prior knowledge of, or preference for, an existing brand, is a strong argument for the use of blind tests. There is also a strong argument for including competitors' brands in tests in order to achieve realistic results by testing the proposed new brand against proven successes.

A third issue is whether or not respondents can discriminate between brands. If the respondents state that they have 'no preference' between brands under test, this may mean that they cannot detect any difference between the brands, or it may mean that they can detect a difference but like each test brand version equally or that the respondent has 'guessed'. Greenhalgh found that when using triangular tests to assess whether respondents could discriminate between brands, the groups classified as 'discriminators' and 'non-discriminators' each exhibited similar preferences which suggests auto-correlation.[56]

Gruber and Lindberg reported an experiment to determine levels of discrimination by presenting respondents with three items of which two were identical, and asking respondents to pick the brands liked most and least. If a respondent chose the same brand for both, an 'insensitive' classification results. This procedure was repeated to check reliability.[57] This method, reported in 1966, does not seem to have been adopted on any significant scale. Greenhalgh has shown that preference in triad tests of this type tends to be for the 'different' brands.[56] Greenberg and Collins suggested that the greater the number of inconsistent preferers, the more likely it is that brands are non-discriminable and that preferences will be evenly divided, presumably by chance. Their research shows that results of discrimination tests are close to a chance performance expectation.[58] It has also been argued that by aggregation of inconsistent individual preferers, a consistent overall preference may result. This result has not been proved experimentally and chance may play a role in obtaining such results.

Penny, Hunt and Twyman reported an experimental test where respondents were asked their preference from two washing-up liquid brands on four occasions to assess consistency of preference.[29] This test illustrates the probabilistic nature of preference judgements over four repeat tests although the relationship between consistency of preference and level of preference is itself consistent.

Greenhalgh[37] has commented from case histories studied that there are significant confounding effects caused by the artificiality and complexity of discrimination tests while Roper suggested that inability to discriminate in the artificial situation of triangular discrimination tests in particular, is not a reliable measure of whether a subject can discriminate in the more natural setting of real life use.[59]

Batsell and Wind insisted that:

> . . . if a product test purports (or is intended) to measure only preference then the ability of subjects to discriminate between options must be verified. On the other hand, verifying discrimination requires extra respondent time, no approach seems to be uniformly best, and it is not clear what should be done with 'non-discriminators' anyway.[26]

Penny, Hunt and Twyman presented a probabilistic model of discrimination and preference in which the probabilities of discrimination and preference are assessed. They outline possible implications of particular combinations of probabilities on an a priori basis but without going on to produce an empirically tested categorization procedure using probabilities of respondent discrimination and preference.[29]

Overall, there seem to be few practical guidelines on the issue of discrimination and preference available in published literature. There is also the complication that discrimination tests necessitate comparative testing techniques which, it has already been argued, are of reduced validity as they do not recreate reality.

A fourth issue to be considered, which also applies to concept testing is the questionnaire construction. Some of the problems involved in this issue have already been discussed. Halo effects, in particular, present special difficulties in designing questionnaires. Other problems apply to all forms of questionnaires such as the meaning of specific words used e.g., 'better', 'normally', 'often', may mean different things to different respondents.

Greenhalgh suggested asking both diagnostic questions such as 'why do you prefer . . . ?', 'how can it be improved?' and also attribute questions to assess the importance of each brand characteristic.[25] Gabor and Granger have suggested that to derive a sales revenue forecast respondents should be asked if they would be willing to buy a new brand at a series of prices with one obviously too low and one obviously too high. Prices should be presented in a random order. By using a representative sample, a sales revenue forecast could then be derived.[60] This and other innovative work on pricing research carried out at Nottingham University is reported by Gabor[61] (see pages 49–50).

Rating scales are commonly used to assess the strengths and weaknesses of a proposed new brand in terms of its characteristics and its perceived advantages and disadvantages. Respondents could also be asked what existing brand, if any, it would replace. To gain an insight into repurchase possibilities, product testing questionnaires are often re-administered after home use by respondents. The decisions on questionnaire design involve examining exactly what is to be measured and how this is to be measured. Question wording is also important. Belkin and Lieberman tested two identical product descriptions for a brand of sun-tan lotion on 854 men. Half were asked, 'Would you be interested in any of these products?' and half, 'Which, if any, of these products would you be interested in buying?' Of the group who were asked the first question 53 per cent expressed interest in buying one or more items, but 64 per cent of the group who were asked the second question expressed such interest.[62]

In trying to reduce the impact of halo effects, Brown, Copeland and Millward[34] argued that an overall evaluation question should be placed after the evaluation of individual characteristics questions rather than before, as is more usual. Their reasoning is 'that the housewife is not able to reach a sensible overall judgement so early in the interview and that questions which remind her of relevant considerations are a positive benefit. If the interviewer begins with a question which is unnatural to the respondent and which also forces a commitment whether positive or negative, subsequent answers will tend to be consistent with this early ill-judged response'.[63] They report that this new question order 'appears to have been successful in increasing discrimination'.[64]

A further problem, that of responses being biased towards the positive, has been tested by Clancy and Garsen who used a sequential monadic test of three new brand concepts each tapered to meet opposing consumer needs (mild, safe to powerful, extra strength).[65] Those who expressed a high probability of purchase for all three concepts were assumed to be 'yeasayers'. Not only did the analysis indicate the presence of response bias, it indicated a relationship between the response bias and socio-economic status — individuals classified as of low socio-economic status were much more likely to be yeasayers than those classified as of high socio-economic status. This potential problem should be planned for in any new brand test.

It is clear from this analysis that many pitfalls exist in product testing for new brands. If the brand is thought to be worthy of further development the next stage is often test marketing.

7.2.6 Test marketing

The problems concerned with a lack of realism inherent in concept and product testing can be overcome by a limited market test in which the proposed new brand is made available on a commercial basis. Thus potential customers make an actual purchase choice between the test brand and the existing brands on the market, taking full account of their budget and other constraints.

Test marketing can be viewed as an insurance policy in that it is a final test of a brand's market acceptability before a commitment to full-scale production is made. Test marketing can be used to forecast total market sales by scaling up the results from a representative test area to form a vital input to the final GO/NO GO decision. Also, the marketing mix can be fine-tuned. If one particular aspect of the marketing strategy is found to be less than optimum it may be feasible to amend the variable-setting before a full-scale launch. Technical factors can also be assessed. For example, the shelf life of a consumer food product can be ascertained in practice. For industrial goods, the operation of equipment in a working environment can be analysed. In addition to market data many valuable insights into the efficient, cost-effective production of the brand can be obtained in a practical context. With food products, it is often found that when production is on a large scale rather than from a 'test kitchen' type of facility, there may be slight changes in flavour, texture or colour and it may be necessary to obtain customer reaction to the different versions.

In the UK it is usual for consumer goods to use a TV region as a test market in order to test the planned advertising campaign on a realistic smaller scale. The smaller TV regions such as Tyne–Tees, Anglia and Southern are popular, especially if more than one is to be used to assess any regional variation.

On a retail level, new brands are often tried in particular stores thought to be typical in some way. However, Marks and Spencer test clothes products in their Oxford Street store on the premise that London fashions are ahead of the rest of the country and a success in London can then be launched nationally without 'missing the boat'.

For industrial goods it is common to use specific customers as 'guinea-pigs' for in-use trial of a new product, perhaps at a price discount. The experience of these customers is then used in the marketing launch of the product on a wider scale.

Increasingly, with the growth of 'world brands' discussed in Chapter 9, test marketing is likely to be on a national basis as preparation for an international launch.

The duration of the test market will vary with the product type. A frequently purchased product should be tested over several repurchase periods so that both trial and repurchase rates can be assessed. Industrial goods such as computer software need to be tested long enough for all the 'bugs' to be ironed out of the system.

As already noted the availability of realistic market data is a major benefit from test marketing use. It is common for companies to use representative panels of consumers so that trend data on brand awareness, interest, trial rates, repurchase rates and advertising tracking studies can be gathered. It may also be necessary to conduct retail audits so that the distribution effectiveness can be assessed. In addition in-depth interview with (groups of) consumers may be necessary to obtain detailed feedback on use, user and usage experiences.

A number of problems exist with test marketing. Firstly, competitors are informed that the company is developing a new brand (if they did not already know from other sources). As discussed in Chapter 3, in highly competitive oligopolistic markets, innovation can be a major form of competition and by revealing plans to competitors, more time is given for them to react. The longer the test, the more time they have to react. Competitors can buy market data to monitor the test brand's performance to aid their own decision-making. It is not unknown for competitors to launch a marketing initiative of their own during a test market – this can then lead to unrealistic and unrepresentative sales results occurring.

This leads on to the second problem. It can, for many product types, be extremely difficult to find a representative test market. This can lead to problems in scaling-up results to produce a total market sales forecast for the brand, but in many cases this can be overcome. However where regional sales levels fluctuate absolutely or relative to other regional sales levels then it can be extremely difficult to take account of these variations sufficiently to produce a reliable sales forecast.

A further difficulty is in forecasting the stable market share of the test brand. When a new brand is launched either in a test market or nationally, its novelty value is at its greatest. Curiosity buyers are most likely to try the brand. However if the brand is to succeed it is usually necessary for it to achieve repeat sales without the 'razzmatazz' of the immediate post-launch period. Unless the test market is of sufficiently long duration the sales forecast may take undue notice of initial curiosity sales and overestimate steady-state market demand.

A fourth problem is the need, at least for consumer goods, to obtain retailer co-operation. In the UK and in most other Western economies the power of retailers has grown rapidly over the past two decades, as discussed in the next chapter. A premium may have to be paid to obtain distribution in the test market area with major retailers. The manufacturer cannot guarantee that a national retail chain will only make the test brand available in the designated test area. This could distort results upwards.

A further problem is cost. There are many fixed costs involved in the launch of a new brand. For example, the advertising campaign needs to be professionally produced. In addition, the initial small-scale production levels may be relatively inefficient, leading to high unit costs. The company has a trade-off to make between the cost of the test market operation and the benefits from it in terms of improved market intelligence.

Finally, extraneous factors such as the weather and the economic climate can have an unpredictable effect on test market sales results. Unless the company has some means of using a control group there is little that can be done to offset this problem.

In summary, test markets can be very valuable but there are pitfalls in terms of cost, informing competitors and representativeness. In recent years alternatives to test markets have been developed and examples will be considered in the next section.

7.3 SIMULATED TEST MARKETS

7.3.1 Practical problems on market measurement at the product-testing stage

It is immediately apparent that the more market research information that is available, the more accurate this demand forecast should be. This is a dilemma for the company: more market information usually involves more cost; the company has to effect a trade-off between accuracy and cost. Once the brand is in a test market, for example, the company has access to a wealth of market data on which to base a demand forecast for the national market; it also has the high cost of setting up the test market operation. Once the brand is launched onto the national market, much more market data becomes available. There is much published work which examines growth rate projections of products once launched[66,67,5,68] and which examines the diffusion process for new products amongst buyers.[69,70] However, it is the purpose of this section to concentrate on pre-test markets, market research and evaluation, to attempt to review the cost-effectiveness of demand forecasts at this stage in the development process. If it were possible to produce accurate forecasts at the product-testing stage relatively inexpensively, the test-market stage could be eliminated, saving much time and cost for the company.

How then can an accurate forecast be made at the product-testing stage? There are formidable problems. Tauber, in an article entitled 'Why concept and product tests fail to predict new product results',[71] illuminated these problems:

> Validation work with concept testing and product testing reveals that pretrial intentions (at concept) relate to, though do not necessarily predict, trial purchase behaviour. Post-trial intentions (product tests) relate to early

repeat behaviour. But neither of these techniques helps to predict how many will become loyal users. Neither of these behaviours correlates well with the eventual adoption level.

He goes on to state that:

> in effect, concept tests and product tests fail to predict new product sales results because they do not predict adoption behaviour. Why? Because consumers at the early stage of experience with a product are not able to predict their own ongoing behaviour.[72]

Tauber suggested that the key to success lies in the identification of the correct consumer behavioural responses to measure; for convenience consumer products this involves predicting continued repeat buys: ' . . . precision in forecasting clearly demands more than relating a magic number on an attitude scale to a norm.'[73]

In a later article Tauber suggested four variables that need to be forecast:

1. Trial rate.
2. First repeat purchase rate.
3. Adoption rate — the proportion who accept the brand as 'their' brand.
4. Frequency of purchase.[74]

From these predicted variables, bearing in mind the limitations and imperfections in the market such as the lack of consumer awareness of the new brand, limited distribution and 'wearout' (consumers buying the brand two to three times and then dropping it), it is feasible to produce a forecast of demand for the brand if launched. The problem is in accurately measuring these variables from product tests.

Taylor, Houlahan and Gabriel reported an experiment to test whether or not consumers really intend to buy, carried out at the product-testing stage.[75] In this test, in the Midwest of America, a representative sample of consumers was selected and each housewife was given three samples of the test product. Ten days later, each was telephoned and given a purchase intention test and told that the brand was available in ten local supermarkets. Six weeks later, each was telephoned again and asked if the brand display had been seen and if the brand had been purchased. Results for the 161 respondents are shown in Table 7.1.

There is no significance at the 90 per confidence limit, and Taylor *et al*. concluded that 'attitudes toward the product during the consumer test did not have an effect on subsequent searching

Table 7.1 Test results

		Intention to purchase	%	
	(a)	Definitely would buy	18	
	(b)	Probably would buy	29	
1st Phase	(c)	Might or might not buy	28	
	(d)	Probably would not buy	17	
	(e)	Definitely would not buy	8	

	Intention to purchase	Saw brand in store (%)	Did not see brand in store (%)
2nd Phase	(a) + (b)	52	39
	(c) + (d) + (e)	48	61

Source: Adapted from Taylor et al.[75]

in the market. In other words, it appears unlikely that favourable attitudes toward the product will lead to active searching which might overcome gaps in actual distribution when the product is marketed.'

The final stage of the test was to relate intention to purchase to actual purchase behaviour for those actually seeing the brand in store:

Intention to purchase	No. buying product	No. not buying product	Probability of purchase (%)
(a) + (b)	17	31	35
(c) + (d) + (e)	0	42	0

This suggests that there is a positive relationship between buying intention and purchase behaviour.

Taylor *et al.* supported the use of intention-to-purchase questions, 'a potent if imperfect tool for use in new product development' They also offer rule-of-thumb benchmarks, based on studying 100+ brands, for acceptable levels of favourable response. These, they stated, should be:

Stage in development	Acceptable level of those who definitely or probably intend to buy, (a) + (b), % of sample
Concept test	80−90
Prototype product test	70−80
Finished product test	60−70

The methodology of this text is relatively straightforward. Leaving aside the issue of whether a telephone -based survey can be representative for a consumer product, there appears to be a lack of realism in the test. There is no mention of the use of simulated advertisements or other promotional activity. Tauber argued that the value of these findings is reduced as, in different surveys, different proportions of the 'definitely buy' category actually buy.[74] This has been found by Tauber to vary between 10−50 per cent. Tauber also argued that the great majority of successful new products are adopted by between 2−10 per cent of the population only. This implies a greater difficulty in identifying and measuring these intentions to buy and the relationship between the intention to purchase and actual purchasing behaviour.

Nevertheless, the evidence presented by Taylor *et al.* is a positive step in the process of deriving a suitable method of forecasting new brand sales pre test market, by using intention-to-purchase scales. Crawford hypothesized that 'predicting new product sales and profits is an inherently impossible task' in an article which examined the reasons for the high failure rate of new products.[76] He quotes one leading American marketing director as saying, 'They [the company] may have introduced it [the new brand] as a diversionary tactic for someone else's new product . . . new flavors may cost almost nothing to bring to market, add a little temporary interest to the line and are then withdrawn.'[77] Crawford concluded that there is much room for improvement in new product development processes, as the causes of failure are amenable to market research. He suggested that market research must be objective and unaffected by enthusiasm for the new brand within brand management, and a high wastage rate within the development process must be accepted. A firm with a low new product failure rate, he suggested, is passing up profitable risk.

While this article threw some light on the overall problems in demand forecasting for new brands, it made few specific suggestions apart from intimating that the way to measure success of new brands should involve management expectation for the brands.

Tauber suggested the requirement to measure needs as well as intention to purchase.[71] Concept product tests should, he argued, try to measure the extent to which a product fills significant unmet needs as consumer interest is not equivalent to consumer need.

Tauber reported on attempts to relate purchase intention to an unmet consumer need or to a consumer problem needing solution. This approach was intended to exclude those who try a new product as a curiosity or for its novelty value. Eight concepts were tested with results for two shown in Table 7.2.

Table 7.2 Purchase Intention Test

	Concept A	Concept B
% who definitely intend to buy or probably will buy (*a*)	60	22
% who thought the concept would solve a problem or meet a need (*b*)	18	19
(b) as % of (a)		
Problem importance %		
Very important	26	63
Somewhat important	46	32
Slightly important	28	5

Source: Adapted from Tauber.[71]

Tauber concluded from these results that purchase intent is a poor surrogate measure of the number of people who feel a product solves a problem or unfilled need because some products attract more curiosity triers than others. For example, Concept A, a fancy dessert product, showed a high level of interest but very low adoption; Concept B, which was rejected by market research, had a small but strong market segment with a high need factor. As a result, Tauber supported a need to forecast adoption rates.[71] This is consistent with the work of Parfitt and Collins which stresses the importance of the initial trial rate and the repeat purchase rate in assessing the steady-state brand share of a newly launched brand.[78] It is necessary to examine not only the adoption rate and the repeat purchase rate but also the importance of the test brand in meeting the needs of the consumer.

Tauber's separation of purchase intention from problem importance seems somewhat suspect. It could be argued that this need factor is taken into account by respondents in stating their purchase intention. Presumably consumers will not purchase any brand which does not meet an unmet need or solve a problem. The 'problem importance' may in practice be a surrogate measure of actual purchase behaviour. It is not possible to ascertain this from the published data. Further, curiosity triers could convert into brand-loyal adopters if it is assumed that at least some curiosity triers are innovators in the adoption process, as pointed out in a paper by Bell.[79] On balance the idea of eliminating curiosity triers of a new brand from consideration, as suggested by Tauber's approach, may be better avoided.

Morrison attempted to 'construct a formal mathematical model that establishes the intermediate links between stated purchase intentions and actual purchase behaviour'.[80] This was undertaken in three steps:

1. The respondents' stated intention is transformed into an estimate of the true intention, i.e., the stated intention = the true intention + error.

2. The estimated true intention is transformed into an unadjusted purchase probability estimate by the exogenous events model which takes into account factors unknown to the consumer at the time the estimate is made. For example, the breakdown of an electrical appliance during the forecast period may necessitate renewal.
3. The estimated unadjusted purchase probability is transformed into the estimated purchase probability by the probability adjustment model.

Morrison proceeded to specify an adjustment formula for each step. This appears to be a relatively straightforward mathematical restatement of the problems inherent in the process of moving from purchase intention estimate to demand forecast. The data collection for new brands market research and the problems involved in making product tests realistic, as discussed earlier in the chapter, was not really addressed by Morrison.

To summarize, this chapter has so far discussed some of the published attempts to forecast market demand for a new brand before it is test marketed, in order to highlight the problems involved. Much of the comment has emphasized the difficulties involved, in practice, in making accurate forecasts at this early stage. Nevertheless, the potential rewards for companies in avoiding or short-circuiting the test-market stage are great. The rest of the chapter will examine the attempts made to overcome the practical problems by creating models of the process which attempt to predict success in the market-place by various forecasting methods. Such a model involves a validation process. A suitable link to this next section of the chapter is provided by the seemingly ubiquitous Tauber relating to the problems involved in this validation requirement.

> A correct method for validating any technique would require a sample of products to be tested using the system, having the same products entered in the marketplace and comparing sales results. The error of a technique recommending 'no go' (low sales) when the product could be a winner in the marketplace has not been adequately studied . . . the cost to test market a 'loser' may cost several hundred thousand dollars out-of-pocket, while the opportunity cost of failing to market a big winner can amount to millions over many years. Since the failure rate of new consumer entries is over 50%, a naïve technique which always recommended 'no go' would have a decent track record based on 'correct prediction', but a dismal one when considering 'net dollars'.[71]

While this statement is self-explanatory, it re-records the problem of control groups which needs to be overcome in validating any acceptable model.

7.3.2 Predictive models and new brand performance

Most predictive models are based either on historical data regression or on laboratory tests. There are problems inherent in both approaches. The major problem with using past data is the lack of a suitable cohort in many cases. Even if data from comparable brand launches from the past are available exogenous variable changes are almost inevitable.

There are a number of problems inherent in laboratory test based models. However complex the simulation process, realism can never be totally created. It is also extremely difficult to simulate the social dynamics involved in the realistic adoption process. In common with most market research, but more than with most methodologies, laboratory tests involve testing effects. That is, the behaviour of respondents may be influenced by taking part in an experiment. This may distort the results. There is also the danger of a maturation effect which is especially relevant in tests of repeat purchase simulations. This effect occurs when respondents gain more knowledge about the experimentation process as the test progresses – this may lead to inconsistent results or to a loss of interest over time.

During the course of a laboratory test, especially one involving repeat purchasing behaviour over time, exogenous variables may change and may explain the measured behaviour patterns rather than the controlled marketing stimuli input. This is known as the history effect. To some extent it can be minimized by the use of control groups if this is feasible. An interaction effect of testing may also occur. If respondents are given a pre-test about the product being evaluated, they may become sensitized to the subject and in the actual test may expect information on the product. This can be unrealistic. Similarly, experimental conditions may interact with the product being tested to affect the measured outcome. The Hawthorne studies are a prime example of this effect.[81] Detail of experimental effects as they affect the internal and external validity of tests is provided by Campbell and Stanley[82] and by Moser and Kalton.[83] Any laboratory-based testing method for new products must be critically evaluated in the light of these possible threats to validity.

The typical laboratory test for new brands would involve exposure of consumers to commercials and then allowing them the option of purchase in a simulated store. The product (obviously depending on type) would be used in a realistic situation, often being taken home, followed at a suitable interval by follow-up interviews to measure attribute ratings, satisfaction level and repurchase intention. Data on competing brands would also be collected. The actual trial purchase behaviour would be observed. This process would apply to a representative sample of the widely defined target market, or may be a method of identifying potential heavy-user segments of the intended market. The longer this process is followed up for, the more repurchase situations can be observed, but also the higher the cost. As noted above there are problems of interpretation with stated purchase intentions.

Further realism can be added to this process if the sample of potential consumers who have chosen to purchase the brand in the initial laboratory test, or who have been given samples of the brand to consume at home, are then offered a series of 'chances' to purchase the brand at a special price. This process assumes that by forcing the consumer to pay money for any repeat purchases and allowing a number of repurchase occasions (Tauber recommended four to six) the resulting behaviour will exhibit the realism that would normally occur in the market-place. The eventual adoption rate will be measurable and the problem of a drop-out rate will be overcome. This drop-out rate, also known as 'wearout', occurs with convenience products with a novelty value which attract consumer interest initially but after two to three purchases of the new brand, consumers revert to original brand purchases having 'dropped out' from purchasing the new brand.[74] If this process is known to occur for a particular product type, then the number of repurchase occasions in the test can be set at a higher level. This is obviously very important in practice. If a significant number of 'novelty' purchases occur then initial estimates of steady-state demand may be a considerable overestimation.

This form of test has a high cost and time factor involved. Depending on the type of brand and the length of the typical repurchase period, the test may take up to six months to complete. During this time, respondents will tire and some will drop out, move house, change employment, etc., which, although arguably adding more realism, will affect the measurement of take-up rate and adoption levels. The threats to validity, as discussed above, are likely to be a significant problem in this form of extended test, particularly the history, maturation and interaction effects. Arguably the testing effect will be of short duration and, although affecting behaviour at the beginning of the test, by later stages respondents will have become used to taking part in the test and their behaviour may be more realistic as a result. This can be taken into account in the measurement by, for example, weighting more heavily the implications of the observed behaviour later in the test. The strength of this extended test is, as noted above, that it allows a more realistic measurement of steady-state purchase behaviour to take place and the eventual adoption rate for the brand to be more accurately predicted. This is the important variable to measure at the product test stage if the producer is concerned with marketing a new brand with a considerable life span rather than having only a short-lived novelty effect. It provides a more accurate answer to the question 'Will the brand become an eventual success, in terms defined by the producer, if launched into the market?'

Bearing in mind the above discussion, which will be returned to later in the chapter, there now follows a review of two models of this product-testing process which have been developed to provide pre-test-market estimates of steady-state demand.

7.3.3 The ASSESSOR model

This model was developed by Silk and Urban to provide a pre-test-market evaluation of new packaged goods as, besides the high costs of test marketing, there is a 'distressingly high probability that such an undertaking will lead to the detection of a new product failure rather than a success.'[84]

The structure of the ASSESSOR system is shown in Figure 7.1.

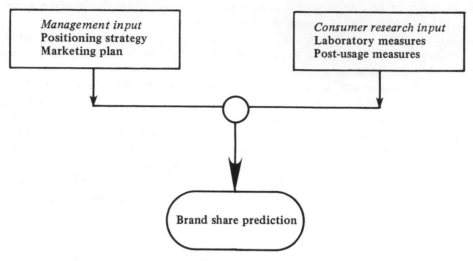

Source: Adapted from Silk and Urban[84]

Fig. 7.1 Structure of the ASSESSOR system

This system is intended to:

1. Predict the new brand's equilibrium or long-run market share.
2. Estimate the sources of the new brand's share — from the firm's other brands or from competitors' brands.
3. Produce actionable diagnostic information for product improvement and the development of advertising copy and other creative materials.
4. Permit low-cost screening of selected elements of alternative marketing plans (advertising copy, price, package design).

The model is based on laboratory simulation. To simulate the awareness-trial stages a sample of consumers are exposed to advertising for the new brand and a small set of the principal competing products already established in the market. The consumers then enter a simulated shopping facility where they have the opportunity to purchase quantities of the new and/or established products. The ability of the new product to attract repeat purchases is assessed by one or more waves of follow-up interviews with the same respondents, conducted after enough time has passed for them to have used or consumed a significant quantity of the new product at home.

This process has been used on samples of about 300 customers selected by personal interview. Advertising materials for five to six established brands plus the new brand have typically been used. For the store stage, respondents are given \$2 as compensation for their time, more than enough to make a purchase, with change. Prices are set at average supermarket levels. Those who do not purchase the new brand are given a quantity of it free after all buying transactions have been completed — this is thought to be equivalent to giving free samples for new brands.

Follow-up telephone interviews are conducted after the average repurchase period and respondents are offered the opportunity to make a repurchase of the new brand, delivered by mail, and asked to rate the new brand and re-rate the established brands. In a study for a deodorant brand, 16.7 per cent of the original sample could not be re-interviewed and a further 16.7 per cent had not used the brand. Measurements were only taken for those established brands which respondents were familiar with, typically three brands.[85]

Brand preference is assessed using a constant sum paired comparison procedure. Such methods have been developed by Axlerod[86] and Haley[87] and by Torgerson.[88] The latter procedure is used by Silk and Urban. Assuming that respondents can provide ratio judgements of paired comparisons between brands, a least squares method for estimating ratio scale values is used.

The assessor model builds on work done on pricing research using laboratory-based simulation procedures by Pessemier[89] also discussed in detail by Palda[90] and early work by Urban in producing the SPRINTER model.[91]

The methodology employed needs to be considered in the light of the discussions earlier in the chapter. The history, maturation and testing effects are all likely to affect the respondents in this form of test. The degree of realism achieved is also debatable. The method of allowing respondents to choose between keeping the small cash reward and buying a brand (test or established competitor) plus change, as used by Pessemier and Silk and Urban seems as close as is possible to realism. The idea of giving those respondents choosing a competitive brand free samples of the test brand is less realistic and seems more concerned with keeping down the cost of the exercise by reducing the sample size. The use of simulation methodologies is likely to be questionable as discussed earlier through lack of realism. Nevertheless, the awareness rate, trial rate and repurchase rate are estimated for the new brand in a competitive environment.

As already noted at length, product testing involving competitors' brands can lead to problems of lack of realism. It is unrealistic to expose respondents to competitive advertising claims in isolation as in the ASSESSOR model. Also the test brand is at a disadvantage because of previous knowledge of established competitive brands by respondents. This can be overcome to some extent by before-and-after measurements. Midgley's criticisms of the lack of explicit consideration of interpersonal communications would also apply to this model. Selecting respondents at random and subjecting them to the simulation tests and follow-up telephone tests is isolating respondents from the day-to-day social interaction with friends and neighbours concerning the proposed new brand which would occur when new brands are available in the market-place. This means that some of the objectives of the ASSESSOR model, especially (3) and (4) may be difficult to achieve. As Midgley noted, there may well be a tendency to overstate the impact of marketing variable changes at the expense of the inter-personal communication variable not specified within the model.

7.3.4 The mini test-market model

The final model to be considered is really a cross between product testing using laboratory simulations and test marketing methods. The model developed by Research Bureau Ltd., a Unilever subsidiary, is described by Charlton, Ehrenberg and Pymont[92] and is discussed further by Charlton and Pymont.[93] The mini-test market 'allows brands of frequently-bought household goods to be tested in repeat-buying terms under fairly natural purchasing conditions, but on a much smaller scale and in a more controlled manner than is possible with normal test marketing procedures.'[94] The aim of the mini-test market is 'to expose a new product to test market evaluation, which means whether or not in a competitive environment consumers will pay real money for it, at a cost comparable with that of product testing.'[95]

As with the ASSESSOR model, there is a determined effort to evaluate repeat purchase rate as a primary determinate of success of new brands. The system of measurement used is a consumer panel of households. Test brands, together with the range of competition they will encounter in the market-place and other consumer items to establish credibility, are exposed to panel housewives using a door-to-door retail operation. Weekly calls are made and all the products for sale are displayed in a colour catalogue with advertising copy. Consumers fill out an order form and items are delivered immediately from stock. Although this is an abnormal buying situation, Charlton *et al.* claimed a high degree of predictive accuracy which is supported using a number of case histories involving 21 brands in four product fields:

> The main conclusion is therefore that buying behaviour under stable conditions in the test situation tends to be realistic. Aggregate macro-measures such as brand shares and sales could conceivably differ from real life because of the selection of brands stocked, the different 'marketing' effort put behind them, and the fact that one is analysing purchases from only a single outlet – the Mini-Test van itself.[96]

The sales forecasts for new brands are derived after mini-testing for 16, 20 or 24 weeks. The method used to deal with repeat purchases is the NBD model derived by Ehrenberg.[67] This model measures sales as a product of penetration, the percentage of households who buy a given brand at least once in a given time period, and the average buying frequency, the average number of times those buyers buy that brand in the same time period.

As Silk and Urban pointed out:

> the home delivery arrangement does not permit the television commercial and product display exposure that can be effected in a laboratory facility and hence trial usage can be expected to accumulate more rapidly under the latter approach. However, if extensive usage experience is required for consumers to learn about the new product or if its frequency of purchase differs from that of established brands, then one or two waves of post-usage interviews conducted soon after the laboratory session will not provide a reliable basis for estimating its repeat buying rate, and the home delivery panel becomes a preferred and necessary alternative.[97]

The validation results reported appear to overcome the argument of lack of realism and the testing, history and maturation effect. Midgley's criticism again applies: there is no specific allowance made for the effects of interpersonal communications. As implied earlier, the repeat purchase rate can be seen as a summary statistic which is determined in part by the effects of interpersonal communications in practice, the overall results obtained by the mini-test market model may therefore be accurate but any sensitivity analysis of the overall results from variation of input marketing variables may prove inaccurate.

7.4 COMMERCIALIZATION

7.4.1 The need for co-ordination

Whether a test market or a simulated test market is used, the final stage of the development process is commercialization. The launch of the new brand is planned, co-ordinated and controlled and all the elements of the marketing plan must then be operationalized in a synchronized process covering such elements as:

— Production of sufficient quantities of the brand.
— Selling-in to distributors.
— Advertising campaign and associated promotion and publicity.
— Product quality control.
— Packaging.
— Brand name.
— Product size, shape, colour and other variant determination.
— Plans for after-sales service.
— Salesman and distributor training.
— Sales aids and other literature.

The development and launch of Rowntree's Yorkie was described in Chapter 3. As a continuation of the competitive process in this market it is interesting to examine the development of the Cadbury brand Wispa in this highly competitive market.

7.4.2 Cadbury's Wispa

This brand was conceived from a combination of the urgent need of Cadbury to develop a high-selling new brand to reverse its falling market share (badly hit by Rowntree's Yorkie for example, see Chapter 3), of intensive market research and of research and development efforts to develop textured chocolate, in particular aerated chocolate. It is debatable whether Wispa was seen as an attempt to strike back at Rowntree for hitting a traditional Cadbury market (CDM) with Yorkie, but this was certainly the closest existing competitor.

A pilot production plant at Bournville started producing a particular blend of textured chocolate aimed at being 'creamy and melting' rather than 'dry and crumbly'.[98] Cadbury had the name 'Wisp' registered and simply added an 'a'. Much research went into packaging. Lower-case letters were used to spell out the brand name because 'they are more relaxed; they say pick me up and eat me'.[99] The colours were chosen to convey quality: royal blue, gold and red.

The brand was initially launched into the Tyne—Tees TV region in autumn 1981 with a £56800 advertising campaign over the initial launch period.[100] Reaction was very favourable but the brand was withdrawn. This was most probably because of production difficulties, although Cadbury now claims that it was a cunning marketing ploy to confuse the opposition (presumably Rowntree).[101] This is ludicrous. Rowntree would be carefully monitoring the test market performance of Wispa and would know almost as much about the brand as did Cadbury. This is shown by Rowntree's reaction. Within a year Rowntree had installed a new production line at its York factory and produced a new 'chunky shaped' Aero bar launched nationally in 1982. In 1983, 250 million of the new-shaped Aero bars were sold with sales not being taken from the existing Aero bars. The reason for this is probably that the new shape Aeros, like Wispas, were sold as countlines, like Mars bars and other filled bars rather than as block chocolate such as CDM and Yorkie. Point-of-sale display of the two Aero brands would be separate therefore, in different parts of the stacker units.

A larger scale production plant costing £12 million was ready for operation in 1983 and Wispa was re-launched in Tyne—Tees in October 1983. Again it was highly successful and was launched nationally via a roll-out, region-by-region, basis until national coverage was achieved by late 1984. Advertising support for Wispa has been estimated at £6 million.[102] Sales for 1985 are forecast by Cadbury at £80 million which would put the brand into fourth place in the brand league table.[103]

This would be an amazing achievement. Rowntree claims that sales of Wispa in the Tyne—Tees region dropped by two-thirds one year after the launch. It also claims that sales of Wispa have hit the Cadbury brands of Flake, Double Decker and Star Bars at least as much as they have hit Aero sales.

Overall it is clear that at least in the short term this brand is a success.

7.5 SUMMARY

This chapter has examined the main feature of the economics of new brand development — that of estimating the chances of success of the new brand in the market-place. A number of problems and pitfalls have been highlighted which perhaps explain the high failure rates normally associated with this necessary but complex process.

One of the problem areas is distribution, caused in particular by the growing power of retailers in the distributive process for consumer goods. It is to this area of marketing that the discussion now turns.

REFERENCES

1. Burns, T. and G. M. Stalker, (1962) *The Management of Innovation*, Tavistock, London.
2. Booz, Allen and Hamilton (1982) *New Product Developments for the 1980's*, Booz, Allen and Hamilton, New York.
3. Nielsen, A. C. (1979) *The Nielsen Researcher*, A. C. Nielsen, Oxford, pp. 2–9.
4. Midgley, D. F. (1977) *Innovation and New Product Marketing*, Croom Helm, London, p. 174.
5. Parfitt, J. M. and B. J. K. Collins (1968) 'The use of consumer panels for brand share prediction', *Journal of Marketing Research*, **5**, May, 131–45.
6. King, S. H. M. (1973) 'Identifying market opportunities', in *Creating and Marketing New Products*, G. Wills, R. Hayhirst, and D. Midgley (eds), Crosby Lockwood Staples, London, pp. 65–96.
7. Goldsmith, R. (1981) 'Methodological approaches to new product development', *Proceedings of the Annual Conference of the Market Research Society*, Market Research Society, London, pp. 53–68.
8. Bessis, P. (1973) 'Market research, marketing decisions and creativity,' in *Creating and Marketing New Products*, G. Willis, R. Hayhirst and D. Midgley (eds), Crosby Lockwood Staples, London, pp. 99–106.
9. O'Meara, J. T. (1961) 'Selecting profitable products', *Harvard Business Review*, **39**, January–February, 83–9.
10. Pessemier, E. A. (1966) *New Product Decisions: An Analytical Approach*, McGraw-Hill, New York.
11. Booz, Allen and Hamilton Inc. (1968) *The Management of New Products*, Booz, Allen and Hamilton, New York.
12. Galbraith, J. K. (1967) *The New Industrial State*, Penguin, London.
13. Sampson, P. (1970) 'Can consumers create new products?', *Journal of the Market Research Society*, **12**, 1, 40–52.
14. Gordon, W. J. J. (1961) *Synectics: The development of creative capacity*, Harper and Row, New York.
15. Tauber, E. M. (1972) 'HIT: Heuristic ideation technique', *Journal of Marketing*, **36**, 1, 59–61.
16. Clemens, J. and C. Thornton (1968) 'Evaluating non-existing products', *Admap*, May.
17. Fenwick, I. (1978) 'A user's guide to conjoint measurement in marketing', *European Journal of Marketing*, **12**, 2, 203–11.
18. Green, P. E. and D. S. Tull (1978) *Research for Marketing Decisions*, 4th edn, Prentice-Hall, Englewood Cliffs, New Jersey.
19. Green, P. E., F. J. Carmone and P. J. Robinson (1968) *Analysis of Marketing Behaviour Using Nonmetric scaling and Related Techniques*, Marketing Sciences Institute, Cambridge, Mass.
20. Kruskal, J. B. (1964) 'Non-metric multi-dimensional scaling: a numerical method', *Psychometrika*, **29**, 115–29.
21. Hendrickson, A. E. (1967) 'Choice behaviour and advertising: a theory and two models', *Proceedings of ADMAP World Advertising Workshop*, Southampton. ADMAP.
22. Doyle, P. (1973) 'Non-metric multi-dimensional scaling: a users guide', *European Journal of Marketing*, 7, 2, 82–8.
23. Shocker, A. D. and V. Srinivasan (1974) 'A Consumer based methodology for the identification of new product ideas', *Management Science*, **20**, 921–37.
24. Westwood, D., A. J. Lunn and D. Beazley (1974) 'The trade-off model and its extensions' *Journal of the Market Research Society*, **16**, 3, 227–41.
25. Greenhalgh, C. (1972) 'Research for New Product Decisions', in *Consumer Market Research Handbook*, R. Worcester (ed.), McGraw-Hill, Maidenhead.
26. Batsell, R. R. and Y. Wind (1980) 'Product testing: current methods and needed developments', *Journal of the Market Research Society*, **22**, 2, 115–37.
27. Essex, P. G. and R. Knox (1980) 'Researching marketing needs and action approaches for new products – "To Russchian with love" ', *Proceedings of the Market Research Society Annual Conference, 1980*, Market Research Society, London.
28. Green, P. E. and V. Srinivasan (1978) 'Conjoint analysis in consumer research: issues and outlook' *Journal of Consumer Research*, **5**, September, 103–23.
29. Penny, J. C., I. M. Hunt and W. A. Twyman (1972) 'Product testing methodology in relation to marketing problems – a review,' *Journal of the Market Research Society*, **14**, 1, 1–29.
30. Bengstron, R. and H. Brenner (1964) 'Product test results using three different methodologies', *Journal of Marketing Research*, **1**, November, 49–52.
31. Penny, Hunt and Twyman, op. cit., p. 20.
32. Blankenship, A. B. (1966) 'Let's bury paired comparisons', *Journal of Advertising Research*, **6**, 1, 13–17.
33. Haller, T. (1966) 'Let's not bury paired comparisons', *Journal of Advertising Research*, **6**, 3, 29–30.
34. Brown, G., T. Copeland and M. Millward (1973) 'Monadic testing of new products – an old problem and some partial solutions', *Journal of the Market Research Society*, **15**, 2, 112–31.

35. Ibid., p. 130.
36. Batsell and Wind, op. cit., p. 124.
37. Greenhalgh, C. (1976) 'Discrimination tests and repeated paired comparison tests', *Journal of the Market Research Society*, **18**, 4, 214–15.
38. Belk, R. W. (1975) 'Situational variables and consumer behaviour', *Journal of Consumer Research*, **2**, 3, 157–64.
39. Foxall, G. R. (1983) *Consumer Choice*, Macmillan, London.
40. Kassarjan, H. and M. Nakanishi (1967) 'A study of selected opinion measurement techniques', *Journal of Marketing Research*, **4**, 2, 148–53.
41. Haley, R. I. and P. B. Case (1979) 'Testing thirteen attitude scales for agreement and brand discrimination', *Journal of Marketing*, **43**, 4, 20–32.
42. Holmes, C. (1974) 'A statistical evaluation of rating scales', *Journal of the Market Research Society*, **16**, 2, 87–107.
43. Penny, Hunt and Twyman, op. cit., p. 21.
44. Midgley, op. cit., p. 228.
45. Ibid., p. 56.
46. Ibid., p. 230.
47. Ostlund, L. E. (1974) 'Perceived innovation attributes as predictors of innovativeness', *Journal of Consumer Research*, **1**, September, 23–29.
48. Batsell and Wind, op. cit., p. 131.
49. Ibid., p. 121.
50. Allison, R. I. and K. P. Uhl (1964) 'Influence of beer brand identification on taste perception', *Journal of Marketing Research*, **1**, 3, 36–9.
51. Beckwith, N. E. and D. R. Lehmann (1975) 'The importance of halo effects in multiattribute models', *Journal of Marketing Research*, **12**, November, 265–75.
52. Beckwith, N. E. and U. V. Kubilius (1978) 'Empirical evidence of halo effects in store image research by Estimating True Locations, Working Paper University of Pennsylvania, Philadelphia, PA.
53. Batsell and Wind, op. cit., p. 121.
54. Green, P. E. and Y. Wind (1975) 'New way to measure consumers' judgements', *Harvard Business Review*, **53**, 4, 107–15.
55. Brown *et al.*, op. cit., p. 119.
56. Greenhalgh, C. (1970) 'Discrimination testing: further results and developments', *ESOMAR Conference*, Esomar, Amsterdam, 181–90.
57. Gruber, A. and B. Lindberg (1966) 'Sensitivity, reliability and consumer taste testing', *Journal of Marketing Research*, **3**, 3, 235–8.
58. Greenberg, A. and S. Collins (1966) 'Paired comparison taste tests: some food for thought', *Journal of Marketing Research*, **3**, 1, 76–80.
59. Roper, P. (1969) 'Sensitivity, reliability and consumer taste testing: some "rights" and "wrongs"', *Journal of Marketing Research*, **6**, 1, 102–6.
60. Gabor, A. and C. Granger (1965) 'The pricing of new products', *Scientific Business*, **3**, August, pp. 3–12.
61. Gabor, A. (1977) *Pricing, Principles and Practices*, Heinemann, London.
62. Belkin, M. and S. Lieberman (1967) 'Effect of question wording on response distribution', *Journal of Marketing Research*, **4**, 3, 312–13.
63. Brown *et al.*, op. cit., p. 121.
64. Ibid., p. 130.
65. Clancy, K. and R. Garsen (1970) 'Why some scales predict better', *Journal of Advertising Research*, **10**, 5, 33–8.
66. Bass, F. M. (1969) 'A new product growth model for consumer durables', *Management Science*, **15**, pp. 215–27.
67. Ehrenberg, A. S. C. (1972) *Repeat Purchasing*, North-Holland, Amsterdam.
68. Kotler, P. (1984) *Marketing Management*, 5th edn, Holt Rinehart and Winston, New York.
69. Midgley, op. cit., Chapter 3.
70. Mahajan, V. and E. Muller (1979) 'Innovation diffusion and new product growth models in marketing', *Journal of Marketing*, **43**, 4, 55–68.
71. Tauber, E. M., (1975) 'Why concept and product tests fail to predict new product results', *Journal of Marketing*, **39**, 4, 69–71.
72. Ibid., p. 70.
73. Ibid., p. 71.
74. Tauber, E. M. (1977) 'Forecasting sales prior to test market', *Journal of Marketing*, **41**, 1, 80–4.
75. Taylor, J. W., J. J. Houlahan and A. C. Gabriel (1975) 'The purchase intention question in new product development: a field test', *Journal of Marketing*, **39**, 2, 90–92.

76. Crawford, C. M. (1977) 'Marketing research and the new product failure rate', *Journal of Marketing*, **41**, 2 April, 51–6.
77. Ibid., p. 55.
78. Parfitt and Collins (1968) op. cit.
79. Bell, W. E. (1963) 'Consumer innovators: a unique market for newness', in *Proceedings of the American Marketing Association*, A.M.A., Chicago.
80. Morrison, D. G. (1966) 'Interpurchase time and brand loyalty', *Journal of Marketing Research*, **3**, November, 289–91.
81. Rothlisberger, F. J. and W. J. Dickson (1939) *Management and the Worker*, Harvard University Press, Cambridge, Mass.
82. Campbell, D. T. and J. C. Stanley (1966) *Experimental and Quasi-Experimental Designs for Research*, Rand McNally, Chicago.
83. Moser, C. A. and G. Kalton (1971) *Survey Methods in Social Investigation*, Heinemann, London, pp. 214–24.
84. Silk, A. J. and G. L. Urban (1978) 'Pre-test market evaluation of new packaged goods: a model and measurement methodology', *Journal of Marketing Research*, **15**, 2, 171–91.
85. Urban, G. L. (1975) 'PERCEPTOR: a model for product positioning', *Management Science*, **21**, 858–71.
86. Axelrod, J. N. (1968) 'Attitude measures that predict purchase', *Journal of Advertising Research*, **8**, 1, 3–18.
87. Haley, R. I. (1970) 'We shot an arrow in the air', *Proceedings of the Annual Conference of the Advertising Research Foundation*, New York, 25–30.
88. Torgerson, W. S. (1958) *Theory and Method of Scaling*, Wiley, New York.
89. Pessemier, E. A. (1975) 'Market structure analysis of new product and market opportunities', *Journal of Contemporary Business*, **4**, 2, 35–65.
90. Palda, K. S. (1969) *Economic Analysis for Marketing Decisions*, Prentice-Hall, Englewood Cliffs, New Jersey.
91. Urban, G. L. (1970) 'SPRINTER Mod III: a model for the analysis of new frequently purchased consumer products', *Operations Research*, **18**, 805–55.
92. Charlton, P., A. S. C. Ehrenberg and B. Pymont (1972) 'Buyer behaviour under mini-test conditions', *Journal of the Market Research Society*, **14**, 3, 171–84.
93. Charlton, P. and B. Pymont (1975) 'Evaluating marketing alternatives', *Journal of the Market Research Society*, **17**, 2, 90–103.
94. Charlton *et al.* (1972) op. cit., p. 171.
95. Charlton and Pymont (1975) op. cit., p. 92.
96. Charlton *et al.* (1972) op. cit., p. 182.
97. Silk and Urban, op. cit., p. 177.
98. Huxley, J. (1985) 'Bars wars', *Sunday Times*, 6 January, quoting C. Lodge.
99. Ibid.
100. MEAL (1981) Quarterly Digest of Advertising Expenditure, Media Expenditure Analysis Ltd., London.
101. Huxley, J., op. cit., quoting N. Hawkins.
102. Ibid.
103. Ibid.

EIGHT

DISTRIBUTION OF BRANDS

8.1 THE EVOLUTION OF DISTRIBUTION

It is clearly of little value to a manufacturer to produce a well publicized, researched brand of a desirable quality at an acceptable price without making it available to potential consumers. The economics of production increasingly require highly centralized, specialized large-scale production processes to minimize unit costs. A distribution system is required which enables the brand to be made available conveniently for would-be buyers.

The history of distribution in the UK is a story of shifting power structures. In the late nineteenth century, the wholesalers dominated the distributive trades. Manufacturers would be expected to produce wholesaler-patented designs to order and the wholesalers dictated terms to retailers who wished to stock these 'brands'. However, from the turn of the century until the 1960s the power of the manufacturers grew as the size of their operations increased. This was primarily due to innovations in productive processes. Gradually the quest for economies of scale in production became dominant in seeking competitive advantage. Consequently manufacturers needed larger markets than single wholesalers could offer and manufacturer-designed 'brands' were offered more widely.

Inevitably this process went too far and by the early 1960s many markets were characterized by the overcapacity in supply, and the emphasis switched towards a marketing rather than a production orientation to reflect the nature of this business problem. The growth of supermarkets which began in the UK in the late 1950s was limited by retail price maintenance which enabled manufacturers to determine the retail price of their brands. With the Resale Prices Act of 1964 the growth of supermarkets became dramatic because they were able to make full use of buying power to reduce their cost price of stock which they could then pass on to customers in the form of lower prices, which led to an increase in sales throughput which further increased buying power. Multiples have increased their share of the grocery trade (and indeed of most other retail trades). Among other implications this has enabled retailers to make increasing demands on their suppliers and to dictate terms to them.

This evolutionary process has also had implications for the performance of the distributive functions. These functions have to be performed but whether they are performed by specialists, by manufacturers integrating towards the market, or by retailers integrating towards the source of supply, has varied over time and between product types. These functions will now be briefly considered.

8.2 DISTRIBUTIVE FUNCTIONS

The number of types of distributors involved in a particular system will depend on various factors including, importantly, the type of product. It is possible, and is for many industrial goods and services probable, that the manufacturer will supply direct to the final user. It is also feasible that various types of intermediary, notably wholesalers and retailers but increasingly, with the internationalization of business, import and export agents, can be involved. The performance of the various distributive functions will be carried out by any one or more of the parties involved in the system and will vary over time and between product types, making generalization difficult.

Transport This function can be provided by the manufacturer, by an intermediary, by a specialist or by a combination of these. It is common, especially for perishable goods, for the manufacturer to transport goods in bulk from the production plant to a central or regional storage depot (owned either by the manufacturer, retailer or specialist firm). This depot is commonly used as a bulk-breaking centre and smaller transport units are used from this point to retail outlets. In some product markets it is usual for specialist transport firms to be involved, for example in the distribution of cars and the movement of coal by railway.

Breaking bulk and storage This is a traditional wholesale function but increasingly has been taken over by retailers, especially multiples who are able to take over this function easily as part of their bulk-buying programme. With the increasing power of retailers in many product markets it is feasible for retailers to insist that manufacturers store their brands until the retailers need them. This avoids the cost of holding large stocks in retailer-owned depots.

This whole process can be made very efficient by using microtechnology in the reordering process. For example Sainsbury's used a system in which each store, at the end of each day's trading, electronically reordered the amount of stock necessary to replenish shelf stocks after the day's sales. These data were collected automatically by a computer-controlled telephone link and processed in the same evening with an order sent to the relevant regional depot. This order was loaded overnight on to a delivery van which was then despatched in the early morning to the store. Thus, by the opening time of the next day's trading, the shelves would be fully stocked again. Importantly this saves the cost of storage space in the expensive town-centre-sited retail stores.

With the growth of point-of-sale systems which have stock control capabilities under computer control, the use of efficient reordering systems is likely to develop rapidly. Electronic links with suppliers could be used for immediate ordering which is likely to reduce the need for large stock-carrying within the distribution system.

Credit Besides the physical movement of brands, their legal ownership changes and payment has to be made. These events do not necessarily coincide in time. It is usual in some product markets for credit facilities to be provided by specialist financial services firms, either directly or indirectly, to finance overdraft facilities for manufacturers or intermediaries.

Local knowledge Another traditional wholesaling function was to keep suppliers informed of changes in local conditions and demand factors. This function has largely been taken over either by retailers or by specialist market research firms.

Many changes have occurred in shopping habits over the past few decades which have reflected such factors as:

— The increase in the number of women in full-time paid employment.
— The increase in ownership of freezers.
— Increasing concern with health and diet.
— The trend towards husband-and-wife shopping expeditions (leading to the growth in 'one-stop' shopping and longer opening hours).
— The increase in car ownership (leading to a growth of out-of-town locations for retail outlets with easy parking facilities).
— The decline in the importance of the nuclear family associated with an increase in the divorce rate.

All these and other associated trends need to be monitored on a local, national and international level. This service is most efficiently provided by specialist market research services. Table 8.1 (pages 128–9) gives an example of the type of basic information on retailing which can be obtained from government publications.

Display The layout of brands in an enticing display for potential consumers (either intermediate or final) has become a complex issue. Window displays, once the traditional preferred alternative for goods are no longer an option in many product markets. The psychology of store layout in the increasingly popular self-service style dictates that window space is minimized (or covered with advertising copy). This is because it has been found that by reducing daylight, by having a warm comfortable environment and by playing background music, impulse buying is induced. Indeed hidden cameras have been used to show that the eye blink rate of housewives while shopping is half the normal rate, on average, equivalent to the first stage of hypnosis. Interestingly, at the check-out, the eye blink rate increases to twice normal as shoppers anxiously realize that they have to pay for all their impulse selections! This example may not be scientific proof but is illustrative of the thinking at the retail level when planning layout.

So-called 'generators' are strategically sited in the layout plan to entice shoppers to visit all parts of the store. Generators are commonly purchased goods, often at loss leader prices, which are sited alongside high profit margin items in an attempt to attract consumers' interest. In a self-service display, an eye-level siting for a brand is considered the prime spot so that convenience to the shopper is maximized, avoiding the stretching or bending which a high or low siting could involve. The amount of display is also important in attracting shoppers' attention. These issues are treated by Buttle.[1]

As already noted, in self-service situations the manufacturers' main influence is usually through the packaging of the brand, which in this context takes on a predominantly display function rather than a protection-in-transit function. The brand must use packaging (colour, size, lettering, etc.) to attract consumer interest in the competitive context of the self-service store. The manufacturer cannot rely on personal selling at the retail level in many markets although with consumer durables and many industrial goods the personal selling approach is still very important.

Of course the retailer will make profit whichever brand the consumer chooses. The objective of the retailer is to make profits for himself rather than for particular manufacturers and this can cause a conflict of interest. A profitability measure in common use is the level of sales per square foot of space which is achieved. Table 8.2 (page 130) shows that the multiples have been particularly successful on this measure in the last few years.

The task of the manufacturer's sales force (or specialist merchandising force) is not only to ensure the retailer stocks the brand but also provides the best possible display space within the store. The display space allocated has been found to have an important bearing on sales results achieved.

Advertising Local advertising by intermediaries is primarily in local press although the growth of multiples has led to image-building national TV campaigns becoming more popular. Local advertising is often price-based and brand specific. This is an opportunity for manufacturers to generate intermediary loyalty through co-operative advertising. A standard advertisement for local press can be produced which leaves space for a local dealer to add his name and address. National press, and occasionally TV, campaigns by manufacturers often feature lists of stockists of the brand, again to build the relationship with the intermediary.

The increase in branding enables the retailer to 'ride on the back' of established brands by advertising low prices for brands of established and accepted quality. The dangers to manufacturers are that this may reduce the brand's credibility in the longer term and that the retailer may attempt to force extra discounts from manufacturers to finance the offer.

Table 8.1 The retail trades in Great Britain

(a) Analysis by form of organization and broad kind of business in 1980

Kind of business and form of organization*	Businesses	Outlets	Total turnover[1]
	Number	Number	£m
TOTAL RETAIL TRADE	**228 077**	**348 601**	**58 484**
Single outlet retailers	197 884	197 884	18 118
Small multiple retailers	28 932	76 920	8 451
Large multiple retailers**	1 261	73 797	31 915
Of which co-operative societies accounted for	191	8 556	3 869
Food retailers[†]	**81 846**	**118 083**	**22 586**
Single outlet retailers	72 640	72 640	5 414
Small multiple retailers	8 776	23 418	2 358
Large multiple retailers	430	22 026	14 814
Drink, confectionery and tobacco retailers	**39 408**	**54 878**	**5 973**
Single outlet retailers	36 790	36 790	3 018
Small multiple retailers	2 494	6 370	772
Large multiple retailers	124	11 717	2 183
Clothing, footwear and leather goods retailers	**29 884**	**57 069**	**5 281**
Single outlet retailers	23 902	23 902	1 429
Small multiple retailers	5 712	16 076	1 104
Large multiple retailers	270	17 091	2 748
Household goods retailers	**38 864**	**58 267**	**7 987**
Single outlet retailers	32 648	32 648	3 012
Small multiple retailers	6 002	15 418	1 849
Large multiple retailers	215	10 201	3 125
Other non-food retailers	**32 228**	**44 745**	**4 640**
Single outlet retailers	27 230	27 230	2 437
Small multiple retailers	4 849	12 721	1 333
Large multiple retailers	148	4 793	870
Mixed retail businesses[†]	**3 346**	**9 250**	**11 083**
Single outlet retailers	2 520	2 520	2 673
Small multiple retailers	780	2 182	977
Large multiple retailers	46	4 819	7 433
Hire and repair businesses	**2 502**	**6 038**	**936**
Single outlet retailers	2 155	2 155	135
Small multiple retailers	319	734	58
Large multiple retailers	28	3 149	743

[1] Inclusive of VAT

* Form of organization: Small multiples have 2–9 outlets, larger ones 10 or more.

** Larger retail businesses: 'Large' denotes businesses with retail turnover of £8m or more in 1980 at current prices.

[†] Mixed retail business: A business is 'mixed' if less than 80 per cent of its turnover falls inside any one of the specialized broad kinds of business.

Food retailers: In the case of food sales only, this '80 per cent rule' has been replaced by a '50 per cent rule'.

Where food, drink and tobacco together form 50 per cent or more of total sales, with grocery sales predominating, a business will be classified as a grocery retailer.

Source: Business Statistics Office, Business Monitor SDA25, Retailing (1980) edition, published by HMSO).

(b) Analysis by detailed kind of business in 1980

Kind of business and form of organization*	Businesses	Outlets	Total turnover[1]
	Number	Number	£m
TOTAL RETAIL TRADE	228 077	348 601	58 484
Food retailers	81 877	118 083	22 586
Large grocery retailers	116	12 218	13 206
Other grocery retailers	38 814	44 342	3 995
Dairymen	6 362	8 210	1 458
Butchers	15 095	21 332	2 165
Fishmongers, poulterers	2 252	2 721	170
Greengrocers, fruiterers	12 344	15 595	808
Bread and flour confectioners	6 863	13 675	783
Drink, confectionery and tobacco retailers	39 408	54 878	5 973
Retailers of confectionery, tobacco and newsagents	36 508	46 094	4 545
Off-licences	2 900	8 784	1 427
Clothing, footwear and leather goods retailers	29 884	57 069	5 281
Men's and boys' wear retailers	4 226	10 451	1 157
Women's, girls', children's and infants' wear retailers	16 336	25 679	1 863
General clothing businesses	4 831	7 541	940
Footwear retailers	3 512	11 834	1 241
Leather and travel goods retailers	978	1 564	80
Household goods retailers	38 864	58 267	7 987
Household textiles retailers	3 250	4 639	362
Carpet retailers	2 892	4 345	684
Furniture retailers	10 002	13 190	2 200
Electrical and music goods retailers	7 199	13 117	2 388
Hardware, china and fancy goods retailers	10 618	15 025	1 332
Do-it-yourself retailers	4 903	7 950	1 021
Other non-food retailers	32 228	44 745	4 640
Chemists	7 723	11 004	1 526
Booksellers, stationers and newsagents	4 348	5 963	704
Photographic goods retailers	587	1 244	297
Cycle and perambulator retailers	1 380	1 672	111
Jewellers	4 489	7 337	814
Toys, hobby and sports goods retailers	6 094	7 770	631
Florists, nursery and seedsmen	3 862	5 024	323
Non-food retailers (not elsewhere specified)	3 744	4 732	234
Mixed retail businesses	3 346	9 520	11 083
Large mixed businesses	49	4 527	8 069
Other mixed businesses	3 258	4 903	680
General mail order houses	38	91	2 335
Hire and repair businesses	2 502	6 038	936
Television hire businesses	1 304	4 183	840
Other hire or repair	1 198	1 855	96

Table 8.2 Sales per square foot by type of outlet, 1974 and 1981 (UK)

	1974	1981 (sales per sq. ft. in £ per week)
Multiples	2.15	6.20
Co-ops	1.70	3.65
Independents	1.60	3.50
Industry average	1.85	4.85

Source: Trade estimates

Private label branding Although not strictly a distributive function, a nevertheless distinctive feature of recent distribution history is the growth of distributors' own brands (known also as private label brands). These brands, often manufactured to the retailer's specification by independent producers, can be seen as a remarkable parallel to the period of wholesaler domination of distribution in the last century as described earlier in this chapter. Both wholesale (known as symbol wholesalers such as VG, Mace, Spar) and retail brands are common. The incidence of private label varies by product type and by retailer. Recent examples from the UK are shown in Table 8.3.

Table 8.3 The importance of private label in UK retail sales by retailer and by product type

Retailer	% private label of total sales in UK 1983 (by value)
Total market	26.2 (21.8 in 1976)
Sainsbury	54.0
Tesco	32.0
Asda	6.3
Co-op	33.4
Waitrose	45.8
Symbol wholesalers	14.9
Type of good	
Dairy products	34.2
Toiletries	9.5
Bakery products	29.2
Soaps and detergents	10.3
Pet foods	9.9
Beverages	31.6
Household cleaners	19.5

Source: Trade estimates

The differences by retailer are accounted for by differing marketing strategies. Kwiksave, for example, as a matter of policy, sell only manufacturer-branded goods. Sainsbury's promote their high quality range of private label goods. To some extent the differences by product-type reflect the power of manufacturers in these markets and their willingness (as part of their marketing strategies) to supply private label brands.

Because it is very common for retailers not to give any marketing support to private label brands (beyond company-level advertising) apart from packaging and display, these brands are usually cheaper than the manufacturers' brands with which they compete. To some extent the retailers are risking their reputation by supplying private label brands because if the consumer does not like them the image held of the retailer is likely to suffer. It is thus important that the quality level of the private label brands reflects the quality level of the retail company image.

Clearly the growth of the private label brand has added to the power of the retailers in their dealings with manufacturers. To develop this issue further, it is necessary to examine the relationship between the intermediary and the manufacturer.

8.3 THE RELATIONSHIP BETWEEN INTERMEDIARY AND MANUFACTURER

The growth in the power of retailers is illustrated by the data in Table 8.4.

Table 8.4 Concentration of buying points in the UK (1981)

Type of retailer	No. of buying points	% of UK grocery trade controlled
Multiple	49 (Head offices)	61
Co-op	186 (Societies)	14
Symbol independent	40 (Wholesaler groups)	7

Source: Trade estimates

From the manufacturers' viewpoint it is vital that their brands are stocked by each of the major intermediaries, otherwise the brand is not available to all final consumers. For example, if Sainsbury's do not stock a manufacturer's brand then the number of housewives using Sainsbury's for their main weekly shopping trips would not have the opportunity to buy it, unless they also visited other retail outlets which did stock the brand. This then becomes an issue of brand loyalty vs. store loyalty. How does the housewife react if a brand is not in stock in her 'usual' retail store? Does she

— Buy an alternative brand from those in stock?
— Make a separate shopping trip to obtain the brand?
— Switch store loyalty and do all her shopping elsewhere?

The answers to this conundrum aggregated across all consumers will determine the power distribution between intermediaries and manufacturers. If the first alternative is generally chosen, retailers have more power to dictate terms to manufacturers. If the final alternative is common, the retailer is pressured not to be out of stock of the brand for fear of losing sales and profits across a broad range of brands.

By consumer advertising to build up the brand image in consumers' minds, the manufacturer can pressure the retailer to stock particular brands. This issue is perhaps greatest with new brands because manufacturers have to persuade retailers to make shelf space available for the new offering. As retailers do not usually have empty space available this is often achieved only by reducing the shelf space available to existing brands (for the same manufacturer in many cases).

Thus the relationship between the manufacturer and the intermediary is of vital significance both to the selling and to the marketing strategy of the manufacturer. It is thus essential to examine the dimensions of this relationship which can have both formal and informal elements.

Delivery speed As noted above, the retailer can save cost and space by minimizing stock carried. Thus if the manufacturer is responsive to orders received, by shipping the orders quickly, this will create a favourable impression on intermediaries. This is particularly important where the dealer stocks only display models of the brand (e.g., typewriters, microcomputer systems, consumer durables) and orders are taken from these models for delivery when the manufacturer (or his depot) responds to an order received. This is common when there is a wide variety of options which a customer can choose and it would be impractical to stock all types, as with cars for example. With some services, such as insurance policies, the supplier must be consulted before the product is sold as the underwriter needs to agree to the risk which each particular customer represents. In these circumstances, delivery responsiveness is a significant element of the quality of service offered by the manufacturer.

Technical product responsiveness A similar issue to delivery speed for complex brands is the speed with which manufacturers respond to technical queries from customers which cannot be handled by the dealer. With computer software and insurance products, for example, it is common for the manufacturer to offer a 'hot-line' telephone service where consumers or dealers can contact the supplier direct and obtain answers to the product queries. Again this adds to the quality of service offered by the manufacturer. This service can often be informal rather than formal as personal contact can be used to speed response. Informal links can develop over time and if used properly can enhance the reputation of the manufacturer.

Price–discount structure Prices are likely to be negotiated, perhaps from a published rate-card, when large, powerful buyers are concerned and are part of the wider supply contract which formalizes the other elements of the relationship between manufacturer and intermediary in a supply contract. Discounts for quantity may but also may not reflect actual cost savings to the manufacturer from large-scale supply. They may reflect the bargaining power of the large buyer. As an interesting application of buying power, Kwiksave invited suppliers to tender for the supply of three months' stock of each product they stock, making clear their intention only to stock one brand of each product. This puts additional pressure on the suppliers as they are in an all-or-nothing situation. Losing the order would mean a lack of availability of the brand in this outlet for a three-month period. Manufacturers are thus pressured to minimize their offer price.

Manufacturer credibility This element of the relationship is partly corporate-image and partly brand-image determined. The stronger the image of the manufacturer the greater is the pressure on the retailer to stock the brands supplied. Credibility can be fostered both formally and informally by ensuring that the quality of the contacts between the manufacturer and its clients is kept high. For example, speed and accuracy of responses and the quality of dealer support programmes should be maintained.

Documentation Sales aids, technical product manuals and training aids can be used by the manufacturer to build a stronger relationship with dealers. In situations where dealers also stock competing brands rather than being exclusive agents, then sales aids are often valuable guides (if well produced) for the dealer's sales force in understanding the main selling points of the brand in order to demonstrate them to the potential buyer. Technical product manuals can be used to answer common technical queries while training aids may be helpful for new dealer sales team members.

Brochures on brand features which can be displayed at the point of sale for customer information are a valuable way of presenting the brand in its best light from the manufacturer's point of view.

Product training If the brand is complex, as with some electronic equipment and consumer durables and in particular industrial goods, then it may be necessary to provide training courses for sales and/or maintenance of the brand. This can provide a valuable opportunity to ensure that the company and the brand are presented in the best possible way by the dealer's sales force and after-sales service team. The high cost to dealers of releasing staff to attend sales or product training courses may lead to these being offered in the evening and/or on the dealer's own premises.

Value added by dealer For many industrial markets the brand forms only a part of a broader service offered by the dealer which may also include customer staff training, after-sales services, delivery and even custom-designing using the manufacturer's brand as part of a larger system. This is common with computer and communication systems and/or heating systems (for homes, factories or offices) for example.

The ability to add-in extra value at the dealer level may be an important consideration in the relationship with the manufacturer. In particular, fault tracing when more than one manufacturer's equipment is involved can lead to complex interface issues.

Joint sales calls For large customers, the manufacturer may offer a back-up sales support service so that the dealer's representative is accompanied by a manufacturer's product specialist. This can provide extra confidence for the potential customer and, from the manufacturer's point of view, can ensure that the brand is presented in the best possible light.

Thus the relationship between manufacturer and intermediary has a number of dimensions which have both formal and informal elements. The abilities of the dealers will also vary in terms of the range they carry, sales abilities, credibility, location and technical skills.

8.4 DIRECT VS. INDIRECT DISTRIBUTION

In some markets, the manufacturer has the choice, within the marketing strategy, of distributing directly to customers, or using intermediaries, or using a mixed strategy. In this section, this issue is discussed in a particular context to provide specificity. The context chosen is the life insurance business. The insurance company can employ a direct sales force, use direct mail or direct response advertising or can use independent brokers or other agents (e.g., solicitors, building society managers, bank managers) to distribute their life policies. The following discussion explores this choice process. This choice is also available in other markets but in slightly different ways, although the principles remain the same.

There has been an increasing emphasis on the direct marketing of insurance in recent years. This trend can be expected to continue. A 1984 study conducted in the US for LOMA by Arthur Anderson[2] using delphi forecasting techniques foresaw a growing acceptance of direct marketing techniques and expected direct mail to account for 8 per cent of life policy sales by 1990 in the US.

In this section: some of the reasons for this are examined, in particular the growth of direct mail and direct response ('off the page') media advertising. This approach will be contrasted with 'indirect' marketing of insurance through tied or independent agents such as brokers and other professional advisers. Some of the features of direct marketing will be examined, and the section ends with some guidelines concerning the use of direct marketing methods.

Let us begin with a consideration of the advantages and disadvantages of direct marketing in contrast with indirect marketing, but excluding the possibility of a direct sales force.

8.4.1 Advantages of direct marketing

1. By aiming marketing communications directly at the final buyer, the company name and image can be firmly established with prospective customers, helping to 'pre-sell' the services over time.
2. Control of distribution and sales strategy is retained within the company — this should lead to easier co-ordination of marketing effort. There is less dependence on independent intermediaries with their own business objectives, which may conflict with those of the supplier.
3. Once the sale of one of the company's insurance services has been effected, a mailing list of existing customers can be used to interest them in other services.
4. Consumers can be contacted in their homes which increases their convenience of purchase.

5. The company's services are presented to the prospective customer in isolation from competing company advertisements in most cases.
6. Cost saving could be an advantage: the company may save on intermediary commission rates, the cost of salespersons and their support, while incurring extra advertising cost. The sales effectiveness and profit contribution would need to be considered, as would the total distribution strategy. The company may use direct routes only, indirect routes only, or a combination of the two.

8.4.2 Disadvantages of direct marketing

1. The potential customer is reached at a time chosen by the supplier, not by the prospective client. Contact is attained at specific points in time only. If the potential customer instigates a search for information, unless this coincides with direct marketing activity by the supplier, he must visit a retail outlet for information which provides him with convenience of access in this situation.
2. It may be difficult to provide any expert advice as back-up to direct response marketing especially independent specialist advice. It is unlikely that anyone will be to hand to answer any customer queries which arise from the promotional copy. A telephone 'hot-line' service may be of limited value in this regard.
3. The quality of after-sales service may be less with direct response sales than with sales through professional intermediaries.
4. A sophisticated consumer may wish to make an informed choice from a range of alternative brand offerings, which could be achieved, in this example, by visiting the offices of a professional insurance adviser rather than from direct marketing copy.

8.4.3 Features of direct marketing in insurance

The above factors are of necessity generalizations but provide some background to the use of direct marketing in insurance. Moving on to examine the features of direct marketing by mail or media advertising, the following points can be made:

Selectivity Direct marketing offers the opportunity to select carefully the target market for a campaign. This can be done by using computerized lists of existing customers, or by buying in suitable lists, or by careful medium selection and the use of 'split tests' where different copy is used to gauge customer reaction to each. The AA for example, began their direct mail activities by aiming motor insurance sales copy at AA members but then saw the opportunity of offering life policies by direct mail to this customer base. There are a number of ways to develop selectivity. One method is the ACORN classification developed by CACI.[3] ACORN (A Classification of Residential Neighbourhoods) uses 39 types of housing clustered into 12 groups to classify all housing in the UK. By adding further population characteristics to the ACORN classification (e.g., postcodes), valuable insights can be gained into a range of market segments of high value for direct mail approaches.

Timing It is sensible to try to reach prospective clients when they are most likely to need insurance services. Motor insurance quotes could be sent out one to two months before renewal dates (of existing or lapsed customers and of those who responded to previous advertisements but did not buy). It may be feasible to tie the timing in with important 'Life events' of prospects such as 18th (or 21st or 25th) birthday, marriage, childbirth, first home purchase, etc., which are often tied to insurance needs.

Incentives When the AA used a free gift offer of a tyre pressure gauge to 50 per cent of a direct mailshot for motor insurance, with the other 50 per cent not receiving the offer, they found there was a significant improvement in enquiry rate when the gift offer was used. The conversion rate from the enquiries was reported to be about the same in each case. The effect of the offer more than justified the cost.[4]

The use of incentives, with a time limit for response, can focus attention on the marketing message. With life offers, a reduced premium on the first payment can make customer acceptance that much easier and is frequently used in press direct-response appeals.

Personalizing appeals Along with the discussion on selectivity opportunities above, it is feasible to personalize direct mail appeals using computer based word-processing facilities. This can go wrong: one man who was in the habit of adding his recently received honour to his name when signing letters, soon afterwards received a word-processed mailshot addressing him as 'Mr. Mbe'. This can be very offputting. The use of laser printing improves the quality of personalized appeals but the novelty value for recipients from seeing their name in the text may detract from the attention given to the message. The provision of personalized quotes for motor insurance, life cover, etc., is an obvious area for insurance marketing use in particular where client data is already stored and is used as the basis for a direct mailshot.

Conflict Where, as is usual, the user of direct marketing methods also uses indirect marketing methods, there is a great danger of conflict of interest arising. Brokers may be concerned if an insurance company also uses direct response advertising and/or direct mail. This concern can be overcome by involving the brokers in the process, by giving them advance warning, by asking for customer response to be made via brokers, by issuing complementary point-of-sale display material for use in brokers' offices and by giving commissions to intermediaries from the direct business written. This could be seen as buying off possible intermediary conflict and it could be argued that business generated from direct marketing might not have used intermediaries as an alternative. However, the loss of intermediary goodwill is a potential hidden cost in direct marketing which should be considered.

Increasingly, as direct marketing usage grows, intermediaries such as brokers, building societies and banks (with monthly statements) will use their own direct mail.

Customer inertia It is often argued that customers for insurance services have low awareness of, and interest in, the competitive services offered and have little inclination to search for information before buying. In marketing terms they have a small evoked set. The evoked set is the shortlist of alternatives which consumers consider before buying. The size may vary from one upwards, but rarely encompasses all the available alternatives. It is a very important concept in insurance marketing. If the evoked set is on average three or more competitive insurance services then, because these services are often complex, expert advice to guide choice may be needed (from brokers, sales staff, etc.). If the evoked set is only one or two competitive insurance services, then providing customers with a direct sales appeal in their home via mail or media may be sufficient for them to buy, especially for low advice services such as term insurance. There is always the danger that direct mail is seen as intrusive by recipients and may cause a negative reaction against the sender.

Extraneous factors Finally, the impact of direct marketing techniques is always likely to be affected by a range of extraneous factors beyond the control of the insurance company user. The range of other advertisements in the issue used by a direct response advertiser, the mood of the recipient, the degree of preoccupation with other matters, other mail received in the same post as a direct mailshot, the weather, and a range of other factors can affect the reaction to a direct marketing effort. It may well be worth while to keep a record of factors thought likely to affect response rates to particular efforts, so that the evaluation of effectiveness of direct marketing usage can be accurately assessed.

8.4.4 Guidelines for effective direct marketing use

The following is not a definitive guide but a checklist of points which seem to be important in determining the effectiveness of direct marketing use:

1. Think in terms of recipients. Try to predict their likely reactions. Importantly, try a pilot scheme and if possible question these recipients about their reactions to the appeal. Use this intelligence to improve the design of the appeal.
2. React quickly to any customer response by post or by telephone. First impressions often last and a rapid, accurate response can create a very favourable image.
3. Design the application form carefully. It should elicit only the information that is absolutely necessary and be as simple as is possible. Again, think from the recipient's perspective.
4. Design the appeal to gain attention quickly. Making the recipient read the text of the advertisement or open the direct mail envelope is the first objective.
5. For direct mail use an accurate mailing list. If this is bought in, then it may be necessary to cross-check for existing clients. Writing to an existing client as though he were a potential new client will worry him about your efficiency.
6. Evaluate. Keep good records of response rates, take-up rates, claim rates, etc., to provide benchmarks for future use. Most users jealously guard this information along with any tricks of the trade which are learnt only from usage experience. There is little published data on this but much can be gained from carefully monitoring the actions of those who do use direct marketing methods.
7. Remember the three 'Cs': control, co-ordination and conflict. Use the direct marketing methods as part of an overall marketing strategy. Fit the technique into a co-ordinated, controlled marketing plan, aimed at meeting company objectives without conflict with intermediaries.

8.5 CHANNEL DESIGN DECISIONS

So far in this chapter, the major issues concerning the distribution of brands have been considered for both goods and services and for consumer (consumable and durable) and industrial goods. The manufacturer of the brand has to decide on the strategic and tactical use of channels of distribution within the overall brand marketing plan. This section summarizes the influences on this decision and specifies the decision process. The major influences on the process include:

8.5.1 Customers (both intermediate and final)

The brand should as a general rule be distributed in a way which meshes well with consumers' existing shopping habits. This may involve making the brand available as conveniently as possible (convenience products) but could involve consumers being willing to make a special trip to buy the brand after shopping around (shopping goods).

The number of potential customers for the brand is an influence, as is their geographic distribution. An industrial good aimed at the car industry which is located in specific, limited regions in the UK would need distributors centred in appropriate locations to service this market. Alternatively if the brand is purchased frequently in small quantities (e.g., newspapers, sweets) then blanket coverage of the market is a feasible strategy to maximize convenience of access for the consumer.

Finally the susceptibility of consumers to particular selling methods may be an issue. For instance there is an adage in the insurance industry that 'life assurance is sold not bought', implying a strong role for personal selling. Thus the distribution method chosen for a life insurance policy should reflect this principle. Indeed the rapid growth of Hambro (now Allied Dunbar) and Abbey Life over the past two decades in the UK has been based on the use of self-employed sales associates using a direct personal selling approach. This contrasts strongly with the trend towards self-service in many other retailing outlets. If consumers are convinced of the quality of a brand they may buy it from, say, a vending machine for convenience but if they need to be convinced of the qualities of a brand then other distribution methods may be more appropriate.

Customers with limited mobility (rural location, illness, for example) may make more use of mail order distribution or take up the 'off the page' direct response offers which characterize weekend newspaper advertising (presumably on the assumption that consumers have more time to browse through newspaper advertisements at the weekend). The recent UK growth of the glossy Sunday newspaper magazine supplements has exacerbated the trend to direct response advertising for a wide range of merchandise.

8.5.2 Product characteristics

Some product attributes directly affect the choice of distribution channel. An obvious example is perishability which emphasizes the need for speed in the distribution process. Fresh fruit and newspapers thus have well-established rapid physical distribution systems and use large numbers of outlets at the retail level to ensure convenience of access for buyers. In the US with the much greater land mass involved, newspapers tend to be regional rather than national as in the UK, and it is common to use air transport for the distribution of fresh fruit and flowers for example.

If the product is usually customized then there is a pressure to use direct distribution. Where a brand has a range of customer options, it may be sold from a demonstration unit with delivery to follow after customization has occurred at the manufacturer level. BMW cars in the UK which have had a restricted quota from the German head office, have as a marketing consequence attempted to build extra options into each sale to maximize their added value. Elevators are usually specifically designed for the characteristics of the building to be serviced which implies a central design/sales force approach to distributing direct to the client.

If the product is likely to require technical advice, installation services, or after-sales maintenance, then the consequent expertise requirement, which may be provided by the manufacturer or by exclusive franchise dealers or others, can be an important factor in the distribution choice. In this situation the brand is only a part of the wider service which the customer is buying. In order to control the quality of this overall service, the manufacturer may operate a system of exclusive area franchises with controls over the franchise holder in terms of training, staffing levels, stock holding and price levels. Because of the added value opportunities in such a service provision, the franchise is likely to be an attractive proposition to would-be distributors.

With other consumer goods and services franchising has become a popular means of vertical integration for manufacturers. This is because the costs of a retail set-up can be passed on to the franchise holder and because of this direct investment, involvement and motivation is likely to be high. Typically the franchise holder is buying into a multiple-type operation for the price of a single retail outlet although there can be many more controls. The manufacturer may determine the layout of the retail store, design and decoration, product range, supplies of goods, advertising levels and content, and other conditions which give a much stronger level of control than is now usual for a manufacturer to have. The underlying assumption, that self-employment and investment by the franchise holder will be a motivating force, is to some extent dependent on the quality of the manufacturer and the product and/or service to be supplied.

Other product attributes which can be important in channel decisions are unit costs and bulk. The higher the unit cost of the brand, the more likely distribution is to be direct, due to high stock holding costs for intermediaries. Large computer systems, which also tend to be customized, are usually distributed direct to the customer. The bigger the physical size and/or weight of the finished brand, the stronger will be the economic pressure to minimize the transport distance.

8.5.3 Intermediary characteristics

As already noted in the discussion of the relationship between manufacturers and intermediaries, intermediaries vary in both strengths and weaknesses. The type of abilities, which can vary, include the following:

- Transport.
- Advertising.
- Storage.
- Contacts and range of customers.
- Training and staff capabilities.
- Frequency of orders. + size
- Range of competitive products carried.
- Locations.
- Number of branches.
- Size.

The decision of a channel of distribution for a brand, besides taking into account the degree of flexibility the manufacturer enjoys, must assess the relevant abilities of the intermediaries who may be suitable partners in the distribution process. The need to build a strong long-term formal and informal relationship with intermediaries has already been stressed and is of the utmost importance in a successful distribution strategy.

8.5.4 Competitive channel choice

It is necessary to take account of competitors' distribution strategy in planning the optimum choice for a brand. It may be that the same route is chosen and typically the brand will be presented side by side with competitive brands within distributors' outlets. In such a situation the marketing strategy must include methods of ensuring that the brand will be chosen by sufficient numbers of potential customers from the competitive array. This may be by price advantage, successful brand image creation, personal recommendation by the distributor, merchandising or other methods which are perceived as valuable by the potential consumer.

In some cases it is possible to take an alternative route to the final consumer. Avon cosmetics shunned the traditional chemist—department-store outlet route in favour of direct-to-home distribution.

If the competitor has an exclusive distribution strategy in which only one distributor is chosen in each area (possibly with the condition that competitive brands are not stocked), the remaining available intermediaries may be of lower quality (either in situation or abilities). In this situation, there is pressure to choose an alternative route or to try to persuade the competitor's exclusive distributors to switch brands or to cultivate alternative intermediaries. This problem made entry into the UK car market difficult for new entrants as the primary intermediaries were already contracted to existing manufacturers. Since the 1960s importers have overcome this problem slowly, although they were helped by marketing, labour and production problems which the UK manufacturers suffered during this time.

The intermediary can be in a position to play off one manufacturer against others to get better deals especially if in a local monopoly position. This then limits the power and the freedom of choice of the manufacturer.

8.5.5 Manufacturer characteristics

Given some of the problems that manufacturers can face in dealing with independent intermediaries, there may be pressure to integrate towards the market by providing intermediary functions. In the

UK a prime example is Boots the Chemists which has a strong manufacturing base, a well established private label policy and a range of prime site retail outlets.

The cost of such an option makes it available only to financially strong companies (or ones which could, by merger or take-over, become capable of or achieve vertical integration). There is the possibility also of conflict with independent distributors if both are to be supplied.

The market position of the manufacturer is also a significant factor. Many intermediaries will be keen to be associated with a market leader but the third, fourth or a new brand in a market may not be such an attractive proposition to a profit-seeking intermediary.

Much of this section has implicitly assumed that the channel is to be set up by a new supplier. Of course, in practice the manufacturer is likely to have existing relationships with intermediaries which may be strong or weak and this past experience must be taken into account. Loyalty to existing intermediaries must be weighed against alternative distributive options.

8.5.6 Summary

The above influences on the choice of a distribution channel for a brand can be summarized as a number of decisions which must be made:

1. What types of intermediaries are to be used (if any)?
   - Will agents be used at all?
   - Will wholesalers/retailers be used?
   - If so, what types are most appropriate (department store, hypermarket, co-op, etc.)?
2. How many of each type will be used at each stage? This covers the degree of market exposure and could be:
   (a) Intensive – blanket coverage of all available outlets.
   (b) Exclusive – appointed intermediaries for exclusive areas.
   (c) Selective – a mixture of (a) and (b) with some but not all of the available intermediaries chosen at each stage.
3. Allocation of specific marketing tasks:
   - Who will provide which specific marketing tasks such as transport, merchandising and display, and advertising?
4. What are the terms of trade?
   - An identification of mutual responsibilities must be made concerning:
     - Price policies.
     - Conditions of sale.
     - Credit provision.
     - Order size and frequencies.
     - Delivery.
     - Territorial rights.
     - After-sales service.
     - Training.
     - Stock holding and display.
5. Evaluation of channel intermediaries:
   The choice must be made by balancing economic criteria such as cost (trade margins, delivery costs, etc.) and sales level expectations through alternative channel rates, against control and flexibility to change as conditions change.

8.6 DISTRIBUTION STRATEGY FOR BRANDS

This chapter has examined the economic and other influences on the distribution of brands. A particular feature of the distribution scene is the rapid rate of change which characterizes the recent history of distribution in the Western world. For this reason the chapter has not identified characteristics of each type of outlet as these are changing rapidly, not least in terms of their adoption of new technology. This is particularly true in the combination of sales registers and stock control within a computer controlled system which has vast potential for the provision of information on sales trends. These data will be available very quickly to enable rapid reactions to occur to changing situations. Thus a feature of distribution strategy should be flexibility, the ability to adapt quickly to changing conditions of supply and demand.

Distribution strategy should form an integral part of the brand-marketing strategy, but most of all should reflect consumers' needs. Distribution strategy can make or break a brand and is of vital significance, especially in the highly complex and competitive grocery markets. Here, the co-operation from large multiples is by no means automatic and may involve high-level negotiation to ensure that a brand attains or retains a sufficiently high level of distribution to make the brand available to consumers who may well put store loyalty before brand loyalty.

This chapter concludes the consideration of the major marketing strategy variables. The final chapter draws these strands together in a consideration of the economics of marketing strategy along with a brief look at the future of the brand.

REFERENCES

1. Buttle, F. (1984) 'Merchandising', *European Journal of Marketing*, **18**, 67, 104–23.
2. Arthur Anderson & Co./LOMA (1984) *Changing Horizons for Insurance: Charting a Course for Success*, Life Offices Management Association, Atlanta, Georgia.
3. CACI (1984) *ACORN: Today's Approach to Market Analysis*, CACI London.
4. Thomas, D. R. (1984) 'Direct Marketing – the Challenge', *Foresight*, May, 14–18.

NINE

THE ECONOMICS OF MARKETING PLANNING

9.1 THE BRAND AS A PROFIT CENTRE

In this final chapter the individual elements of the marketing plan for the brand in a competitive environment are drawn together. The brand itself, the brand image creation process, the price structure and the distribution strategy should be integrated into a meaningful whole.

The brand can be seen as a profit centre. As a major asset to a firm, built over time into a valuable item as perceived by consumers, the brand is of necessity the focus of attention within the firm. The sales of the brand are easily measurable in absolute terms. It may be difficult to define competitive brands but if this is done then estimates of the market share can be made using a market definition in brand terms. Sales level by brand is often protected information jealously guarded by firms. Cost data may be difficult to allocate exactly between brands in a multibrand firm but estimates can be made so that the profitability of a brand can be assessed using the sales and cost data.

This profit calculation is usually the key to marketing planning. Demand forecasts can be made and costs estimated so that profit projections result for future periods. This planning process is extendable to production planning, resource planning and financial planning.

The within-firm planning process involves two major steps in decision terms:

1. How much should the firm spend on marketing?
2. How should this budget be allocated between marketing activities?

The first of these decisions, the size of the marketing budget, has been considered already. In essence it concerns the relationship between market response (in sales terms) and marketing input. If this relationship can be estimated then, for a planned output, a market budget is determined as shown in Figure 9.1. Thus if OY_1 is the planned sales level for the brand then it follows that OX_1 should be the size of the marketing budget if the relationship is estimated by the fitted curve OZ_1. Of course, as noted already, the great difficulty is in forecasting the shape of OZ_1. If for example OZ_2 is a more appropriate curve then the planned sales level OY_1 can be achieved with a marketing budget of only OX_2.

The practical difficulties concern the isolation of the marketing effects on sales from other effects such as the economic climate and competitive action. Nevertheless, attempts to model this relationship could have significant pay-offs in the planning process.

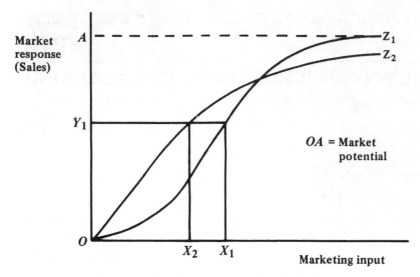

Fig. 9.1 Relationship between market response and marketing input

The second question concerns the allocation of the marketing budget between the alternative marketing decision areas. This is considered in the next section.

9.2 ALLOCATION OF THE MARKETING BUDGET

This section examines the allocation of marketing money (the total amount of which would have been determined by the corporate planning process) between the available marketing instruments so as to maximize returns for this expenditure in terms of sales. The theoretical analysis is an extension of the basic economic norm for profit maximization, setting marginal cost equal to marginal revenue.

9.2.1 The Dorfman–Steiner theorem

The Dorfman–Steiner theorem provides this extension:[1]

Let Q = sales

C = cost

P = price

D = distribution and selling effort

F = fixed costs

Z = profit

A = advertising and other promotional activity (which could be further divided if appropriate)

R = brand quality

If demand is determined by marketing variables then the demand for the brand is:

$$Q = q(P,A,D,R) \tag{1}$$

Costs can be variable or fixed and will vary with Q and R directly and with F, D and A indirectly, giving:

$$C = c(Q,R)Q + A + D + F \tag{2}$$

In other words, unit costs (c) vary with output (economies of scale) and brand quality.

Dorfman and Steiner use these functions to formulate a short-run profit function of the form:

$$Z = PQ - C \tag{3}$$

Substituting from (1) and (2):

$$Z = P_q(PADR) - c(Q,R)Q - A - D - F$$
$$Z = P_q(PADR) - c[q(PADR)R]q(PADR) - A - D - F \tag{4}$$

The necessary (but not necessarily sufficient) condition for marketing mix optimization is found by finding the partial derivatives with respect to each of the marketing variables (P,A,D,R) and equating them to zero. This is the first order condition. The second order condition for a maximum is that the second derivatives are negative.

Thus the condition for short-run profit maximization is:

$$\frac{\partial Z}{\partial P} = \frac{\partial Z}{\partial A} = \frac{\partial Z}{\partial D} = \frac{\partial Z}{\partial R} = 0 \tag{5}$$

the response of profit to a small change in any (and all) of the marketing variables is equal to zero and profit is maximized (assuming the second derivatives are negative).

By taking the partial derivatives from equation (4) and substituting in equation (5) the Dorfman–Steiner theorem* shows that the profit-maximizing position is achieved when:

$$e_p = MRP_A = MRP_D = e_R \frac{P}{C} \tag{6}$$

where:

$$e_p = \frac{\partial Q}{\partial P} \cdot \frac{P}{Q} = \text{price elasticity of demand}$$

$$MRP_A = P \cdot \frac{\partial Q}{\partial A} = \text{marginal revenue product of advertising}$$

$$MRP_D = P \cdot \frac{\partial Q}{\partial D} = \text{marginal revenue product of distribution}$$

$$e_R = \frac{\partial Q}{\partial R} \cdot \frac{\partial R}{\partial C} \cdot \frac{C}{Q} = \text{product quality elasticity of demand}$$

Thus, as a necessary condition for profit maximization, the values of price, advertising, distribution and product quality must be set at such levels that price elasticity, the marginal revenue products of advertising and distribution, and product quality elasticity, multiplied by the ratio of price to unit costs, are all equal.

This condition can be written in terms of elasticity measures as:

$$e_p = \frac{PQ}{A}e_A = \frac{PQ}{D}e_D = \frac{P}{C}e_R$$

* The proof of this theorem is also shown by Kotler.[2]

Thus the theorem does not directly give the optimal values of the marketing variables but rather the conditions that will be satisfied when the optimal values are found.

Attempts to empirically test the Dorfman–Steiner theorem have been made by Palda[3] and by Lambin[4] with limited success. There are a number of problems involved in applying the theorem to budget allocation for brands.

Firstly, the empirical problem of measuring elasticity. The many attempts to do this seem to be much more successful the greater the level of aggregation. Thus at the industry or the product-group level of analysis there is a reasonable amount of success. At the brand level the difficulty of disentangling the effects of other marketing variables seems to set a limit to the accuracy that can be achieved. Chapter 7 explored in detail the great difficulties of accurately measuring consumer reactions to new and proposed brands, in particular relating to price. However, estimates can be made using accumulated past data and a multiple regression model for example.*

The use of advertising as a fixed cost can also be seen as a problem, although one which could be overcome relatively easily. In Chapter 5 the section on the advertising budget determination showed that advertising budgets in practice are often set as a percentage of sales (either achieved or anticipated). This leads to a complexity in the relationship between sales and advertising known as two-way causation. Thus it is likely that advertising levels affect sales levels but the reverse is also likely, albeit lagged by one period in some cases. In the Dorfman–Steiner theorem, advertising could be incorporated as a variable cost.

A third problem is that there is no explicit incorporation of competitive effects in the model. Although it could be argued that the elasticity measures implicitly incorporate competitive effects there is no outright incorporation of the level of prices, advertising, product quality and distribution for competitive brands. To overcome this, Lambin developed an approach in which each of the marketing variables are defined relatively, thus taking explicit account of competitive action.[6]

A fourth problem is that the Dorfman–Steiner theorem (and the Lambin extension) is essentially a static model in that sales in the period are a function of the levels of the marketing variables in that period only. To be of empirical value, a longer-term, dynamic model may be necessary. As noted above, if advertising has lagged effects in relation to sales then a dynamic model formulation is necessary to take account of this. As discussed in Chapter 5 the Nerlove and Arrow model, using the concept of advertising goodwill, produced a dynamic model.[7]

A further problem is that all the variables are assumed to be continuous functions (and hence capable of being differentiated). In practice this is unlikely to be the case, for example to increase advertising expenditure may involve a minimum increase of the cost of an extra insertion in the press or on TV. This is discussed further in the next section.

Finally, the acceptability of a model to practising marketing managers involves their confidence and understanding of the principles and of the technique. The complexity of the theorem and of the measurement difficulties may make the model less acceptable to managers faced with the practical task of marketing-budget allocation.

9.2.2 Geometric optimizing techniques

Two-variable case Kotler outlines a two-variable model which examines sales levels which result from various levels of advertising and distribution. This process could then be repeated for other combinations of two marketing variables to form a profit function.[2]

The major problem is still the need to predict sales response to the various levels of marketing variable settings, i.e., to isolate the effects of each variable.

Four-variable case Verdoorn proposed an interesting diagrammatic approach.[8] Using the four mar-

---

* See Fitzroy[5] for examples of the use of multiple regression in marketing.

keting variables used by Dorfman and Steiner, none of which are assumed to be continuous, the assumptions are made that:

1. Production cost is a function of the quantity sold and product quality.
2. Beyond a certain threshold point, all variables will be subject to diminishing returns.

Then for a given price (if total revenue varies directly with sales levels) the assumption is made that there are three possible levels of product quality being considered. The model then evaluates the effects of a number of combinations of advertising outlay and distribution channel expenditure on sales and costs.

For a specified price and product quality, the sales and cost effects of a number of combinations of promotional outlay and channels are estimated.

A diagram is then used to fill out all the technically and economically feasible configurations of marketing mixes with given price and three quality levels. These combinations are not continuous and there will emerge a 'desert and oasis' map in which the filled-in dots represent oases in the desert of technical and practical impossibilities as shown in Figure 9.2. C represents the minimum cost of each combination for each sales volume with OQ_1 representing the sales volume which maximizes profit at this price and would involve product quality 3 and the assumed combination of advertising and distribution outlay that this dot represents.

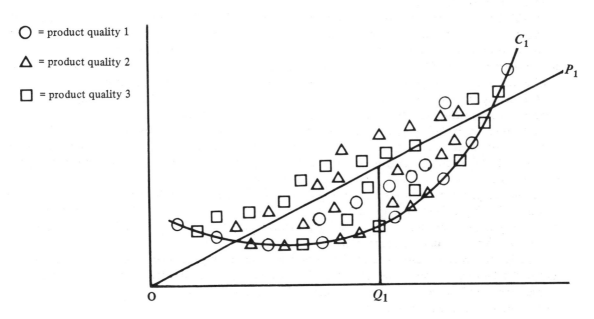

Fig. 9.2 Desert and oasis map — one price level

This process could then be repeated for different price levels to give a series of price (revenue) lines and their corresponding minimum cost (C) lines. An example is shown in Figure 9.3. OQ_1 represents the maximum profit with price P_3 and the implied levels of the other three variables.

Thus this approach deals with both marketing and production aspects of the brand although the concentration is on marketing variables and non-continuous variation in inputs is incorporated.

In an attempt to make the model dynamic, Verdoorn suggested that the maximization of the present value of future profits can be viewed as present (short-run) profit maximization under the constraint that the present value of future profits is not impaired. This could include such items as no loss of control by the owner through increased borrowing, and discouragement of potential

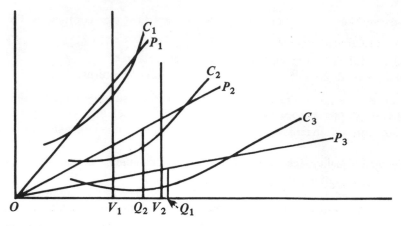

Fig. 9.3 Desert and oasis map — various price levels

competitors. These conditions can be viewed as limits (maximum or minimum) on output shown as V_1 and V_2 in Figure 9.3. For example the conditions could:

— Limit investment (to avoid loss of control), thus affecting the maximum sales level achievable.
— Limit sales price (threat of new competition).
— Limit market share (threat of government intervention).
— Put a minimum level on production (maintaining present labour force).

If V_1 and V_2 are the minimum and maximum (respectively) boundaries on output then the profit-maximizing output is constrained to OQ_2 from OQ_1 (assuming that P_3 is an acceptable price level).

Both this and the Dorfman–Steiner models can be further refined by taking into account the effectiveness of marketing expenditure. Both models concern themselves with the amount of expenditure only and, in practice, firms will differ in the efficiency with which marketing expenditures are made. For example the creative content of an advertising campaign may vary widely for the same expenditure and this could be reflected in sales effectiveness.

This could be incorporated into the models by adding a coefficient to each marketing variable based on an index of effectiveness (e.g., making the effectiveness of the average firm = 1 with those being more highly effective than average, having a coefficient > 1, and both below, having a coefficient < 1). Again the problems of measuring effectiveness remain. The methods of advertising effectiveness measurement outlined in Chapter 5 and the methods of measuring reaction to new brands in development discussed in Chapter 7 could be used to assess effectiveness. The opinions of experts or a selected representative audience or simulated sales tests could be used in this context.

9.2.3 Brand share models

It is very common in marketing practice for brand share to be the major focus of attention for managers. This perhaps reflects the intense rivalry which is a feature of modern business. A number of models have been developed which attempt to forecast brand share. Some of these models concentrate on new brands (Parfitt–Collins,[9] for example) others on repeat buying (Ehrenberg[10]), while others take a market-wide view (see Kotler,[11] for example) which compares marketing expenditures for competitive brands. This latter approach is expressed by Kotler as:

$$s_i = m_i = \frac{k_i - aX_{1i} + bX_{2i} + cX_{3i} + dX_{4i} + eX_{5i} + \ldots nX_{ni}}{\sum_i (k_i - aX_1 + bX_2 + cX_3 + dX_4 + eX_5 + \ldots nX_n)}$$

where s_i = brand share of brand i

m_i = brand i share of total marketing effort

X_{1i} = price of brand i

X_{2i} = promotion expenditure of brand i

X_{3i} = distribution effort of brand i

X_{4i} = sales effort of brand i

X_{5i} = product quality of brand i

∴ X_n = other marketing variable effort of brand i

$a-n$ = constants determining the particular effectiveness of each marketing variable

This assumes a linear relationship between the variables and brand share.

Other forms of the relationship could be used, for example an exponential relationship could be:

$$s_i = m_i = \frac{kX_{i1}^{-a}X_{i2}^{b}X_{i3}^{c}X_{i4}^{d}X_{i5}^{e} \ldots X_{in}^{n}}{\sum_i (k_i X_1^{-a} X_2^{b} X_3^{c} X_4^{d} X_5^{e} \ldots X_n^{n})}$$

This approach can be criticized both for the difficulty of objectively determining the coefficients of effectiveness and in terms of the static analysis. The model takes no account of accumulated goodwill, a critical variable in the brand image formation process. Thus the model applies only to the current period although it would in theory be possible to add a dynamic dimension.

9.2.4 Summary

This section has examined the allocation of the marketing budget in terms of market effects of the individual marketing variables. The overriding difficulty is in terms of measuring market response.

In practice companies have to make these decisions. It is likely that they evolve from custom and practice, by discussion, or by adjustment from existing (last period) allocations. The decision-makers may use an intuitive model of the process but there is little published evidence to show that the use of explicit market models is widespread. There are some exceptions to this: a market model for motor oil has been published, for example.[12]

It would seem that as marketing decisions become more complex the use of market modelling is likely to grow. One reason for this complexity is the increase in the use of marketing information brought about by improvements in technology. The next section examines the growth of marketing information systems being brought about by the supply-side influence of technology growth. This is included as an indication of a major future trend in marketing practice and addresses the issue of the economic value of information to a brand manager.

9.3 MARKETING INFORMATION SYSTEMS – ECONOMIC AND ORGANIZATIONAL ISSUES

9.3.1 Introduction

The importance of information in marketing decision-making has grown as business complexity has increased: 'good information is a facilitator of successful marketing action and indeed, seen in this light marketing management becomes first and foremost an information processing activity.'[13] This trend is likely to continue: 'the 1980's will see a profound transformation in the working environment of marketing and sales management . . . the most successful companies will be those who have decided to make efficient use of information systems as a control tool.'[14]

The reasons for this increasing reliance on marketing information are many but can be summarized as being concerned with:

1. The growth in size of organizations and centralization of operations to gain economies of scale which has distanced manufacturers, in both spatial and temporal dimensions, from their customers.
2. Increasing amounts of competition due to the internationalization of business.
3. The tendency for organizations to become multiproduct, multimarket concerns.
4. Technological change, especially pertaining to information technology.
5. Changes in consumer behaviour, increasing affluence reducing the importance of price competition and widening choice, for example.

A marketing information system (MKIS) is an attempt to formalize and centralize the provision of data within an organization. It has been rather verbosely defined as 'a structured, interaction complex of persons, machines and procedures designed to generate an orderly flow of pertinent information collected from both intra- and extra-firm sources for use as the basis for decision making in specified responsibility areas for marketing management.'[15] This definition identifies the three important components of the MKIS as data collection, data interpretation and data usage.

It is argued by Piercy and Evans that an MKIS is not the same as market research, indeed that the latter should be seen as an integrated part of the former.[16] They make the comparison between the MKIS as a 'candle' providing continuous illumination, and marketing research as a 'flash-bulb' (providing specific insights over a short period) but this is a simplistic approach. Churchill identified control as the major MKIS feature: 'The concept of a MKIS parallels that of a thermostat in that the emphasis is on continually monitoring business activities, for example, sales, profits and market share, to make sure the process is in control.'[17] In practice the amount of marketing research within an MKIS will vary between organizations, in some cases providing the vast majority of data, in others very little, in bursts, to meet specific needs.

Certainly there has been much academic interest in MKISs, developing in the US in the late 1960s in the work of Berenson,[18] Montgomery and Urban,[19] Cox and Good,[20] and Smith, Brien and Stafford,[15] which seemed to predict a bright future. Empirical work at this time by Armstutz[21] and by Boone and Kurtz[22] found relatively little usage in US industry.

In the UK there is a dearth of published material until the early 1980s when books by Piercy and Evans[16] and by Foxall[23] appeared.

This section will progress with a brief examination of the major elements of the MKIS followed by a consideration of problems in their development. The limited evidence on the practical use of MKIS will then be presented.

9.3.2 Elements of the marketing information system

It is obvious that the level of sophistication of an MKIS will vary between organizations according to needs and within the same organization over time. In an award-winning paper Westwood *et al.* postulated six levels of sophistication based on the two dimensions of system capability and the basis for relating files.[24] These are shown in Table 9.1.

They clearly identity a progression within a company from a very basic system to a complex control system.

Kotler's model concentrates on the information gathering, processing and utilization aspects of MKIS within what he calls a Marketing Information and Analysis Centre (MIAC). This centralizes the process, drawing on sources and outputting to users.[25]

Howard builds a model which develops an MKIS system from a simple user-interrogation system

Table 9.1 Levels of sophistication in marketing information systems

Level/dimensions	System capability	Basis for relating files
Level 1	Retrieval	None
2	Intuitive analysis	Cross-referencing
3	Mathematical analysis	Aggregation over files
4	Synthesis	File amalgamation
5	Prediction	Statistical model
6	Learning	Behavioural model

Source: Adapted from Westwood *et al.*[24]

by adding in a feedback loop and then a control and evaluation system to a complex paradigm capable of decision-making.[26] A practical model developed for Mead Johnson in the US is discussed by Adler[27] and a computer-based simulation system is developed by Armstutz.[28] The essential elements of the MKIS are:

1. The sources of information.
2. The manipulation of data into usable forms.
3. The use of data in marketing decision-making.

9.3.3 Limitations to the use of marketing information systems

The starting point here is the economic value of information. Do managers need more information? While it is possible to attempt to assess the value of information, using Bayesian statistical theory,[29] in practice the views of individual managers are likely to vary. It seems sensible to relate information needs to the decisions which have to be taken. King has suggested that 'the major reason for this focus on the user is a very practical one: evidence suggests that managers will simply not use systems which are not designed from such a perspective.'[30] It is difficult to assess whether or not extra information would lead to better decisions and more effectiveness. There is also the issue of the speed of provision of information. The rapid growth of information technology enables an MKIS to produce up-to-date analyses but again at a cost which relates directly to the speed of provision. This growth is often technology-led rather than market-driven. The assumption is that because it is available it will be used, but in practice there is a 'cultural lag' before managers will adapt their working practices to fully utilize available technology. At least in the short term, a new MKIS may have a negative effect on the quality of decision-making by reducing the use of a manager's accumulated experience, intuition and creativity. An MKIS should supplement rather than replace these factors. Further, as managers do not necessarily make decisions in the same way, the effectiveness of standardized reports is limited.

The implicit assumption to date is that the MKIS is centralized. This may not be the case, especially as the cost of computer hardware reduces, and the feasibility of a system which is based on intelligent rather than dumb terminals increases, thus saving data communications costs, especially if multiplexing can be used. The decision on how to distribute the intelligence in a computer system will depend on the exact use and usage rate of the system. However, if the MKIS is centralized then a further organizational issue is raised.

Piercy has addressed the issue of the neutrality of information, arguing that information represents organizational power.[31,32] This is exacerbated with a centralized system. Anderson and Cundiff postulated that, 'in every organization one individual or occasionally more than one, serves as a communication centre for exchanges of information relating to each important marketing decision area'.[33] A

wed that this 'gatekeeper' tended to introduce selectivity into the flow of
potentially powerful position. Pfeffer has argued that 'secrecy or the limita-
mation is used strategically by power holders to enhance and maintain their
n the organization'.[35] Thus information is power and can be used to further
tal interest at the expense of overall company goals.

Bowersox identified the concept of *executive fear* in this context: for selfish
managers might obstruct the flow of information for their own self-protection.[36]

between marketing and other departments was highlighted by Kotler[37] and was
recog... yert and March[38] view of organizations in which the total goals are seen as a
coalition of independent goals for factors such as profit, sales, market share, production and inventory.

One possible solution to this potential problem in the use of MKISs is shown by Cox and Good's empirical study where they found that 'in every case, at least some members of top management have seen the promise of the technique and have viewed its development as a top management responsibility'.[39] Such backing would ease the introduction of MKISs into organizations. The introduction of an MKIS would need careful management to avoid conflict and suspicion using a detailed analysis of the information needs of each manager, and the turning of these needs. When operational, the changing information needs should be monitored and access to the system for input and output needs to be controlled.

9.3.4 The use of marketing information systems — US and UK evidence

As already mentioned the studies in the US in the late 1960s by Armstutz[21] and by Boone and Kurtz[22] found little evidence of usage on any sophisticated level. A UK study by Jobber and Rainbow in 1975 (published in 1977)[40] and repeated by Fletcher in 1981 (published in 1982)[41] found very similar results with little change in the six-year period. Using a similar methodology and a random sample of the top 500 UK firms, a response rate of 153 (35 per cent) was achieved by Jobber, and 117 (58 per cent) by Fletcher.

In the four studies noted, the number of respondents claiming to have an MKIS were

1. Armstutz (1969) — 47 per cent (39 out of responses from 83 firms) with a further 29 per cent developing a system.
2. Boone and Kurtz (1971) — 39 per cent (77 out of responses from 193 firms) with a further 38 per cent developing a system.
3. Jobber (1975) — 50 per cent (74 out of responses from 153 firms) with a further 9 per cent developing a system.
4. Fletcher (1981) — 54 per cent (63 out of responses from 117 firms) with a further 9 per cent developing a system.

In the UK the major uses of the MKIS were (most popular to least popular, 1981 study):

1. Improved speed/quality of planning and decision-making.
2. Sales forecasting/monitoring.
3. Improved retrieval of information.
4. Cost saving.
5. Competitor analysis.
6. Sales force control.
7= Profit analysis.
7= Customer analysis.

The major reasons given for non-use were:

1. No real need.
2. Lack of staff appreciation.
3. Budget constraints.

Finally, the major problems encountered in the introduction of MKISs were:

1. Poor quality and inconsistencies in input data.
2. Defining management information needs.
3. Educating users in the potential of the system.
4. Technical computer-related problems.

The MKISs had relatively limited scope, being used for data retrieval (100 per cent of 1981 responses), monitoring (65 per cent), exception reporting (56 per cent), making recommendations (37 per cent) and predictions (68 per cent). They were also relatively unsophisticated with 90 per cent carrying out arithmetic calculations, 75 per cent statistical analyses, 35 per cent using mathematical models and 22 per cent computer-aided simulation analysis.

Westwood *et al.* conclude their article on 'integrated information systems' by identifying a number of guidelines for the introduction of MKISs. This is a useful conclusion for this section: their guidelines were:

1. Begin with the needs of managers, not with computer capability.
2. Lay out relationships for integrating data measures. Start with commonsense models and then build on this foundation.
3. Aim to provide basic documents for company marketing planning.
4. Decide how files are to be organized and the system's functions before passing the design to the computer department.
5. Present the reports well, ensure that they are expressed in telling and meaningful ways, e.g., use exception reporting, graphs, short reports, etc.
6. Adopt a staged approach to development. Don't be too ambitious initially.[24]

Thus the economics of MKISs for brands are not clear-cut and a careful analysis of needs and costs must be undertaken before taking a programmed step-by-step approach to the development of a user-orientated and friendly system which is a valuable contribution to brand marketing management.

9.4 THE FUTURE OF THE BRAND – GLOBALIZATION

The last section was concerned with future developments in brand management; this section adds to this by exploring how the role of the brand may change in the future. In particular we consider the growth of 'global brands'. Global brands are not new. Examples include Coca Cola, IBM Computers, Marlboro. There is an increasing emphasis on the use of advertising to create a global brand. A recent article by Levitt[42] notes this trend but emphasizes the global company and differences between countries, a point also noted by Porter, 'ignoring country differences can be suicidal to international companies. But forgoing the opportunity to find or create common worldwide demand for a standardized product can be equally devastating.'[43] Thus the trend is perhaps towards worldwide multinational companies rather than brands although brand names may be standardized for global use but with subtle variations in the brand marketing to reflect country differences. An obvious example is that language differences lead to labelling differences but, more subtly, colours have different connotations in different cultures. Climate differences may lead to different packaging needs, while differing shopping habits may lead to different size, shape or display aspects.

The clear need is for market research to understand differences between markets and to take account of these differences by variations in the marketing strategy for the brand.

In the UK attention has been focused on global brands by Saatchi and Saatchi Compton World-wide, the advertising agency. In the 1984 Review of Advertising Operations, part of their annual report, they emphasize some of the problems facing brands:

1. Population is static in the developed economies, meaning static markets which mean increased competition for market share.
2. Product quality is converging with increasing technological parity among major marketers.
3. The influence of the retailer and retailer's own brands is growing in many parts of the world.
4. Marketing expenses are growing as manufacturers respond to the ever-higher cost of reaching the consumer.

These influences, they claim, increase the advantages of the global brand gained from international economies of scale.

They argue that progress is occurring for both organizational and economic reasons:

(*a*) Organizational progress:

    (i) Company starts to operate in its own country.
    (ii) Starts to export.
    (iii) Opens marketing companies overseas with their own manufacturing plant.
    (iv) Co-ordinates marketing and production across different countries.
    (v) Centralizes production/distribution/marketing by continent.

(*b*) Economic progress:

    (i) Pressure of cost-inflation in static markets.
    (ii) Need to be low-cost producer to win market share battle.
    (iii) Search for more efficient business structure.
    (iv) Economies of scale.
    (v) World brands.

The other major influence on the progress to world brands is, they argue, 'consumer convergence in demography, habits and culture are increasingly leading manufacturers to a consumer driven rather than a geographic driven view of their marketing strategy'. This reflects such worldwide trends in developed economies as:

— The decline of the nuclear family.
— The increase in the number of women in paid employment.
— The increase in divorce, with fewer marriages.
— The rise in living standards.
— The increased penetration of TV.

It is clearly thought that it is possible to market a standard brand world-wide but that not all brands are potential world brands. This focus of attention will only serve to make the brand even more important to the company. This importance is often shown through the use of brand management as a form of organizational structure as discussed in Chapter 1.

The global advertisement has been made possible by the use of advanced telecommunication systems which give 'live' access to broadcasts across the world. It is estimated that the 1985 FA Cup Final in the UK was seen by a world audience of 600 million in 56 countries, with about 40 taking the programme live. The use of advertising hoardings or sponsorship can be used to communicate a brand name world-wide on these occasions. This may well be desired.

The man living in Knightsbridge is more like the man living near Central Park, Manhattan or off the Champs-Elysees than a person living in some drab London suburb. That means there is a certain logic in aiming the same advertising at people even though they are physically thousands of miles apart.[44]

Multinational companies are increasingly targeting their advertising on a continental, or even wider, scale. The 1985 British Airways advertising has been seen in 40 different countries. Consequently multinational advertising agencies have grown in importance. In 1976 13 per cent of global advertising was done by multinational agencies; by 1983 it was 21 per cent. In 1984 world advertising was estimated at £100 billion. Global advertising has the additional advantage that competitive accounts can be handled by different agencies within a multinational agency conglomerate, thus conveniently avoiding conflict-of-interest problems.

However, individual country differences should not be ignored. Brooks gives three examples:

1. An agency ran an international advertisement for Scotch Whisky in which the whisky was shown in a decanter. It was shown in Japan but went down very badly because the Japanese decant only poor whiskies.
2. Saatchi and Saatchi produced a famous advertisement for Silk Cut cigarettes in which the pack is not shown: there is merely a piece of crumpled silk with a cut in it. Because of the subtlety of this appeal, it was decided in some countries that a pack of cigarettes would be shown coming through the cut in the silk to clarify the message.
3. An advertising campaign for the Opel Kadett motorcar had one advertisement for Italy (where Opel market share is very low), one for Spain and one for the rest of Western Europe.[45]

The main reason for the trend to globalization is perhaps not so much the need for a worldwide message but the need to save money. Globalization means simpler co-ordination of the advertising appeals and resultant economies of scale. In the British Airways case, making one advertisement rather than 40 (one for each country) has an obvious appeal and the use of visual, musical or other non-verbal messages can create brand image claims which transcend national boundaries.

This is a complex subject. The cultural, language, economic, social, legal and other differences between countries must obviously be taken into account if brand marketing is to have maximum effect on a global scale. Nevertheless, this is clearly an area for the future development of brands which can only grow in importance. Among other things, extra pressure would be put on the marketing information system of a company to take into account different demand conditions in different markets on an international basis.

9.5 CONCLUDING COMMENTS

This book has sought to explore the relationship between economics and marketing through the medium of the brand. The practice of marketing has been emphasized, although concepts, principles and techniques have been presented which have added a theoretical element.

Where necessary a wider view has been taken of brand marketing. The economic influences have thus been contrasted with the other influences on the brand. The orientation of the book has been towards the demand side rather than the supply side and many instances of the role of market research for the brand have been explored in both theoretical and empirical terms.

The initial intention in writing this book was to clarify the value of economics in the context of brand marketing. Therefore this is not purely a book about economic principles but a book about brands which takes a pragmatic view of marketing theory.

The reader should be left with a clearer view of brands as a focus of company interest and of the influences on the brand, both economic and non-economic. The reader should have an analytical framework for examining the practice of brand management.

REFERENCES

1. Dorfman, R. and P. O. Steiner (1954) 'Optimal advertising and optimal quality', *American Economic Review*, **64**, 5, 826–36.
2. Kotler, P. (1974) *Marketing Decision Making: A model building approach*, Holt Rinehart and Winston, New York, p. 684.
3. Palda, K. S. (1964) *The Measurement of Cumulative Advertising Effects*, Prentice-Hall, Englewood Cliffs, New Jersey.
4. Lambin, J. J. (1969) 'Measuring the profitability of advertising: an empirical study', *Journal of Industrial Economics*, **17**, 2, 86–103.
5. Fitzroy, P. T. (1976) *Analytical Methods for Marketing Management*, McGraw-Hill, Maidenhead, pp. 17–25.
6. Lambin, J. J. (1970) 'Optimal allocation of competitive marketing efforts: an empirical study', *Journal of Business*, **43**, 4, 468–84.
7. Nerlove, M. and K. J. Arrow (1962) 'Optimal advertising policy under dynamic conditions', *Economica*, **29**, 129–42.
8. Verdoorn, P. J. (1956) 'Marketing from the producer's point of view', *Journal of Marketing*, January, p. 230.
9. Parfitt, J. H. and B. J. K. Collins (1968) 'Use of consumer panels for brand share prediction', *Journal of Marketing Research*, **5**, May, 131–45.
10. Ehrenberg, A. S. C. (1972) *Repeat Buying*, North-Holland, Amsterdam.
11. Kotler, op. cit., p. 92.
12. Talmage, P. A. (1981) 'A market model for price/advertising decisions', *Proceedings of Market Research Society Annual Conference*, p. 150, Market Research Society, London.
13. Christopher, M., M. McDonald and G. Wills (1980) *Introducing Marketing*, Pan, London.
14. Graf, F. (1979) 'Information Systems for Marketing', *Marketing Trends*, **2**, 1, 1–3.
15. Smith, S. V., R. H. Brien and J. E. Stafford (eds) (1968) *Readings in Marketing Information Systems*, Houghton Mifflin, New York.
16. Piercy, N. and M. Evans (1983) *Managing Marketing Information*, Croom Helm, London, p. 22.
17. Churchill, G. A. (1976) *Marketing Research: Methodological Foundations*, Dryden, Hinsdale, Illinois.
18. Berenson, C. (1976) 'Marketing Information Systems', *Journal of Marketing*, October, 32–39.
19. Montgomery, D. B. and G. L. Urban (1969) – *Management Science in Marketing*, Prentice-Hall, Englewood Cliffs, New Jersey.
20. Cox, D. F. and R. E. Good (1967) 'How to build a marketing information system', *Harvard Business Review*, **45**, 3, 145–54.
21. Armstutz, A. E. (1969) 'Marketing orientated management systems: the current status', *Journal of Marketing Research*, **6**, 16, 481–96.
22. Boone, L. E. and D. L. Kurtz (1971) 'Marketing information systems: current status in American industry', in *Proceedings: National Conference of the American Marketing Association*, A.M.L., Chicago.
23. Foxall, G. R. (1981) *Strategic Marketing Management*, Croom Helm, London.
24. Westwood, R. A. *et al.* (1975) 'Integrated information systems', in *Journal of the Market Research Society*, **17**, 3, 127–81.
25. Kotler, P. (1974) *Marketing Decision Making: A Model Building Approach*, Holt International, London, p. 570.
26. Howard, J. A. (1973) *Marketing Management*, 3rd edn, Irwin, Homewood, Illinois, pp. 147–58.
27. Adler, L. (1967) 'Systems Approach to Marketing', in *Harvard Business Review*, **45**, 3, 111.
28. Armstutz, A. E. (1967) *Computer Simulation of Competitive Market Structures*, MIT Press, Cambridge, Mass.
29. Elliott, K. and M. G. Christopher (1974) *Research Methods in Marketing*, Holt Rinehart and Winston, London.
30. King, W. R. (1979) 'Strategies for success in MIS', Working Paper WP–333, Graduate School of Business, University of Pittsburgh, quoted by Piercy, N. (1981) in 'Marketing information – bridging the quicksand between technology and decision making', *Quarterly Review of Marketing*, October, 1–15.
31. Piercy, N. (1979) 'Behavioural consideration on marketing information systems', *European Journal of Marketing*, **13**, 8, 261–70.
32. Piercy, N. (1982) 'Marketing information: the corporate battleground', in *Proceedings of the Annual Conference of the Marketing Education Group*, Lancaster, Marketing Education Group, pp. 376–99.
33. Anderson, R. G. and E. W. Cundiff (1965) 'Patterns of communication in marketing organisations', *Journal of Marketing*, **29**, 7, 30–4.
34. Pettigrew, A. (1972) 'Information control as a power resource', *Sociology*, **6**, 2, 187–204.
35. Pfeffer, J. (1981) *Power in Organizations*, Pitman, Marshfield, Mass.
36. Staoudt, T. A., D. A. Taylor and D. J. Bowersox (1976) *A Managerial View of Marketing*, 3rd edn, Prentice-Hall, Englewood Cliffs, New Jersey.
37. Kotler, P. (1965) 'Diagnosing the marketing takeover', *Harvard Business Review*, **6**, 70.

38. Cyert, R. M. and J. G. March (1963) *A behavioural theory of the firm*, Prentice-Hall, Englewood Cliffs, New Jersey.
39. Cox and Good, op. cit., p. 152.
40. Jobber, D. and C. Rainbow (1977) 'A study of the development and implementation of marketing information systems in British industry', *Journal of the Market Research Society*, **19**, 2, 104–11.
41. Fletcher, K. P. (1982) 'Marketing information systems: a lost opportunity', in *Marketing: Bridging the Gap between Theory and Practice*, M. J. Thomas (ed.), Lancaster, Marketing Education Group, pp. 421–38.
42. Levitt, T. (1983) 'The globalization of markets', *Harvard Business Review*, May–June, 92–102.
43. Porter, M. (1984) *Competitive Strategy*, Free Press, New York.
44. Brooks, R. (1985) 'Rise of the global persuaders', *Sunday Times*, 19 May, quoting M. Waterson.
45. Ibid.